A Whole New Game

A Whole New Game

Off the Field Changes in Baseball, 1946–1960

by JOHN P. ROSSI

McFarland & Company, Inc., Publishers
Jefferson, North Carolina, and London

Front cover: Hank Aaron (Brace Photo)

British Library Cataloguing-in-Publication data are available

Library of Congress Cataloguing-in-Publication Data

Rossi, John P.
    A whole new game : off the field changes in baseball, 1946–1960 /
by John P. Rossi.
        p.   cm.
    Includes bibliographical references (p.) and index.

    ISBN-13: 978-0-7864-0651-7
    (softcover : 50# alkaline paper) ∞

    1. Baseball — United States — History — 20th century.   I. Title.
GV863.A1K67   1999
796.357'0973'09045 — dc21   99-21308
                                                                  CIP

Manufactured in the United States of America

McFarland & Company, Inc., Publishers
    Box 611, Jefferson, North Carolina 28640

For Frances and Monica

Acknowledgments

Anyone researching baseball history in the modern era is blessed with wonderful material. In my view, the level of writing about baseball peaked over the last two generations. Harold Seymour and David Voigt broke new ground by placing baseball within the context of historical developments in America. Bill James' books, especially his *Historical Baseball Abstract*, showed how to get beyond a recitation of statistics by looking inside the game.

Among recent scholarly studies I found three particularly useful: Bruce Kuklick, *To Everything a Season: Shibe Park and Urban Philadelphia, 1909–1976*; James Miller, *The Baseball Business: Pursuing Pennants and Profits in Baltimore*; and Neil Sullivan, *The Dodgers Move West*. These monographs are characterized by solid research and lively writing. They are models of scholarship in baseball.

I have also drawn heavily on the great sports writers and journalists who have specialized in baseball history. Books that stand out in my mind include Leonard Koppett's *The Man in the Dugout* and Roger Kahn's *The Era*, his highly personal view of the years from 1947 to 1957 when New York teams ruled baseball. Peter Golenbock has written three books which I found useful: *Dynasty: the New York Yankees 1949–1964*; *Bums: An Oral History of the Brooklyn Dodgers*; and *Fenway: An Unexpurgated History of the Red Sox*.

The Sporting News and the *Sporting News Guides*, 1946–1960, were valuable sources of information and insight into baseball. The fifteen years after World War II may not have been baseball's Golden Age, but they constituted a great era for the *Sporting News*. The detail about baseball is breathtaking and shows better than anything I know of how baseball dominated America's thinking about sports in those years.

The following former Major Leaguers kindly answered questions for me: Buddy Lewis, Eddie Sawyer, Vern Law, Bob Kuzava, Andy Seminick, Jack Banta and the late Del Ennis.

I wish to thank a number of people who helped me with my research. First, the administration of La Salle granted me a sabbatical at the perfect time when my research was finished and I was ready to write. The reference librarians of La Salle's Connelly Library, in particular Eithne Bearden and Stephen Breedlove, located obscure material for me and made it a pleasure to do my research. Francine Lottier, secretary of the English Department, saved me again and again when I had computer problems. Without her help, it would have taken me much longer to finish. My brother, Angelo Rossi, a lifelong baseball fan, patiently listened to me as I tried out my ideas on him.

Finally and most importantly, my wife Frances encouraged me for years to write this book. She said (and as usual she was right) that I was fortunate in having an avocation, the history of baseball, that I loved as much as my vocation. For putting up with my obsession with baseball for almost 30 years, I dedicate this book to her.

Contents

Introduction

Some years ago sportswriter Harold Rosenthal wrote a charming book, *The Ten Best Years of Baseball: An Informal History of the Fifties.* His title said it all. "The fabulous fifties" were a time of high excitement when baseball reached its peak of development. Others have made the same point. A. B. "Happy" Chandler, commissioner from 1945 to 1951, believes that this was baseball's greatest era. This period is often labeled a "golden era," but I contend that the years from roughly the end of World War II until the first wave of expansion in the early 1960s saw Major League baseball confront a series of crises that have been overlooked or that were little understood at the time. As the public focused on the superstars of the period — Ted Williams, Stan Musial, Joe DiMaggio, Robin Roberts, Jackie Robinson and Willie Mays (to name a few) — they failed to notice that the game of baseball was being transformed.

Baseball recovered impressively from World War II and shared initially in the enormous prosperity that characterized the United States for a generation. Attendance at the major and minor level reached all-time highs. The Major Leagues peaked at 20,921,000 in 1948, more than double the figure for the last year of the war. Attendance then declined for five straight years before rising slightly again. The overall decline was 6,600,000, a drop-off of 30 percent — a sure sign that baseball was in trouble. The minors attracted 31,000,000 in 1946 and then began a decline that continued precipitously for the next 20 years, reducing the number of minor leagues from 59 in 1948 to 22 twelve years later.

The fall in attendance was symptomatic of the problems confronting baseball. At the Major League level people were losing interest in the sport because it was dominated so completely by New York–area teams. Between 1947 and 1961, the first expansion period, the Yankees, Dodgers and Giants won 21 pennants and 12 World Series. Some of these pennant races were exciting, and a handful of the World Series were among the most dramatic in baseball history. But overall the dominance of these three teams robbed the sport of its competitive edge. The three New York teams themselves suffered at the gate. In 1947 they attracted 5,591,000 fans. Ten years later the figure was 3,179,000, a decline of 43 percent!

Another factor that contributed to baseball's loss of fans was the growth of new leisure-time activities for the males who constituted the largest part of baseball's audience. Hunting, fishing, boating, golf, bowling and tennis all boomed in the two decades after the war. The prosperity of these years, exemplified by real disposable income that increased by 38 percent, enabled people to follow activities that before the war had been limited to the wealthy.

The enormous growth in popularity of television also served to keep people from the ballpark. The impact of television caused baseball problems similar to those posed by radio in the 1930s. The baseball owners didn't know whether to embrace or spurn the new medium because it seemed to threaten their conception of the game. The owners were afraid that TV would keep people at home. They failed to realize that television would create new fans, especially among young people, just as radio had. Nor did the owners recognize the enormous economic possibilities of television. Even so, by 1960 each Major League team received $783,000 from a national television contract, a figure that would grow slowly in the 1960s, speed up in the 1970s and explode dramatically in the 1980s.

The deterioration of the neighborhoods in which many of the older ballparks were located further contributed to baseball's problems after the war. With the suburbs booming and car ownership becoming commonplace, the public began avoiding the older ballparks, especially those located in decaying or racially changing neighborhoods. Most of the ballparks were built or rebuilt between 1909 and 1923, a time when the inner cities housed a majority of the urban population. These parks were built to take advantage of the new trolley, bus or subway systems created in the first quarter of the twentieth century.

Ebbets Field, the holder of the National League attendance record for almost a decade after the war, had exactly 700 parking spaces. Shibe Park, located in a declining neighborhood, had space for less than 1000 cars. The problem was duplicated all over the Majors.

All of these factors came together in the early 1950s to create the first franchise moves since the reorganization of the Majors in the opening years of the twentieth century. The Boston Braves, St. Louis Browns, and Philadelphia Athletics, plagued by terrible attendance, moved to what they hoped could be greener pastures between 1952 and 1954 — Milwaukee, Baltimore and Kansas City respectively. They were followed in 1958 by baseball's greatest restructuring — the move of the Brooklyn Dodgers and New York Giants to California — making baseball truly a continental game for the first time.

These franchise shifts reflected deep problems for baseball and created a sense that the game had lost its direction. For two teams the franchise move proved transitory. Within a few years the Milwaukee Braves and Kansas City Athletics were preparing to move again. Only the Baltimore Orioles were a long-term success. The California experiment was a success waiting to happen once transcontinental air flights became possible. The movement of the Dodgers to Los Angeles was shrewdly managed by Walter O'Malley and eventually made them the most successful franchise in all sport. The Giants were marginally successful in San Francisco. The city never took to them the way New York had or the way Los Angeles embraced the Dodgers. Still, the continental shift of baseball was long overdue. Larry MacPhail had talked about the concept for years, arguing for the creation of a truly representative sport for all of North America, including Canada, Mexico and even Cuba.

The franchise shifts came at a time when baseball suddenly seemed like an old, slow game. The game as played in the late 1940s and most of the 1950s had virtually no movement. Hit-and-run plays were rare, bunting was used only occasionally, and there was virtually no base stealing. The game consisted of waiting around for someone to hit the long ball, preferably the home run. Home runs rose to all-time highs in the 1950s. A total of 1000 homers had been hit in 1945 by both leagues, and 1215 were hit in the first season after the war. In 1961 that figure reached 2700, or an increase of 270 percent over 1945. At the same time base stealing stagnated. In 1950 Dom DiMaggio led the American League with just 15 steals. Even fast runners like Jackie Robinson, Richie Ashburn or later Willie Mays stole a base only when they had to. The game revolved around moving one base at a time or circling all four behind the home run.

Baseball in this fifteen year period was in danger of losing its audience to sports like football, which was better adapted to television and seen as a much livelier game, especially following the dramatic Giants-Colts championship game of 1958. Together with other leisure-time activities in this affluent era, baseball was a big loser.

Even some of the positive developments of this era in baseball history did not benefit the sport. The long overdue integration of the game, which began in 1947 with the arrival of Jackie Robinson, was at too slow a pace to affect the game. As late as 1953 there were only 23 blacks out of 400 players in the Majors. Some very successful teams like the Yankees, Red Sox, Tigers and Phillies held off signing blacks until well into the 1950s. Aside from Jackie Robinson and Willie Mays, no black players were major gate attractions. Nor were there any Latin players to lure new fans to the game until Roberto Clemente became popular in the early 1960s.

Baseball was cursed by unimaginative ownership in this era. The cleverest magnates — MacPhail, Branch Rickey or Bill Veeck — were on the outs with the baseball establishment. Major League baseball's dominant figure was

Walter O'Malley, a shrewd businessman with sound baseball sense but a cold-hearted pragmatism. MacPhail left baseball after the 1947 season and had no input into the sport he had helped to revolutionize in the 1930s and early 1940s through ideas like night baseball and radio broadcasting. Veeck had great success for a couple of years with the Indians, then failed to revitalize the Browns, only to surface again in the late 1950s for a brief success with the White Sox. But he had to fight the establishment at every point. Rickey was ousted in a power play by O'Malley in 1950. He resurfaced with the Pirates and eventually built them into a forceful franchise by the end of the decade. But by then he was out of the Majors. He reappeared late in the decade as one of the powers behind the new concept of a third Major League, the Continental League, which was largely responsible for baseball's first expansion since the formation of the Major Leagues. There was no place in baseball during the fifteen years after World War II for any kind of maverick.

By 1960 Major League baseball was on the brink of a new era of expansion and popularity, but it would not have the sport field to itself as it had in the 1920s. Professional football threatened baseball's popularity and would overtake it by the late 1960s and early 1970s. But Leonard Koppett, the baseball writer and keen student of the sport's history, has observed that 1960 was as distinct a dividing line in baseball history as 1920, when Babe Ruth launched the lively-ball era. Around 1960, he argues, baseball "became entirely different...ending for all time the neat patterns of the eight team, 154 game leagues" (Koppett, 1995). In that sense, the fifteen year period after World War II constitutes, if not a Golden Era of baseball, the end of the game's first phase, which had begun in 1903 with the emergence of the two, eight-team leagues.

1

Baseball Recovers
from the War, 1946

Back to Normalcy

On September 2, 1945, as the Japanese signed the surrender document aboard the USS *Missouri* to end the worst conflict in human history, the Philadelphia Phillies beat the Boston Braves 6–3. In the starting lineup for these two teams that afternoon were ten players who would be out of the Major Leagues before the start of the next season, a reflection of the low level of professional baseball during the last year of the war.

Baseball barely survived World War II. Most of the game's greatest stars were lost for three years or more: Joe DiMaggio, Ted Williams, Hank Greenberg, Bob Feller (to mention just a few). Of 565 wartime Major Leaguers, 509 served in the military in some capacity, leaving the game to 4F types, teenagers and over-the-hill veterans. Two of the youngest players in the game's history appeared during the war. Joe Nuxhall was 15 when he pitched two-thirds of an inning for the Cincinnati Reds in 1944, and 16-year-old Tommy Brown played 46 games for the Brooklyn Dodgers that same year. Among veterans who played during the war, the great Babe Herman was in 37 games for the 1945 Dodgers. He hadn't played in the Majors since 1937 and still was able to hit .265. More incredibly, Hod Lisenbee appeared in 31 games for the Reds, winning one and saving another at age 45. He had last pitched in the Majors in 1936. Two Major Leaguers — Harry O'Neil and Elmer Gedeon — were killed in the war, and a number were injured (Turner, 83). The level of baseball during the war years was low, the quality of player marginal at best.

Of those injured in the war, some suffered shortened careers. Cecil Travis, an outstanding shortstop–third baseman for the Washington Senators, had his feet frozen in the Battle of the Bulge and never recovered his prewar level of play. He had hit .359, second to Ted Williams' .401 in 1941. A lifetime .314 hitter, Travis played a season and a half, hitting .252 and .216, before retiring at 34. He believed that it was his frozen feet as much as the loss of youth that shortened his career. "You didn't have to be off but just a hair and you couldn't play" (Kindred, "Baseball Legend," *Philadelphia Inquirer*, 1/1/95, sect. C, p. 5).

His teammate Buddy Lewis, a career .300 hitter before the war, flew the Hump in Burma. He came back to baseball prematurely gray-haired at 29 and was out of baseball after two and a half years at age 33. Lewis just lost the taste for baseball. The game no longer seemed important to him. Despite what the war cost him, Lewis says it was a great experience that he would not want to have missed (Lewis to author, 1/22/95). Phil Marchildon, one of Connie Mack's brightest pitching prospects, had been a prisoner of war. He had a couple of good years, including winning 19 games in 1947, but his teammates believed his career was shortened by his wartime experiences (Crissey, 43–44). The other Major Leaguer whose career was effectively ended by the war was John Grodzicki, a big, highly regarded right-handed pitcher for the Cardinals, who suffered from shell fragments in his leg. He spent most of 1946 on the disabled list and never became the pitcher the Cardinals expected him to be. He was out of baseball by the end of 1947.

Major League baseball, like the nation itself, looked toward the postwar period with a combination of optimism and trepidation. There were predictions of labor strife, runaway inflation and widescale unemployment as millions of people tried to adjust to a new society. This view alternated with a growing confidence that the prosperity of the war would continue while the nation converted its wartime industries to peacetime uses. On the positive side, weekly earnings had risen by 80 percent since Pearl Harbor, to $44.39. Total wartime savings reached the staggering figure of $136 billion. (To get some idea of how this would translate into modern purchasing power, 1946 figures should be multiplied by eight.) And even more important, the GI Bill promised veterans a college or technical education at the expense of the nation. The government also allowed returning veterans $20 per week for a year, the famous "52-20" club. It was hoped that all of these factors would hold off hard times and banish the haunted memories of the Great Depression.

The 1945 season, with attendance approaching 11 million, surprised the baseball owners and indicated that the public had a growing thirst for baseball. Attendance figures had stagnated since the golden days of the 1920s. In fact, baseball attendance had dipped by 12 percent during the depression decade. The figures for the early 1940s were not much better. The Boston Braves drew 208,000 fans in 1944; the St. Louis Browns attracted 188,000 the year before. No Major League team drew one million fans in 1943 or 1944, and only one, the Dodgers, did so in 1942. The owners looked to 1946 with enthusiasm, especially because they would have their stars back. Will Harridge, the dull and sober president of the American League, was uncharacteristically enthusiastic during spring training. He estimated that the American League would have 260 of 300 players with Major League experience discharged from the military (*NYT*, 1/19/46, p. 18; 4/14/46, p. 2).

Demobilization of baseball players had actually begun in 1945. Bob Feller came out of the Navy in 1945 and resumed his domination of American League hitters. His record was 5-3 with an ERA of 2.50. In 72 innings he struck out 59 batters. Even more significantly, Hank Greenberg, after almost four years in the Army, was instrumental in helping the Tigers win the pennant and World Series in 1945. In half a season Greenberg clubbed 13 homers, drove in 60 runs and batted .311. His homers sealed the pennant for the Tigers that season. Others, including Joe DiMaggio, could have played toward the end of the 1945 season but preferred to use the off-season to get into shape. Some baseball players and owners feared that the players would find it difficult to return to prewar quality of play. This was especially true of those who lost key years out of their careers, players 30 to 32 years old when the war broke out. In many cases these fears were well founded.

Baseball also recognized that wartime play had deteriorated badly by 1945 and worried about the consequences for the next season. A comparison of the records of some key players in 1945 with 1946 tells much about what baseball was like in the last year of the war. About a dozen players who had fine 1945 seasons flopped badly in 1946. For example, John Dickshot and Tony Cuccinello, who were second and third in the 1945 American League batting race, did not make a Major League roster in 1946. In the National League, the third-leading hitter at .325, Goody Rosen of the Dodgers, slipped 44 points in 1946 and was out of baseball after the season. Elvin "Buster" Adams of the Cards was fourth in RBIs with 109 and third in homers with 22 in 1945. He dropped to 22 RBIs and 5 homers the next year and was finished as a ballplayer at 32 in 1947. The second-leading home-run hitter in the league with 25, Chuck Workman of the Braves, hit exactly four homers in 1946 and was out of baseball by the end of the year. Among pitchers the two biggest flops from 1945 to 1946 were Charles "Red" Barrett, who won 23 with the 1945 Cards and dropped to 3 wins the next year, and Roger Wolff, the Senators' knuckleballer, who won 20 games in 1945 and exactly 6 the rest of his career.

Even some talented players had difficulties adjusting to the postwar environment. Johnny Vander Meer, author of the only back-to-back no-hitters in baseball history, found the first year back from the war difficult from a physical standpoint. He said it took him "another year to get back into shape. We had to build up our stamina again" (Gilbert, 266).

Other players like Warren Spahn, Johnny Sain and Ralph Houk believed that the military experience had matured them. Houk felt that his service in the Army gave him more understanding of the "problems young men have and the pressures they go through, not only in war, but in baseball" (Gilbert, 266).

Along with adjustment to new playing conditions the baseball owners confronted the postwar era with a new untried commissioner, former senator Albert "Happy" Chandler. Chandler had succeeded the legendary Kenesaw Mountain Landis, who died in 1944. Chandler was an unknown quality. A skilled pol who had served as governor and senator from Kentucky, he was a notorious gladhander who had been campaigning behind the scenes for the commissioner's job for years. The baseball establishment had no intention of allowing him the kind of authority that Landis had developed after he became commissioner at the height of the Black Sox scandal in 1920.

What also foreshadowed problems for Major League baseball was the anger of many returning players at the way the owners had taken advantage of the wartime wage freeze to keep salaries artificially low. In 1941 Hank Greenberg had been baseball's highest paid player at $55,000. In 1944 Bill Dickey, the Yankees' great catcher, had that honor but with a salary of just $22,500 (Voigt, 3: 261). For some salary comparison, Cary Grant earned $150,000 in 1946 (Steinberg, 68). Given the growing union militancy in the country, this situation would create problems during the 1946 season.

In fact 1946 turned out to be the worst year of labor strikes in recent American history. The buildup of savings with no place to spend the money drove prices up and combined with the ending of the Office of Price Administration controls led to runaway inflation. One estimate had the cost of living rising by 75 percent at times during 1946. At various times 5,000,000 men were on strike in what one historian called a "spontaneous backfire to the end of war time austerity" (Manchester, 400).

Murphy Money

During spring training, Robert Murphy, a 35-year-old Harvard-trained lawyer and former examiner for the National Labor Relations Board, attempted to organize a union of professional baseball players, the American Baseball Guild. Rumors abounded throughout 1945 that the CIO was going to unionize the Major Leagues after the war. Murphy beat them to it.

On April 14, 1946, he formally registered the Guild as an independent union in Suffolk County, Massachusetts. He announced that the Guild would not be affiliated with either the CIO or the AFL. During February he had visited spring training camps trying to sign players for his guild. He continued through the opening weeks of the season, claiming eventually to have substantial membership on ten or eleven Major League teams and a simple majority on four or five teams. He hinted that several "big name players" were among the signees.

Murphy outlined a five-point program for the Guild, stipulating among other things that any money from a player's sale was to be divided equally among the player and his team, no player would receive less than a $6,500 wage, and disputes over salary and playing conditions would be subject to collective bargaining. Because he wanted to wait until the Guild was solidly established, he avoided a frontal attack on baseball's bastion of power, the reserve clause.

Murphy argued that past efforts to organize baseball had failed because conditions were not propitious. But World War II changed all that. "Back in the old days," he said, "there was no National Labor Relations Act. Today we have the law behind us." Even people as anti-union as political columnist Westbrook Pegler understood Murphy's case. Pegler argued that if baseball was unionized the owners would only have themselves to blame. "Not all, but enough of them, have been harsh and arrogant, mean in money matters and completely ruthless in imposing on the players"("Strike One," *Business Week*, 4/26/46, pp. 92–94; "Baseball Strikes Out," *Newsweek*, 6/7/46, pp. 90–91; and Gould, 135–137).

Murphy's efforts to form a union came at an opportune time. Along with increased union activity in 1946 two other unrelated developments gave him increased leverage. New, younger owners like Dan Topping and Del Webb of the Yankees, Lou Perini of the Boston Braves and Robert Carpenter of the Philadelphia Phillies, although not sympathetic to unionism, understood the changing times better than did older dinosaurs like the Comiskeys, the Wrigleys or Connie Mack. The younger owners were willing to accept some changes in player-owner relations. Murphy also benefited from the growing threat of the Mexican League, which began raiding Major League baseball in late 1945 and early 1946 with enough success to scare the owners. Players sensed that for the first time since the outlaw Federal League days they had some bargaining power.

Baseball's owners recognized the seriousness of Murphy's challenge from the first. In an article that appeared in the *New York Times* early in the 1946 season, Clark Griffith, one of the game's senior owners and a notorious penny-pincher, spelled out baseball's case against Murphy. All the familiar arguments were trotted out. Unionization would destroy the reserve clause, which Griffith said was the heart of baseball. All the game's stars would also wind up on one team, the same argument used thirty years later when the reserve clause was finally declared illegal.

Griffith also resorted to good, old-fashioned Americanism to thwart Murphy. "Eventually collective bargaining," he said, "would put a ceiling on salaries and destroy initiative. The better players would go into some other business." He argued further that baseball was fair with rookies, thus obviating the need for a $7,500 minimum. They made between $4,500 and $5,000 according to Griffith, up from about $3,000 before the war (*NYT*, 4/22/46, p. 27).

Murphy decided to concentrate on one team as a way of demonstrating to the baseball establishment that his union effort was serious. He chose the Pittsburgh Pirates because Pittsburgh was such a strong union town that pressure might be brought to bear on Pirates ownership. Murphy believed that by successfully threatening a strike or walkout he could force management throughout the Majors to meet his specific demands and gain recognition for the Guild. His tactics backfired.

He initially issued some confusing statistics. Early in the 1946 season he claimed that pay levels for Major League baseball were horrendous despite an obvious boom in attendance. Citing the Boston Braves as an example, he said that 40 percent of the players were making less than $5,000 a year. Ford Frick, president of the National League, contradicted him and pointed out that only 29 of 250 National League players earned less than $5,000 and the league average was $9,500 (Scully, 105). Murphy was forced to admit that his figures were wrong (*NYT*, 7/16/46, p. 31).

In fact, baseball salaries in 1946, although good compared to other professional sports, were still low. Of 480 Major Leaguers only 15 made $20,000, and six (DiMaggio, Williams, Greenberg, Dick Wakefield, Feller and Lou Boudreau) made $25,000. Nineteen National League players and 31 American Leaguers made less than $5,000 (Turner, 56).

Murphy then tried to step up the pressure on the owners by issuing statements designed to show the growing popularity of the Guild among the players. He told the *New York Times* that 80 percent of the Pirates had signed with the Guild. Besides the Pirates he had 90 percent of the players on one unnamed American League club and 60 to 70 percent of the members of four National League teams signed up. Murphy's figures were totally exaggerated. At that same time he tried to make his case seem more honest by admitting that he was having difficulties with certain teams: "The New York Yankees, Detroit and Boston Red Sox are proving pretty tough to crack." But he wasn't downhearted. "We intend to get some of the (unionization) done this season. We're not going to be tossed about" (*NYT*, 6/5/46, p. 27).

Murphy was bluffing. He hoped for that one dramatic success that would start an avalanche in favor of the Guild. But the danger was that if his bluff failed the whole concept might collapse.

Murphy informed William Benswanger, president of the Pirates, that because a majority of his players supported the Guild, a collective bargaining election was called for. Benswanger was part of the Dreyfus family that had owned the Pirates since 1900. He was an elderly, kindly gentleman-owner genuinely liked by his players (Turner, 139). If Benswanger did not allow an election, Murphy said he would seek a hearing before the National Labor Relations Board (NLRB). He also set early June, while the Pirates were on a homestand, as the date for a test strike vote. President Truman, who recently had unsuccessfully tried to seize the steel industry, was jokingly asked by a reporter if he would now try to take control of baseball. The Missourian joked by saying if he had his way he would put all the baseball stars on the two St. Louis teams ("Baseball Strikes Out," *Newsweek*, 6/7/46, p. 91).

The baseball establishment didn't see any humor in the situation. They planned to meet the challenge head-on by forming a joint player-management committee to prepare a new contract for the Major Leagues.

On June 7 Murphy suffered a major setback when the Pirate players voted at a closed two-hour meeting against going on strike. The players, coaches and trainers had actually voted 20–16 to strike, but Murphy had agreed to a ⅔ rule before a strike would be called. Before the vote Pirate manager Frankie Frisch told them to stick by the team. He also said that rather than forfeit he would field a team of coaches including himself and 72-year-old Honus Wagner. Murphy appealed his defeat to the NLRB charging intimidation of the players. But it was becoming clear that he could not deliver on his threat to paralyze baseball (*ibid.*, p. 92; *NYT*, 6/8/46, p. 24; 6/9/46, III, p. 1).

After the NLRB refused to intervene on the grounds "that professional baseball did not fall under its charge to oversee labor management relations in interstate commerce," Murphy turned to the Pennsylvania NLRB, which agreed to set a formal election for the Guild later in the summer (Jennings, 11). This was a tactical victory for Murphy, but it gave the owners time to undermine the Guild.

Murphy miscalculated. He thought that the extra time would convince wavering players to support the union. He also believed that he would win his case before the Pennsylvania NLRB (Lowenfish, 145). The owners had gotten the word out to the players that they were going to issue a new charter for the Majors that would effectively answer Murphy's complaints. On August 20 the Pirate players met again and this time voted by 15 to 3 to reject the Guild as a bargaining agent. Only 18 of the eligible players voted. Among the team starters Billy Cox, Al Gerhauser, Frank Gustine, Lee Handley and Al Lopez didn't vote. Rip Sewell, the veteran blooper-ball pitcher and one of the highest paid Pirates at $10,000, spoke for the majority: "I'm in favor of any union for men who can't help themselves — like in the coal mines and in steel mills...but I'd hate to see baseball unionized as a player has no limit on what he can earn in this game." Chandler had helped defuse the crisis. He informed Pee Wee Reese and Dixie Walker that the players would have access to his office and the offices of the two league presidents to present any complaints they had. Reese and Walker relayed that information to Sewell, who used it in his argument against going on strike (*SN*, 4/7/51, p. 4).

The individualism that Griffith had put his finger on in his piece in the *New York Times* summed up the attitude of most Major Leaguers. The very individual nature of the game, pitcher versus batter, batter on his own against the eight men in front of him, made players think not as a unit but as isolated figures. Seventy years of this mentality, reinforced by an American suspicion of unions as protecting the unworthy, undermined Murphy's efforts to organize the players.

Murphy was furious at being so completely outmaneuvered. He attributed his defeat to the "pretended fairness of the owner-dominated player management committee. ... They will give the players an apple instead of an orchard." He predicted that the Guild idea would eventually triumph. "The players will realize that the club owners who have had seventy years to change...never acted until the American Baseball Guild threatened the very foundations — sometimes rotten — of their baseball empire"(*NYT*, 8/21/46, p. 30). He was correct, but he was making a case that too many players were unable to absorb in the face of the great changes sweeping the nation after the war. It would take time for Murphy's views to sink in.

Although Murphy continued his efforts on behalf of the Guild, he was beaten, and he knew it. In late November the *New York Times* reported that he was trying to unionize professional hockey players — quite a comedown from America's premier sport to a game that many Americans considered foreign and minor. Rip Sewell had been right. Baseball players didn't see themselves as miners or steelworkers. They viewed themselves as professionals and profoundly accepted the concept that there was no limit on their financial future.

In one sense Murphy was right. He laid the groundwork for the organization of ballplayers that would begin feebly in the anti-union Eisenhower years, grow stronger in the more radical 1960s and then culminate in the Marvin Miller era, when power would pass to the players as completely as it had once rested with the owners.

The threat of unionization did gain the players a new deal from the owners in 1946. During July and August the owners on seven different occasions invited 26 players, representing all teams, to meet with them to draft a new players contract (Lowenfish, 148). Called with typical overblown rhetoric baseball's "Magna Carta" (the term was coined by New York writer Dan Daniel), the new standard players contract did meet some of their demands (Turner, 197), but as Murphy had predicted, it was a basket of apples, not the orchard. It established a minimum salary of $5,000, provided players with $500 for moving expenses if they were sold or traded to another club, guaranteed full payment should a player be injured while playing, allowed greater barnstorming where players could make lucrative sums in the off-season and, most significantly, established a pension program for players, coaches and even trainers. The new contract was funded with $650,000 from the All-Star Game and $150,000 from radio broadcasting rights.

The new deal for players postponed unionization of baseball for two decades. The pension plan was particularly popular with the players. As Jim Brosnan noted some years later, even if you lost a game, "Well, at least, it's one more day in the pension plan" (Miller, 13). The Chicago sportswriter John C.

Carmichael, who was sympathetic to ownership, hailed the new contract as heralding "a better era for the game. Everything considered," he said with vast overstatement, "the new contract leaves the players holding all the aces" (Carmichael, 52).

The new contract remained the basic one for the Major Leagues until the demise of the reserve clause in the 1970s. Despite protests over the years the new approach kept player discontent largely under control. To some extent the new contract was an example of enlightened thinking on the part of the owners. But the real lesson from this incident was that ownership would do nothing until their hand was forced.

Mexican Hay Ride

At the same time that the baseball solons were dealing with the threat of unionization, they were challenged from south of the border — a good neighbor policy in reverse. Five Mexican brothers, all famously wealthy, the Pasquels, of whom Jorge was the guiding genius, laid siege to baseball's monopoly in the most serious confrontation since the founding of the Federal League thirty years earlier.

The Pasquels' wealth was derived from vast holdings in land, cattle and a hugely successful customs brokerage business. More significantly, they were close to the immensely corrupt ruling political establishment, the Institutional Revolutionary Party, that had run Mexican politics since the 1911 revolution. As a result they got federal patronage, and their customs business handled more government shipping than any competitor. It didn't hurt that they were on a first-name basis with the president of Mexico, Miguel Aleman. The Pasquels knew their way around the corrupt Mexican political system, which was good training for challenging the baseball establishment.

The Pasquels' wealth was estimated at between $20 and $60 million, depending on whom Jorge, the family spokesman, was talking to. He had a con man's talent for exaggeration. By any measure the Pasquels were rich, and in 1946 they set their sights on the Major Leagues as a pool of talent to upgrade Mexican baseball.

The Mexican League had done well in 1945, earning profits of over $400,000, but the Pasquels knew that the return of the prewar American stars would turn the baseball-mad Mexican fans' attention to north of the border. They also grasped the potential profits that could be made if they could gain recognition for the Mexican League as equal to the American Majors.

Beginning just before spring training, the Pasquels began peddling lucrative contracts to various players. Their plan was to lure about 30 to 40 name Major League players to Mexico over a couple of years, thus improving league play gradually. In order to spread the talent fairly, the Pasquels put a limit of seven American Major Leaguers on the roster of any Mexican team much in the way Japanese baseball did later. Their initial signees were marginal players, often Latins, like Nap Reyes of the Giants and Roberto Estalella of the Washington Senators, mixed in with a handful of wartime successes like outfielder Danny Gardella of the Giants. Their biggest catch early in the year was Luis Olmo, the Dodger outfielder who had hit .313 in 1945. Branch Rickey, who had made a career of outsmarting his competitors, expressed disgust at the foul deeds of the Pasquels. He threatened lawsuits and other forms of revenge if Olmo went south of the border. Jorge smiled at Rickey's protests and said he just "liberated" Olmo from the Dodgers for $40,000 for three years (*Time*, 5/11/46, p. 89).

The baseball establishment first became concerned when the Pasquels switched their attention to more name players like catcher Mickey Owen of the Dodgers and Vern Stephens, the star shortstop of the desperately poor St. Louis Browns. Rickey was furious to discover that the Pasquels had even set their sights on Jackie Robinson, who was about to break the color barrier in professional baseball by playing with the Triple-A Montreal team. Fortunately for Rickey and for baseball, Robinson rejected a lucrative offer and remained with the Dodger organization (*NYT*, 5/20/46, p. 26).

The Pasquels reeled in Owen before the 1946 season with a bonus of $12,500 and an offer to be a player-manager. Stephens signed a five-year deal but after playing just two games in Mexico decided to return to the Browns. They rewarded him with a nice raise, and he returned his bonus money to the Pasquels. Showing that if nothing else he had a Major League sense of humor, Jorge now began to outmaneuver the baseball owners with a series of clever public-relations ploys. He lured Babe Ruth, still the biggest name in baseball and on the outs with the Major League owners, to Mexico for a two-week tour. The tour included batting demonstrations and an opportunity for Ruth to see the quality of play in Mexico. Jorge hoped that Ruth's presence would lend validity to Mexican baseball.

Ruth responded to Jorge's handling favorably. He complimented the Pasquels, saying that they were making a fine contribution to baseball. They deserved credit according to Ruth because "baseball is a game that should be played all over the world. It keeps kids out of trouble and develops them into better citizens (*ibid.*, 5/16/46, p. 25).

Ruth was cheered everywhere he went in Mexico. He had trouble hitting because he was now over fifty and in terrible shape. Occasionally he hit a ball out of the park, and the fans went wild. One of Mexico's leading matadors, Edmundo Zepeda, even dedicated a bull to Ruth (*ibid.*, 6/1/46, p. 17).

Jorge's gamble with Ruth paid off. Not only did the Babe say nice things about Mexico, but he appreciated the royal treatment he was shown in comparison to the cold shoulder he had received at the hands of the baseball establishment in America. The Mexicans thoroughly enjoyed the Major Leagues' embarrassment at Ruth's tour. Jorge had touched on a deep sense of satisfaction in Mexico by tweaking Uncle Sam's nose. Jorge was a St. Jorge slaying the dragon of Yankee baseball.

Jorge used some other public-relations gimmicks. He leaked a report that he had offered Commissioner Chandler an extra $50,000 to also serve as president of the Mexican leagues while continuing to lead the Majors. Jorge recognized that this had the effect of equating the two leagues.

Chandler, whose ego was as large as his sense of humor was tiny, responded by announcing that any Major Leaguer who signed a Mexican contract would be banned from American baseball for five years. This didn't stop the bleeding. More players left the Majors almost every week during spring training and the early weeks of the season. The most important signings the Pasquels made were from the Cardinals: Max Lanier, a first-class pitcher, and Fred Martin, a capable outfielder.

Jorge kept up the pressure all spring by leaking to the press huge offers in the range of $100,000 to $150,000 to name players like Phil Rizzuto and Snuffy Stirnweiss of the Yanks, Pete Reiser of the Dodgers, Whitey Kurowski of the Cards and Johnny Pesky of the Red Sox. Stan Musial, then making $13,500 for the Cards, was offered a contract worth six times that salary to desert to Mexico. The Pasquel brothers offered him five certified checks for $10,000 each. He was tempted but refused. Hal Newhouser, the winningest pitcher in baseball over the past two seasons, was approached with an offer that seemed inconceivable — $300,000, to be deposited in a bank of his choice, and a three-year contract worth $200,000. At the time he was among the highest paid players in baseball at $45,000. He told the Tiger management that he didn't want to go, but "the money meant a lot." The Tigers convinced him to stay by promising to take care of him in the future (Jordan, 174).

The Pasquels kept Major League baseball off balance throughout the 1946 season, but in the end, reports that leaked back from Mexico painted a grim picture of playing conditions: awful playing fields, no showers, strange foods. The Pasquels put up a brave front while admitting that all the contracts to American players had wiped out the profit the Mexican League had made in the past. They argued that this was temporary and predicted that 1947 would see a further upgrading of the Mexican game. They set their sights higher for the next year and included Ted Williams among their targets. In fact, the Pasquels' dream was over. The Mexican League challenge would fade before the 1947 season ended. The Major Leagues had proven resilient and showed enough adaptability to survive. A combination of a better contract for the players in 1946 and bad reports from south of the border saved American baseball from the Pasquels. Many American players showed little sympathy for those who deserted to Mexico. When Mickey Owen tried to return to the big leagues, Marty Marion, the Cardinal shortstop, remarked, "Owen jumped his team to go down there for that big money; now let him stay there" (*NYT*, 9/8/46, p. 25).

The Pasquels had given the baseball establishment a scare. They managed to sign 18 Major League players, although the majority were marginal at best. Only Max Lanier and perhaps Olmo would be considered first-line players. One future great, Sal Maglie, later admitted that he learned his profession pitching in Mexico.

Chandler's five-year suspension was not lifted until 1949, when one of the blacklisted ball players, Danny Gardella, brought a lawsuit against the Majors. When Gardella settled out of court for $60,000, Chandler was willing in his words "to temper justice with mercy" and lift the ban (Dworkin, 59). This was a wise move because it made baseball look good in the eyes of the public and the press, and the teams lost nothing and even got back a few good ballplayers. It also was better than letting the courts get involved in baseball matters. After the Gardella case was settled, Chandler told the press, "I feel so relieved. If I were a drinking man I'd get drunk" (Lowenfish, 157).

In the final analysis the Majors survived the threat from the Pasquels because baseball had such a phenomenal year in 1946, with record-breaking attendance figures reflecting an enormous thirst in the country for having its game back from the war.

The Pasquels picked a bad time to deliver their challenge to the American game. There was a great deal of talk after the war about better relations between the United States and Latin America, but in reality Americans did not take the Latinos seriously. A deep prejudice about the competence and abilities of the Mexicans ran through American society. The flashiness of the Pasquels only confirmed the American view that Mexicans were not reliable.

The Stars Are Back

The 1946 season proved to be both a great success and something of a letdown. It witnessed a huge boom in attendance but was not particularly competitive. Almost from the start of spring training the crowds were extraordinary, as though the fans were saying that they couldn't wait to see their heroes and return baseball to normal. The great crowds continued into the season itself as one team after another shattered attendance records. The owners were thrilled as the money poured in. The attendance boom even extended to the minors, where teams thrived as never before. Baseball had entered a period of success not seen since the golden age of the 1920s.

Eventually the Majors drew a record-breaking 18 million fans, and the figure for the minors was an astounding 31 million. For the Majors the gain over 1945 was seven million, the largest single season increase in baseball history. The minors drew 20 million more than the previous year. It appeared that fans were starved for baseball of any kind. Money was unimportant because of the huge savings accrued during the war. Ticket prices remained low. According to one study the price of an average baseball ticket in 1988 dollars for the first postwar season was $2.39 (Scully, 105). Many of the Major League teams still set aside parts of their stadiums for wounded soldiers, although they gradually dropped other World War II gimmicks, such as free admission to men or women in uniform (*SN*, 6/12/46, p. 6). A contributing factor to the rise in attendance was the growth of night baseball. The Yankees and Boston Braves added lights in time for the 1946 season, leaving only the Red Sox, Tigers and Cubs without them. Gas rationing had ended, and this made it easier for some fans to get to the ballpark. Finally, the demobilization of the military returned 10 to 12 million young males to civilian life. They constituted a natural audience for baseball at all levels that hadn't been available for three and a half years.

The most successful teams in 1946 in attendance were not necessarily the best. The lowly Phillies broke the one million mark for the first time in their history with a team of older players mixed in with a few younger future stars, such as Rookie of the Year designee, Del Ennis. The Phillies' increase over 1945 was in excess of 800,000. The club rewarded the faithful by giving a car to the one millionth fan in late September.

The Phillies' success in 1946 marked the beginning of a shift of fan loyalty in Philadelphia from Connie Mack's Athletics to the National League club. The Phillies, now backed by DuPont money, not only outdrew the A's that year but continued to do so for the next decade, despite some better-than-average Athletic teams. Ultimately the Phils' success spelled the end of the A's in Philadelphia and prepared the way for their flight to Kansas City in 1955 (Kuklick, 92).

Other sharp increases were recorded by the third-place Yankees, who jumped from 882,000 to 2,265,000 to become the first team to break the two million mark, and the Red Sox, whose increase was 800,000 fans over 1945. The Detroit Tigers, despite failing to repeat as pennant winners, increased their attendance by over 440,000 fans. Other than the Phillies, big gains in the National League were recorded by the Dodgers, whose increase over 1945 was 700,000, Boston for a net gain of 590,000 and the pennant-winning Cardinals, who drew almost a half million more in 1946 than in 1945. In all, 11 of the 16 Major League franchises set attendance records in 1946.

On the field the two pennant races were a study in contrasts. *The Sporting News* picked the Cardinals and the Yankees to win the pennant in 1946. They expected the Braves, Dodgers and Cubs to compete in the National League, whereas the Tigers and Red Sox were regarded as threats to the Yanks in the American League. The choices made sense in that both the Yankees and Cardinals had dominated baseball in the years just before the war.

The Sporting News was right about the nature of the competition. They couldn't have foreseen the collapse of the Yankees or the intense level of play of the Dodgers. The American race was over for all practical purposes by the middle of May, after the Red Sox swept 15 games in a row between April 25 and May 10. The Red Sox opened a six-game lead over the second-place Yankees by Memorial Day, with Washington and the Tigers lagging ten games back. The Red Sox gradually widened the gap until by Labor Day their lead over the second place Yankees was 13½ games.

The Red Sox coasted home behind a superb pitching staff led by Dave "Boo" Ferris's, Cecil "Tex" Hughson and Mickey Harris, who together won 62 games. The Red Sox also had the most solid hitting team in the American League, led by Ted Williams, Bobby Doerr, Johnny Pesky and Dom DiMaggio. Rudy York, who came from the Tigers early in 1946 for infielder Eddie Lake, drove in 119 runs, and Doerr was steady at second and also drove in 116. Williams lost the batting title to the surprise winner, Mickey Vernon of the Senators, but still hit .342, drove in 123 runs, led the league in runs scored with 142 and hit 38 homers. Pesky led the league in hits and was third in hitting with a .335 average.

When the Red Sox got off to a fast start, the Tigers were not worried. Their manager, Steve O'Neill, said that once the Red Sox settled down, the rest of the pack would catch up to them, especially as the Red Sox were notoriously poor outside of Fenway Park. O'Neill was wrong. The Red Sox played close to .700 ball all season (*SN*, 5/16/46, p. 7).

The Tigers failed to get untracked until too late in the season. They staggered for the first two thirds of the season and then put on a rush in August. Eventually they won 92 games, four more than 1945, but were a distant second, 12 games behind the Red Sox. Hal Newhouser proved that he wasn't just a war-time fluke by winning 26 games tying Bob Feller for most wins in the Majors. In fact, Newhouser had a shot at 30 victories. He had 16 wins by the All Star break and won his 20th on July 26. Then elbow chips flared up and he won only 6 games the rest of the way. Still for the second straight season his ERA was under 2.00, not rare today but unheard of in those days of solid, contact hitting. He also struck out 275 while holding the opposition to a .201 average (Jordon, *Newhouser*, p. 178). Newhouser attributed his success to the fact that many returning players hadn't seen him since the war broke out. He was a changed pitcher, no longer the wild man who you could wait on for a fat pitch to hit. "I think I caught them all by surprise because my pitching technique had changed. Instead of ball one, ball two, it was strike one, strike two. Then ball one. So the whole pattern changed" (*ibid.*, p. 177). In fact, Newhouser like many southpaws had matured late. After struggling for five years he became an accomplished hurler when he was 25. Between 1944 and 1949 he would average over 20 wins a season.

Newhouser was helped by Dizzy Trout, Virgil Trucks and Fred Hutchinson to give the Tigers a solid rotation. But aside from Hank Greenberg the

Tigers hitting fell off badly. George Kell, obtained from the Athletics had a good year at third, hitting .327 but Dick Wakefield failed to regain the hitting stroke he showed before going into the service. Wakefield hit just .268, nowhere near the .300-plus seasons he had in 1943 and 1944. Greenberg opened the 1946 season with a homer against the Browns. By the All-Star break his batting average was only .275, but he had 55 RBIs and 22 homers, one behind Williams. Greenberg came on with a rush to win both the home-run and runs-batted-in titles with 44 and 127 respectively. No other Tiger hit more than 15 homers or drove in more than 59 runs. Of Detroit regulars in 1945 only Greenberg, Newhouser, Dizzy Trout, Al Benton and Virgil Trucks were starters one year later (Mead, 240).

Greenberg was clearly a tired player. He admitted that he had lost his enthusiasm for baseball after four years in the Army. "I wasn't physically in the same condition as I had been before I left. … Baseball wasn't that important. I had seen a lot of things happen in the world and I didn't think that baseball was the only thing in my life." Toward the end of 1946 he told a reporter for the *Boston Traveler* that it had been a tough season for him. "Playing baseball isn't fun anymore. It's hard work" (Berkow, 165–166, 169).

The collapse of the Yankees was the surprise of the 1946 season. The Yanks played fairly solid ball for the first half of the season. They were 7½ games out of first place on July 4. But they were suffering from too many injuries and internal problems by then. They collapsed in the second half of the season.

The team lost their manager, Joe McCarthy, in May. After 15 years as Yankee skipper, the so-called push-button manager called it a day. He had been losing interest in baseball since the end of the war. He was also drinking heavily. When Joe Page, then a starter, blew a game against the Cleveland Indians, McCarthy erupted on a plane trip to Detroit. The next day he flew home to his farm in New York state and resigned. Bill Dickey took over, but he was ill at ease managing people he had played with, and his relations with the new Yankee ownership were strained. He quit toward the end of the season and was succeeded by Johnny Neun, a coach (Golenbock, *Dynasty*, 19–20; Golenbock, *Fenway*, 171).

Part of the Yankee problem had to do with the difficulties that key players had recovering their prewar form. Joe DiMaggio opened the season with a homer against the A's and was tied for the home-run lead for about a month. But then, showing signs of poor conditioning, he gradually wore down, ending the year for the first time in his career under .300 at .290. He also failed to drive in 100 runs for the first time. He hit just 25 homers, the second-lowest total of his career at that point. The year 1946 was when DiMaggio published his autobiography, *Lucky to Be a Yankee*, but 1946 was anything but lucky for him.

Of the other Yankee regulars, only Charlie Keller approached prewar form. He hit 30 homers and drove in 101 runs. Tommy Henrich hit just .251, which was far below his career average. Even more shocking was the drop-off of Snuffy Stirnweiss. The 1945 batting champ hit 58 points below his league-leading average, hit no homers and drove in a grand total of 37 runs.

Joe Gordon, the Yanks' flashy second sacker, was even worse. The MVP of 1942 hit .210 with just 11 homers and 47 runs batted in. He was traded to Cleveland by Larry MacPhail at the end of the season for Allie Reynolds as the Yanks sought to prop up their weak pitching staff. It was a daring move by a daring baseball man. Gordon was a darling of the New York sportswriters, whereas Reynolds was largely an unproven pitcher with a slightly better than .500 record. He would help turn the Yankees into an American League power for the next decade. The Yankees' two biggest winners in 1946, Spud Chandler and Bill Bevens, were suspect. Chandler, who won 20 games, was 38 at the end of the year, and Bevens, with 16 wins, had only 1½ wartime seasons under his belt. Only one other Yankee pitcher, the unheralded Randy Gumpert, had more than ten wins.

MacPhail and his dour general manager, George Weiss, had started to lay the groundwork for the Yankee dynasty that would dominate baseball for the next 20 years. MacPhail was an executive genius who had already rebuilt two sagging franchises, Cincinnati in the 1930s and Brooklyn in the late 1930s and early 1940s. He bought into the Yankees in 1945 along with Del Webb and Dan Topping and immediately showed his sure touch. He ranks with Branch Rickey and Bill Veeck as one of the most innovative figures in baseball history. He introduced Red Barber to Major League broadcasting, inaugurated night baseball and was among the first executives to recognize the potential of television. He inherited a fine organization from Ed Barrow and continued running a first-class minor league system modeled after Rickey's St. Louis Cardinals. Out of many minor leaguers would come the future Major League stars: quantity leads to quality as Rickey had predicted.

MacPhail had a violent temper, drank heavily and was always fighting with someone, whether partner, sportswriter or his manager. Leo Durocher, when he was manager of the Dodgers, was fired literally hundreds of times by MacPhail. MacPhail was difficult to love, but he was respected. Weiss on the other hand was a cool establishment type. Naturally he survived long after MacPhail's career in baseball ended in 1947. Weiss wound up as general manager of the zany Mets, where he was constantly bewildered by a franchise that became more popular as it lost more games.

Except for the Red Sox, Tigers and Yanks no other teams in the American League finished over .500. The talent looked thin and concentrated at the top. More revealing was the seeming dearth of rookie talent. For example, no rookie finished in the top five in any hitting or pitching category. The American League was dominated by prewar players, some of whom, like Greenberg, were on their way out, or players like Newhouser, who had developed during the war. When John C. Carmichael in his popular summary of the baseball year, *Who's Who in the Major Leagues*, singled out the best American League rookies, he was left with Hoot Evers of the Tigers, the forgettable Chuck Stevens of the Browns and Hank Edwards of the Indians. This is not exactly a collection of future Hall of Famers. Edwards had one good year, 1946, when he hit .301, and Evers was a solid performer for a few years. He was also an enigma. He hit .300 for three straight years, 1948–1950, and then suffered one of the greatest declines in batting average in baseball history. After hitting .324 in 1950, he dropped to .223 the next year and never again hit better than .264. His teammate, George Kell, believed that Evers was afraid of success and didn't enjoy being in the spotlight. Stevens was out of the Majors by the end of the next season. To some extent this listing was not accurate. Those three may have played the most games of any rookies, but a number of really talented players got their feet wet in 1946. Vic Raschi won the first two games of his distinguished career late that year, and Yogi Berra came up briefly and at bat showed flashes of the skills that would take him to the Hall of Fame.

The problem for baseball and sports in general was that World War II had changed the thinking of many young men. Baseball still seemed a lucrative outlet to be sure, but returning vets had new horizons before them. The government not only guaranteed them a year with some pay, the 52 weeks at $20 per week program, but it also opened up an aspect of the American dream long denied many Americans — college. Millions took advantage of the GI Bill and flocked to colleges and universities, with the nation becoming the eventual winner in the process (Voigt, 3: xv–xvi).

Statistically the 1946 American League season was unremarkable. Team hitting was .001 better than 1945, whereas home runs increased by over 200 from 430 to 653. Team ERA was slightly higher than 1945 but still at 3.50, the lowest it would be until the great hitting slump of the late 1960s. The American League had returned to the brand of play that had characterized it before the war: lots of home runs, plenty of solid hitting and virtually no stolen bases. George Case, the Cleveland outfielder, led the league with 28 stolen bases. No other player had 20.

Mickey Vernon, first baseman for the Senators, beat out Ted Williams for the batting championship, .353 to .342. Only four players hit better than .320, in contrast to eight in 1941, the last true peacetime season. Hank Greenberg's 44 home runs were the most by an American Leaguer since 1938, when he hit 58 and Jimmy Foxx hit 50. Probably the single outstanding performance of the season was Bob Feller's 348 strikeouts, which broke the record established by Rube Waddell 40 years before. Feller also pitched the second no-hitter of his career, this time against the Yankees. Team hitting was off by 11 points from 1941, and pitching ERA was over a half run lower.

For the National League the first postwar season was remarkable. There was an exciting pennant race unlike in the American League. The favored Cardinals battled the underdog Dodgers in a seesaw battle the entire season. The Cubs and Braves, the other highly regarded clubs, failed to compete and wound up a distant third and fourth.

The Cards, with returning veterans like Stan Musial and Enos Slaughter, were easily the class of the league under their rookie manager, Eddie Dyer. The great organization created during the 1930s by baseball's most original thinker, Branch Rickey, was still producing quality players. The great Cardinal teams of the early to mid-1940s would soon wear out without Rickey's skilled hand directing them.

The Dodgers' success owed much to Leo Durocher's aggressive managing, especially his handling of a thin pitching staff led by the hard-throwing, hard-drinking southerner, Kirby Higbe. Durocher got double figures out of five men on the staff, but only Higbe won more than 15 games. Other than Higbe none of the Dodger starters were as effective as the Cards' big three: Howie Pollet, Harry Brecheen and Murray Dickson, who won 51 games among them. Durocher also used his everyday players to maximum advantage. On paper the Cards and Dodgers were not even close. A comparison of their starting lineups makes Durocher's managing job even more impressive.

	Dodgers	*Cards*
1B	Stevens .242	Musial .365
2B	Stanky .273	Schoendienst .281
3B	Lavagetto .242	Kurowski .301
SS	Reese .284	Marion .253
LF	Walker .319	Slaughter .300
CF	Furillo .284	Walker .237
RF	Reiser .277	Dusak .240
C	Edwards .267	Garagiola .237

Of the Dodger starters, Stanky, Reese and Furillo still had solid careers ahead of them. Peter Reiser was almost at the end of his tragic career at 27, the result of injuries brought on by his aggressive brand of play. He would never again get to bat 400 times in a season. Dixie Walker was still a fine hitter, but he was 35. Bruce Edwards seemed like a potential star, but he would hurt his arm in 1948 and never again be a first-class catcher. He lost his job in 1948 to Roy Campanella.

The Cardinal players had their best years ahead of them. Musial would dominate the National League for another decade. Enos Slaughter played quality baseball for the Cards into the early 1950s, and he was still a solid hitter into his late 30s for the Yankees. Marion and Schoendienst formed one of the National League's best double-play combinations. Both were solid hitters,

Howie Pollet. The stylish left-hander led the St. Louis Cardinals to a pennant in 1946, winning 21 games. He averaged over 200 innings and 15 wins between 1946 and 1950. During a 14-year career in the majors, Pollet won 131 games and hurled 25 shutouts. He twice led the National League in ERA, once with an incredibly low 1.75, a figure not topped until Sandy Koufax in 1964. (Brace Photo.)

especially Schoendienst. Harry Walker would win a batting title the next year with the Phillies. Even Joe Garagiola was a solid backstop despite his later jokes about his mediocre career.

During 1946 the Cards outhit the Dodgers by five points, slugged 26 more homers and had a slightly lower ERA. They had the league's leading hitter in Musial and the RBI champ in Slaughter. Slaughter was also third in homers.

Defensively the Cards were the best in the league, making only 124 errors for the year.

For most of the season the Cards and Dodgers exchanged the lead, staying within a few games of each other. A Brooklyn margin of five games on July 4 was transformed into a Cardinal lead of two games by Labor Day. The teams played close ball through September right up to the last day of the season. The Cards knew the Dodgers had been shut out by Mort Cooper of the Braves, 4–0. A Cardinal victory would have clinched the pennant, but a five-run inning by the Cubs beat them 8–3 and forced the first play-off in modern baseball history. Both teams finished with 96-58 records. This was the first of four play-offs in the period 1946–1962, a reflection of the close quality of the National League play in those years.

The 1946 play-offs were a letdown. Durocher won the toss and chose to start the best of three series in St. Louis, with the final two games to be played in Brooklyn. Ever the gambler, Durocher hoped to steal the first game and then take the Cards into Ebbet's Field, where the fanatical Dodger fans would give his team an advantage. His hunch backfired.

The Cards swept both games handily, largely because of their superior depth of pitching and more timely hitting. Howie Pollet beat Durocher's surprise starter, 20-year-old Ralph Branca, winner of exactly three games, in game one, and Murry Dickson stood off a late Brooklyn rally to win the second game, 8–4. The fact that the Dodgers were forced to use a 20 year old, the winner of exactly eight games in his brief career, in the biggest game of the year tells all you need to know about their pitching depth. The Dodgers were humiliated. Rickey, ever since he came over from the Cardinals in 1942, had been stockpiling talent in the minors even during the war years (Durocher, 219). He was laying the groundwork for a future dynasty that would pour talent into Brooklyn over the next decade. In fact, the Dodgers had 25 minor league teams in their system in 1946. Jackie Robinson, Gil Hodges, Duke Snider, Roy Campanella and Don Newcombe would come out of the Dodger organization between 1947 and 1949, enabling the Dodgers to dominate the National League for the next dozen years.

There is some evidence that Rickey never expected to compete in 1946. He believed that the Dodgers would begin to close the gap on the Cardinals in 1947 and then dominate the National League for the foreseeable future. He was as surprised as anyone that Durocher was able to drive the Dodgers to a pennant tie.

The World Series proved a letdown. The underdog Cards won because they had a hot pitcher, Harry "the Cat" Brecheen, who copped three games and compiled an astounding 0.45 ERA. Brecheen had the perfect tools to foil the Red Sox. He "threw a little screwball, a little sliding curve and he mixed speeds," according to Doerr. "He wasn't overpoweringly fast. Our ball club was a fastball hitting club, a pull hitting ball club, and what we should have done with him was to hit him through the middle. But we didn't" (Golenbock, *Fenway*, 160). The vaunted Red Sox lineup didn't produce — Boston scored just 20 runs in seven games. In his only appearance in the World Series, Ted Williams hit a woeful .200 with just five singles. Williams's poor performance wasn't a case of slumping or choking. While waiting for the Dodger-Cardinal play-offs to end, the Red Sox tried to keep sharp by playing a three-game series against a group of American League All-Stars. During the first game the Senators' Mickey Haefner hit Williams on the tip of the elbow. The elbow swelled and Williams was unable to swing comfortably. The Red Sox wisely canceled the remaining games. His counterpart as the dominant hitter of the postwar years, Stan Musial, didn't do much better. He hit just .222.

The most celebrated incident of the Series, and perhaps its only dramatic moment, was Enos Slaughter's dash in the seventh inning of the seventh game from first base to score the winning run on Harry Walker's double to left center.

The winner's share was $3,757, the equivalent of $30,000 today, a good payday in those pre–free agency days.

The National League did better than their American League counterparts as far as rookies were concerned. The 1946 season saw the arrival of one future Hall of Famer, Ralph Kiner, who led the league in homers with just 23. Another quality player was Del Ennis of the Phils, who hit .313 and was *The Sporting News*'s choice for rookie of the year. Other quality players who made their first appearance that year were Ewell Blackwell and Grady Hatton of the Reds, Carl Furillo of the Dodgers and Eddie Waitkus of the Cubs. Blackwell won 22 games in 1947, and Furillo would become one of the great right fielders in the league. His throwing arm was legendary. He was also a solid hitter, winning one batting title and hitting .300 five times. His lifetime batting average was .299. Waitkus was a consistent .300 hitter until he was shot by a deranged female in 1949, when he played for the Phils. Hatton was a steady, unspectacular third baseman who gave the Reds nine years of solid play at the hot corner.

Overall, 1946 was a great success for baseball. Once again the game proved its importance to the nation, or at least to its white majority. It provided a sense of continuity amid the vast cultural and social changes occurring in the years after the war.

Aesthetically, the return of the prewar stars was satisfying, even if some of them did not live up to their past stats. The quality of play was clearly superior to the war years, but there was little exceptional about the season except the enormous boom in attendance.

The enthusiasm of the fans was amazing. Attendance figures broke every imaginable record and would continue to rise for three straight years before dipping slightly in 1949. Every team in the Majors drew more fans in 1946 than in the last year of the war, including a staggering Yankee net gain of 1.4 million over 1945.

Baseball looked to the future with renewed optimism. The war was quickly forgotten. The owners were convinced that they had dealt with the major problems facing baseball when they created a new contract and beat back the challenge of the Mexican League. Although the American economy was still trying to shake off the remnants of World War II–fueled inflation and return to normality, economic conditions improved throughout 1946. Politically, the Republican party, out of power since 1930, regained control of both Houses of Congress. Like the Republicans who were optimistic about the future, with dreams of recapturing the White House, baseball dreamed of a new golden era to match the great prosperity of the 1920s. Matters took a different, if interesting, course.

2

The Baseball Boom, 1947–1948

Rickey and Robinson

On October 24, 1945, the *New York Times* announced the Brooklyn Dodgers had signed Jackie Robinson to a professional contract. The usually authoritative *Times* for once got things wrong when it noted that Robinson would be the first "negro ever admitted to organized baseball." In fact, blacks had played for a variety of professional teams in the early history of the game. In the 1870s, as baseball developed, blacks played the game without causing too much comment. Some college teams used black players. But in the 1880s, as America's racial attitudes hardened into something approximating separation of the races, blacks were gradually ousted from professional baseball at any level. The final blow came in 1887 when Adrian "Cap" Anson, one of the game's most popular stars, refused to allow his Chicago White Stockings to take the field against a team with a black player. Just as Jim Crowism took root in America, it also took hold in baseball with the usual convenient justifications about the two races going their "separate but equal" ways.

Robinson's signing ended 60 years of baseball segregation and also inaugurated a new era in the history of the sport. In baseball's long evolution only a few changes have truly reshaped the game — establishing the pitching distance at 60' 6", Byron "Ban" Johnson's successful establishment of the American League, Babe Ruth's inaugurating the home-run era are examples that come to mind. Breaking the color barrier ranks with them in importance.

Jackie Robinson's signing opened baseball to one of the last great pools of untapped talent in America. Within a decade first the National League and then the American League would be reshaped by quality black players like Willie Mays, Hank Aaron, Ernie Banks, Frank Robinson and Reggie Jackson. Baseball would never be the same.

None of this was on Branch Rickey's mind when he signed Robinson that autumn day. Rickey believed that blacks constituted "the greatest untapped reservoir of raw material" in baseball's history. They will make the Dodgers winners for years to come. For that, Rickey said, "I will happily bear being called a bleeding heart and a do-gooder" (Tygiel, 43). Rickey, the closest thing baseball had to a resident intellectual, was a shrewd businessman and a famous judge of baseball talent. Among other accomplishments he created the concept of the farm system when he was with the Cardinals. "Rickey's Chain Gang" it was called. He was looking not only to end an injustice in the sport but also for a way to help the Dodgers outdistance their rivals. He was not averse to making some money while doing so. And so the story of the ending of baseball's sordid era of racial segregation is another wonderful mix of American motives: justice and profits.

Rickey chose Robinson carefully. He scouted the Negro Leagues, looking for someone who could play professional baseball at the Major League level but also someone who would serve as a model to open the way for others. There were more talented black players in the Negro League than Robinson, but none better represented the qualities that Rickey wanted: skill, intelligence, poise. There was enormous pressure on Robinson to succeed because he was seen as representing his whole race. For this, Rickey, in his usual generous terms, gave Robinson a $3500 bonus and paid him $600 a month to play for the top Dodger farm club, the Montreal Royals (Robinson, 46–47).

Robinson's performance during the 1946 season exceeded Rickey's expectations. He led the International League in hitting with a .349 average and in runs scored with 113. He also showed his great speed by stealing 40 bases and helping the Royals win the pennant. For his performance Robinson was voted the League's most valuable player.

Despite this record some players, managers and writers doubted he would make a Major Leaguer. Bob Feller claimed that he was too tightly muscled in his upper body to get around on a Major League fastball. "If he were a white man, I doubt if they would consider him big league material," Feller stated (Golenbock, *Bums*, 144). An interesting comment considering that upper body muscles didn't seem to handicap Jimmy Foxx or Lou Gehrig. Bucky Harris, fresh from his appointment as Yankee manager, also said that he thought Robinson wouldn't be ready for the jump to the Majors in 1947.

Cy Kritzer in *The Sporting News* argued that Robinson was playing over his head in his rookie year and "that his crusading zeal to pave the way for others of his race into pro baseball actually increased his ability" (*SN*, 1/8/47, p. 54). Kritzer didn't believe that Robinson could maintain that level of play. Why if this was true at the AAA level it wouldn't hold up in the Major Leagues he never made clear. *The Sporting News* believed that Rickey had signed a black as a way of satisfying political pressure groups in New York (Tygiel, 74).

When spring training 1947 rolled around, Rickey was preparing to move Robinson to the Major League roster. To ease the pressure Robinson would face, Rickey switched the spring training site to the more racially tolerant community of Havana, Cuba. He wanted to keep Robinson away from the limelight for a while.

Rickey knew that the baseball establishment opposed his policies. As early as 1943 he had wisely secured the support of George McLaughlin, the conservative director of the Brooklyn Trust bank, which controlled the Dodgers, for his plan to sign black players. There had been talk for years about ending baseball's policy of racial segregation, but as long as Judge Landis was commissioner this was impossible. Landis was a racist who would not even allow Major League players to wear their team uniforms when they barnstormed against black teams. By the time that Landis died in 1944 the racial atmosphere in the United States was slowly beginning to change. During World War II the United States emphasized that it was fighting to end an intolerable racist regime in Nazi Germany and all it stood for. All the talk about the Four Freedoms, while the United States maintained its own unique racial segregation policy, raised questions about America's honesty and motives. A sense of fair racial play began to take a tenuous hold in the country.

Landis's successor, the former governor and senator from Kentucky, A. B. "Happy" Chandler, represented a more enlightened southern populist viewpoint. He believed that "if a black boy can make it on Okinawa and Guadalcanal, hell he can make it in baseball" (Polner, 174). He could see no rationale for banning blacks from baseball. Overall, Chandler's role in ending the color bar in baseball was a relatively minor one, although after the fact he made it seem that he played a central part in the affair. Even with Chandler's support Rickey still had his problems. In 1946 Major League owners voted 15 to 1 (Rickey was the one) against formally ending baseball's racial segregation. Part of this opposition was pure prejudice, part fear of the future. Ford Frick, president of the National League, believed that there would be problems throughout the South during spring training if blacks played against whites (Wiggins, 12). It should also be kept in mind that at the time that Robinson signed his contract, 60 percent of Major League players were southerners, with all the ethos of the South that that entailed.

Some owners had special reasons for opposing baseball integration — they made money by renting their stadiums to the Negro League when the Major League teams were not playing. Connie Mack of the Philadelphia Athletics and Calvin Griffith of the Washington Senators, both owners without a great deal of capital, made tidy sums from the Negro Leagues. But even rich teams like the Yankees engaged in this profitable venture. In 1943 the Yankees made $100,000 renting the House that Ruth Built plus assorted minor league parks to the Negro Leagues (McPhail, 205). Integrating baseball would eventually doom the Negro Leagues and end that lucrative business.

During the 1947 spring training Robinson became the focal point of protests by some Dodger players led by Dixie Walker and including Kirby Higbe, Bobby Bragan and Carl Furillo among others. Robinson believed that Hugh Casey, the top Dodger reliever, was the group's ringleader. Rickey expected this. He passed the word that he was willing to trade anyone who felt strongly about playing with blacks, adding the typical Rickeyesque proviso, "as soon as he could make a good deal"(Higbe, 103–104). Rickey never gave anything away. In fact, Rickey was hoping that his players would work the matter out among themselves and see that Robinson had the kind of talent that could help them win the pennant. Rickey always tried to appeal to both decency and selfishness at the same time.

Leo Durocher, the Dodger manager who was having his own difficulties, which would see him banned for the season, got wind of the protests and called a late-night meeting of the team. Arrayed in beautiful silk pajamas, he laid out his thinking in typical Durocherese to squelch the protest. To win a pennant Durocher said he would play an elephant. As for the petition circulating against Robinson, the players, in Durocher's delicate phrase, could "wipe their asses with it." Robinson, he argued, was going to "put money in your pockets and mine." Just in case they missed the point he noted that these black players are hungry. "They're good athletes and there's nowhere else they can make this kind of money. They're going to come, boys, and they're going to come scratching and diving. Unless you fellows lookout and wake up, they're going to run you right out of the ball park" (Durocher, 205).

Between Durocher's warnings and Rickey's threat to trade any dissidents, the Dodger players dropped their protests. Robinson did his part by playing well during spring training. In games between the Dodgers and the Montreal Royals Robinson hit .625. Because the Dodgers already had a talented second baseman in Eddie Stanky Robinson moved to first base, where the Dodgers had a serious gap — in 1946 Dodger first basemen hit just .249. But the turmoil for Robinson had just begun.

Robinson's first year in the Majors was a nightmare. For the longest time he was, in the words of writer Dick Young, the loneliest man in baseball, shunned by teammates and opposing players alike. According to one of his teammates, Al Gionfriddo, Robinson even waited until the rest of the players showered before he took his own. That he succeeded is a testament to his tremendous drive and ambition as well as a determination to open new careers for fellow blacks.

He started the season fairly well, considering he was playing a new position. Then the lowly Phillies came to Brooklyn for a three-game series. The Phillies manager, southern hothead Ben Chapman, led the Phillies players in a chorus of cruel and abusive attacks, saying that Robinson was only in the Majors to "draw nigger bucks at the gate for Rickey." Chapman claimed that he was only treating Robinson the way rookies had been greeted in the past.

"He must learn to take it like all others," Chapman told *The Sporting News* (*SN*, 5/7/47, p. 6). "Nigger, jungle bunny, snow flake" seemed like reasonable taunts to Chapman.

Robinson got some revenge when he single-handedly won the first game of the series by singling, stealing second, going to third on the throw and then scoring the only run on a single by Gene Hermanski.

Despite drawing huge crowds whenever he played, Robinson slumped after the Phillies series, at one point going hitless in 20 times at bat, which left his batting average at a season low of .241. He was mentally exhausted by the tremendous pressure he was under to please his fans and by the sense he had that he was carrying the black cause on his shoulders. Robinson was inundated everywhere he went by various African American organizations asking him to speak or wishing to present him with some kind of award. Eventually, the Dodgers took over the management of his time. Jimmy Cannon, the sports columnist, was struck by the nature of the pressure on Robinson at this time. "He is the loneliest man I have ever seen in sports," Cannon wrote (Tygiel, 188).

When the Dodgers came to Philadelphia for a four-game series May 9–11, Robinson gradually came out of his slump. He managed five hits including a double in the four games, and his average slowly began to rise. Eventually he hit .385 on this road trip, playing before huge crowds in Philadelphia, Cincinnati and Chicago. For the rest of the season he never really looked back.

Overall, Robinson had a superb season. He played all but three of the Dodgers' games and hit .296. He scored 125 runs with 31 doubles, 12 homers and 29 stolen bases. He also struck out just 36 times in 591 times at bat. For this he was easily elected rookie of the year over some solid competition from two Giants: Larry Jansen, who won 21 games, and Bobby Thomson, who hit 29 homers and drove in 84 runs. More important, it was clear that Robinson played a crucial role in the Dodgers' edging of the Cardinals for the pennant. He was the one player the Dodgers added that pushed them past the Cards in 1947.

Robinson's success paved the way for other black players. Before the 1947 season was over four more blacks made it to the Majors: Dan Bankhead, a pitcher for the Dodgers; Larry Doby, who was signed by the Indians; and Hank Thompson and Willard Brown, who played briefly for the sickly St. Louis Browns. Brown and Thompson, who were signed out of the Negro Leagues, were in the lineup at the same time in a July 20 game against the Red Sox, the first time that two blacks started a game together in the Majors. Both men faded back into the minors, although Thompson returned to the big leagues as a starter for the Giants in 1949, giving them seven years as a competent third baseman (Kleinknecht, 102). Brown, who couldn't handle the racial taunting, never made it back to the Majors.

Doby's signing was a typical decision by Bill Veeck, the president of the Cleveland Indians. He had long wanted to tap the black talent and was not happy when Rickey broke the ice. Veeck had his own people scouting the Negro Leagues looking for someone who could duplicate Robinson's success. He specifically wanted a young black who could play quality baseball but who also would make a positive impression. He and his scouts decided on Doby, who not only didn't smoke or drink but didn't even use coffee (Moore, 40). Rickey had an opportunity to sign Doby but he was happy to have him go to the American League if for no other reason than it would take some pressure off Robinson (Tygiel, 43).

Eleven weeks after Robinson made his Major League debut, Veeck purchased Doby's contract from the Newark Eagles of the Negro League for $10,000 and $5000 more if the Indians kept him. The Eagles also offered to throw in the contract of a hard-hitting outfielder named Monte Irvin, but Veeck didn't believe Cleveland was ready for two blacks and thus missed out on a future Hall of Famer. Veeck argued that in a decade Negro players would be in "regular service with big league teams. ... The entrance of Negroes into the Majors is not only inevitable — it is here" (Moore, 44). Veeck told *The Sporting News* that there would be a scramble for the best black players, with baseball being the ultimate beneficiary (*SN*, 7/16/47, p. 9).

Veeck proved a good prophet. It took about a decade for blacks to make the roster of all Major League teams. With the Dodgers leading the way, adding Roy Campanella in 1948 and Don Newcombe in 1949, the rest of the Majors with varying degrees of hesitancy and hostility caught up. The Giants, pressed by the success of the Dodgers in attendance and baseball success, were the next franchise to add quality black players: Irvin and Thompson in 1949 and finally Willie Mays in 1951, the first black superstar. The National League, perhaps because of Robinson, had greater success in tapping the pool of talented blacks than did the American League. Players like Ernie Banks with the Cubs in 1953, Hank Aaron with the Braves one year later and Frank Robinson with the Cincinnati Reds in 1956 foreshadowed not only the coming of the black superstars but the domination of the National League over the American League from the mid-1950s to the late 1970s.

The American League lagged behind the National League for a variety of reasons, of which the reluctance of the dominant franchise in the League, the Yankees, to sign black players was probably the most significant. If the Yankees had aggressively pursued blacks the way the Dodgers did, other American League teams probably would have done so. In fact, the Yankees did not have a black on their roster until 1955, when they added the quiet, efficient and proper Elston Howard, eight full seasons after Robinson broke the color barrier. The Yankee general manager George Weiss didn't want any blacks. He believed that they would attract the "wrong" kind of fans (i.e., blacks) and would thus offend the Yankee clientele. It didn't matter. The Yankees won because of their superb minor league system and had no need to reach into the Negro Leagues.

A look at the black players in the American League in the decade after Robinson broke the color barrier reveals largely marginal talent. Aside from Doby, who eventually became a topflight outfielder, Minnie Minoso and perhaps Luke Easter, who played briefly with the Indians in the early 1950s, the first blacks in the American League did not turn their teams around the way Aaron or Frank Robinson did.

One can grasp the importance of blacks in baseball, specifically the National League, by just glancing at their statistical success in the fifteen years after Rickey signed Robinson. Blacks won five batting titles in the National League and just one in the American League. They also led the National League in homers five times. Doby did it twice in the American League. Blacks were also rookie of the year ten times, beginning with Robinson in 1947. In contrast, no black won that award in the American League. Most impressively, blacks won the coveted MVP Award ten times between 1949 and 1961, including a stretch of seven straight years, from 1953 to 1959.

Despite this success blacks still faced prejudice in baseball. In the 1950s in spite of their impressive record blacks never made the cover of the popular baseball statistical guide, *Who's Who in Baseball.* Instead, in a variant of "the back of the bus" scenario, three blacks — Campanella, Bobby Avila and Newcombe — were put on the back cover (Rosenthal, 109). There was an unspoken agreement among Major League owners to keep the number of blacks limited. In 1950, of 400 players in the Majors, only nine were black. Ten years later the number had risen to 75: 54 in the National League, 21 in the American League. Even this figure isn't accurate, though, because many of the players on the 40-man roster didn't play any significant time in the Majors (*S&S,* 1960, pp. 78-93). The imbalance in favor of the National League is obvious in these figures. Closer analysis shows further that most blacks were outfielders. Only a handful played the so-called crucial position of shortstop, catcher or even pitcher. Even a study done in 1986 reveals that 70 percent of blacks in the Majors were outfielders, whereas only 25.5 percent were infielders and 7.7 percent pitchers (Scully, 177). Still, compared to the record of the rest of society, baseball at least made some effort to integrate blacks into the game.

Bonus money, which was spent lavishly by many teams in the 1950s, virtually never went to a black player. Why should it when they could be gotten cheaply? (Miller, 67) Interestingly, the last two teams in each league to sign blacks — the Phillies in the National League, who didn't play a black until 1957, and the Red Sox, who waited until 1959 — were among the teams who spent the largest sums on bonus babies. Neither team had much success in the mid-1950s; both became competitive in the 1960s when they reached into the pool of black talent: Richie Allen for the Phillies, George Scott for the Red Sox.

Buttoning "the Lip"

Before the 1947 season had even begun, the already-divided Dodgers confronted another crisis. This time it revolved around four men with huge egos: Rickey, Durocher, Chandler and Larry McPhail of the Yankees.

Durocher had been a highly successful manager for the Dodgers since he took over the team in 1938. With the help of McPhail he transformed the moribund franchise into one of the most successful teams in the Majors. The two men had a stormy relationship, which included McPhail's firing Durocher dozens of times and even a fistfight between them. But they formed a brilliant team. They won Brooklyn its first pennant in 21 years in 1941 and came in a close second to a great Cardinal team in 1942, winning 104 games. In 1946, after McPhail had left the Dodgers, Durocher surprised the baseball world by leading an unheralded Dodger team into a tie for first place against a highly regarded Cardinal squad.

The Dodgers bore all the qualities of Durocher-led teams. They were aggressive, always played for an edge, baited umpires ruthlessly and were tightly focused on winning. It was said that Durocher lost interest with a poor team but was a brilliant field manager with a team that had some talent. He could always squeeze a few extra wins out of a decent team.

After McPhail left the Dodgers in 1942 to go into military service, Durocher was teamed with Branch Rickey. This was baseball's original odd couple, the hard-drinking, womanizing, foul-mouthed, street fighter and the pious, Bible-quoting baseball intellectual. The relationship worked because in a strange way each man respected the other's talents. Durocher, who was a master con man, always said that Rickey was the only man he never lied to because he always felt that somehow Rickey would know. On the other hand, Durocher constituted Rickey's constant reclamation project. He was always trying to save Durocher from his baser instincts (Golenbock, *Bums*, 108). It was one of Rickey's few failures.

Rickey respected Durocher's baseball knowledge and paid him accordingly. He had a base salary of $20,000 and a guarantee of $50,000 if the Dodgers drew over a million fans. Durocher says he never made less than $50,000 in the years he was with Rickey (Durocher, 216).

Durocher was looking forward to the 1947 season because he believed that the Dodgers were a younger, better balanced team with Robinson than the Cardinals, whose dynasty was beginning to show the first signs of owner Sam Breadon's tight-fisted financial policies. After Rickey left the Cardinals, Breadon failed to nurture the farm system. It was too costly. The Cardinals had been the most successful franchise in the National League for a 15-year period, 1931–1946, because of Rickey's astute development of talent — quality from quantity he called it.

In 1946 Durocher had fallen in love with the Hollywood actress Laraine

Day. In typical Durocher fashion he courted her while in her home at the invitation of her husband. Durocher and Day were married after she secured a quickie divorce. The publicity surrounding their relationship caused problems for the Dodgers, who derived considerable support from the Catholic Youth Organization of Brooklyn, whose knothole gang numbered better than 50,000 boys. The director, Fr. Vincent Powell, labeled Durocher's actions as "undermining the moral and spiritual training of our young boys" (*ibid.*, 244). This was dangerous because Rickey was disturbed by the divorce publicity and feared a threatened boycott.

Durocher probably could have survived that threat, but he became a target of "Happy" Chandler — that "Hamfat politician," as Durocher always called him — at the same time. Chandler was trying to establish himself as a commissioner in his own right and not just as a cornpone version of Landis. In the midst of the uproar over the divorce, an incident took place during a spring training game between the Dodgers and Yankees that gave Chandler his opportunity to target Durocher.

Durocher and McPhail had carried on a war of words for a couple of years, each one accusing the other of being a blowhard who took too much credit for the success of the Dodgers. Durocher said to anyone who would listen that McPhail had tried to lure him away to the Yankees after Joe McCarthy quit in 1946. McPhail's response was to hire Chuck Dressen, Durocher's right-hand man, as a Yankee coach.

McPhail was also angry that Rickey had broken the color barrier in what he believed was an underhanded way. It is possible that McPhail wanted to be involved so that he could add this innovation to his already impressive credits: the first to use lights and the first to see the possibilities of baseball broadcasting

Durocher and McPhail were both loud, and in Durocher's case crude, but neither really held a grudge for long. When stories circulated that Durocher fraternized with gamblers and hoodlums like Bugsy Siegel and questionable Hollywood types like tough guy George Raft, McPhail said that Durocher was a menace to baseball. Durocher reciprocated in kind, using a newspaper column in the *Brooklyn Eagle* entitled "Durocher Says," which appeared under his name but was in fact written by Harold Parrott, to attack McPhail.

Before a spring training game between the Yankees and Dodgers on March 2, Durocher pointed out to Dick Young of the *New York Daily News* two gamblers with names right out of Damon Runyan — Memphis Engelberg, a well-known bookie, and Connie Immerman, former owner of the famous Cotton Club — whom he claimed were sitting in McPhail's box. In fact, they were sitting directly behind McPhail's seats. Durocher told Young that if he had anything to do with them he would be out of baseball. Parrott repeated that story in his newspaper column the next day, and all hell broke loose.

McPhail, whose temper was legendary, fired back by saying that Durocher was a liar and should be thrown out of baseball. Rickey came to the defense of his manager and chided McPhail, with whom his relations were strained anyway, for unfairness.

All of this was reported with juicy details in the newspapers, and the incident began to overshadow baseball itself. At this point Chandler stepped in. He claims that he had his eye on Durocher ever since he took over as commissioner. In a self-congratulatory memoir written for *Sports Illustrated* in 1971, Chandler said that even before the spring training fracas he had enough on Durocher to ban him from baseball for life (Chandler, *SI*, 5/3/71, p.52). What Durocher was guilty of Chandler did not specify, but others including McPhail always believed that Chandler used the Durocher case to show that he could be as tough as Landis (McPhail, 190).

Chandler was a sensitive man who wore his heart on his sleeve, and he believed that certain New York writers, among them Dan Parker, Red Smith and Arthur Daley of the *Times*, made fun of him because of his southern background. Parker, then writing one of the most influential sports columns in New York, discovered that a swimming pool supposed to be used by the poor in Kentucky was built for Chandler instead. Parker had a lot of fun with that. Red Smith in the *New York Herald Tribune* came to Durocher's defense, accusing Chandler of throwing Leo a "bean ball." Although Durocher was no plaster saint, Smith asked where "had he behaved any worse than any of the other parties involved?" The harshest criticism came from Daley. Daley was regarded by most sportswriters as a lightweight, but his paper was powerful. If this is Chandler's kind of justice, Daley wrote, "then the club owners could make a good investment for themselves by buying up the remainder of his contract and getting someone who knows what the score is." Daley summed up the situation best: "Leo is like a fellow who passes a red light and gets the electric chair" (McGowen, 36).

With this kind of cold war going on between Chandler and the New York press, the commissioner would use the Durocher case to show them who was running baseball. Chandler's handling of this dispute began the process that destroyed his position as commissioner. Within a few years he would lose support among the owners and eventually be ousted as commissioner.

Rickey tried to moderate the dispute, and even McPhail agreed that the whole incident had been blown out of proportion. After this incident the two men never talked to each other again. As he had done in the past with Durocher, McPhail was ready to forgive and forget and get on with baseball. But Chandler wanted blood. After meeting with all the parties involved, he sent shock waves through the baseball world on April 9 (one day, incidentally, before Rickey announced that Robinson would join the Dodgers) by fining the Yankees and Dodgers $2000 each, which was a lot of money in 1947. He ordered

Parrott to give up his column and fined him $500, which Chandler claims he returned later.

Parrott tells the story of the return of his money in his autobiography, *The Lords of Baseball.* Chandler realized that he had been unfair to Parrott and had the money returned with a warning that if Parrott ever mentioned the fact, he would be fined $5000 (Parrott, 21–22). Chandler also suspended Chuck Dressen for 30 days for signing with the Yankees while he still had a contract with the Dodgers. But in his most shocking action, he banned Durocher from baseball for a year. Chandler also ordered all parties in the dispute to keep silent about the matters or face further disciplinary action. Chandler claims that he was warned by Frank Murphy, the Supreme Court judge, that unless Durocher was removed he would recommend a boycott of the Dodgers by Catholic groups (Chandler, 53). He gives no evidence of this warning, nor is there any found among the Murphy papers.

The "Baseball Bible," *The Sporting News,* was divided over Chandler's actions. The editor, J. G. Taylor Spink, was in the commissioner's corner. Spink believed that Durocher had disregarded warnings over his behavior in the past and had brought the penalty on himself. Bill Corum, reflecting the opinion of the New York press, took the opposite view. Durocher, he correctly noted, was given no chance to defend himself and was even silenced. Corum said this was against the American way of handing out justice. For the next few weeks *The Sporting News* was inundated with letters on the Durocher case, with most backing him against Chandler.

Time magazine summed up the situation perfectly: "Chandler had done the seeming impossible: he had made Leo Durocher a sympathetic figure." Rickey was furious. He had lost his manager on the eve of the season, a season that already promised to be difficult because of the expected uproar that would accompany Robinson's first year in the Majors. Rickey was mad at Durocher for getting himself into this mess, mad at McPhail and mad at Chandler. He solved the manager problem quickly by asking an old crony, Burt Shotton, who did a variety of jobs in the Dodger organization to take over the team. Shotton was a crafty student of baseball, a man who looked like a kindly old gramps but was tough. One player described him as a "sarcastic Southern son of a bitch" (Smith, 138). Brookyln writers found him hard to deal with at times and often referred to him jokingly as KOBS, "Kindly Old Burt Shotton." Shotton was reluctant to take the job but came to Rickey's rescue.

Durocher spent the 1947 season in California with his new wife and tried to keep a low profile, always difficult for "the Lip." MacPhail refused to keep silent and defended himself in spite of Chandler's threats. But MacPhail was on his way out of baseball. He did say that the commissioner's power would have to be reined in after Chandler's heavy-handed action in Durocher's case.

The Year All Hell Broke Loose

Nineteen forty-seven started on a controversial note, hardly what the baseball establishment wanted. The game was coming off its best season in history and now that was jeopardized by the actions of a few hotheads. The "lords of baseball" were beginning to have second thoughts about Chandler, and he had taken the first of a series of steps that would eventually cost him the job of commissioner.

Before the season began the sportswriters picked the Cardinals and Red Sox to repeat as pennant winners with the Tigers and Yankees challenging in the American League and the Dodgers and Braves in the National. This proved accurate, even if the writers had the wrong teams winning. There were few surprises in either league during 1947. The closest thing to a shock was the Philadelphia A's record of 78-76, as Connie Mack finally put together a winning team for the first time since 1933. The A's had some fine pitchers in Phil Marchildon, Dick Fowler and Joe Coleman; and the team infield defense was strengthened by the addition of two newcomers, veteran Eddie Joost at short and rookie Ferris Fain at first. The team ERA of 3.44 was second in the League. Marchildon was a sad case. He pitched well in 1946 and then won 19 games the next season, but something had happened to him while he was a prisoner of war. Kell described it as "a funny look in his eye that hinted that his thoughts were about the war and not baseball" (Peary, 72). Jimmy Dykes noted that same thing. Marchildon was out of baseball by 1949 for no discernible reason. The League was divided into two sharply contrasting parts during the season. The Yankees, Tigers, Red Sox, Indians and A's played .500 or better baseball. The White Sox, Senators and especially the Browns were terrible.

The White Sox had some competent pitching in Ed Lopat and Joe Haynes, who won 30 games between them. But aside from ageless Luke Appling, who hit .300 for the twelfth time, the team's hitting was feeble and its defense among the worst in the American League. The Senators were almost as bad, winning just 64 games. They had a couple of solid pitchers in Early Wynn and Walt Masterson, but their hitting was awful. Stan Spence led the team in hitting at .279 and was the only Senator to homer in double figures. Mickey Vernon, the 1946 batting champ, saw his average dip 90 points. Buddy Lewis continued to struggle to regain his prewar form, and Cecil Travis was finished, hitting just .216 for the season.

The Senators edged the Browns out of the cellar by just ½ game. The Browns made it on merit. They finished eighth in team pitching and tied for eighth in batting. The franchise was slowly dying, attracting just 320,000 fans at a time when baseball was prospering everywhere. Only one pitcher, Jack Kramer, won in double figures, and he was 11-16 with a 4.97 ERA. Jeff Heath hit 27 homers, and Vern Stephens drove in 83 runs. All three were gone by the end of the season — Heath sold to the Boston Braves, Kramer and Stephens to the Red Sox. The Browns got junk in return: six nonentities, including such household names as Eddie Pellagrini, Roy Partee, Pete Layden and Al Widmar from the Red Sox, plus $310,000 of Tom Yawkey's money. All told, the Browns earned $1,300,000 from player sales between 1947 and 1951. It was the only way the team could stay solvent (Quirk & Fort, 281).

This two-tier division of the American League would last through the 1940s until Mack's A's began to decline into the second division beginning in 1950. Washington and the Browns remained pathetic franchises during this period, but the White Sox began to show signs of improvement in 1951 under the shrewd leadership of field manager Paul Richards and some clever trades by the new general manager, Frank Lane, who was hired in 1949 by the Comiskey family, which still owned the team.

In the National League there were no real surprises. The Phillies dropped back to a tie for the cellar with the lowly Pirates after playing well in 1946. For the Phillies the slippage was only seven games from the previous year, but the team seemed to lack the excitement of the 1946 club. Del Ennis, 1946 rookie of the year, saw his batting average drop 38 points and his home-run total decline by five. Ennis attributed much of his batting decline to a sore back he hurt while sliding (Peary, 31). The Phils had the League batting champ in Harry "the Hat" Walker, who hit .363 (.371 as a Phillie), but they brought up no rookies as the team consisted of over-the-hill vets. In reality, the Phillies' farm system, constructed with loads of du Pont money by Herb Pennock, was about to start paying off. But it would be 1948 before the young blood would begin to transform the Phillies.

Pittsburgh was an odd club in 1947. They only won 62 games, yet they had in Ralph Kiner the greatest young home-run talent to enter the National League since Hack Wilson. Kiner hit 51 homers that year, 48 after June 1, tying him with Johnny Mize of the Giants. He also drove in 127 runs and scored 118, hitting .313. Wally Westlake in his rookie season hit 17 homers and drove in 69 to give the Pirates a hard-hitting duo in the outfield. In the infield Frank Gustine and rookie Billy Cox had good years. For Gustine it would be his last quality season. But the Pirate pitching was awful, with a team ERA of 4.68, easily the worst in the Majors that year. The team's biggest winner, Fritz Ostermueller, was 40 years old. There were no young arms on the staff.

The Cubs and Reds continued to decline. For Cincinnati this had been the case since they were a powerhouse in the late 1930s, early 1940s. What saved the Reds from total embarrassment in 1947 was the incredible season that Ewell Blackwell had. He won 22 games and lost only 8, pitched a no-hitter and then almost duplicated his teammate Johnny Vander Meer's feat of back-to-back no-hitters only to give up a hit in the ninth inning pitching against the Dodgers. The Reds had no outfield, an old infield, with only Grady Hatton providing any speed, and a pitiful pitching staff aside from Blackwell. Only two teams, the Pirates and the Giants, had a higher ERA.

The process of decline was more painful for the Cubs, who as recently as 1945 had won the pennant and taken the Tigers to a full seven games before losing the World Series. Some of the Cub players like Stan Hack and even Phil Cavarretta, who had a good year hitting .302, were past their primes. The Cubs had no shortstop and no third baseman, and their hitting was tied for seventh in the League, despite playing in a great hitter's park.

When the 1947 season started in the National League the prediction that the race for pennant would be between the Dodgers and Cardinals did not pan out. The Cardinals started poorly. Stan Musial was bothered by an inflamed appendix for the first two months of the season. He hit just .312, fine for most players, but for Musial it was a 50-point decline from the year before. Enos Slaughter also had an off year. He hit just ten homers, down eight from 1946 and drove in 44 fewer runs. The Cardinals led the League in ERA, but Howie Pollet dropped from 21 wins to just 9. It was becoming apparent that the fabled Cardinal farm system was no longer producing. No rookie made any impact on the Cardinals in 1947. With Musial playing first, which was not his usual position, the Cardinals needed to develop two outfielders to replace the aging Terry Moore and the ineffective Irv Dusak, who drove in just 28 runs. The Cardinals resorted to stopgap trades for the likes of Ron Northey, a sign the franchise was now paying a price for Breadon's penury.

By Memorial Day the Cardinals were in last place, seven full games behind the pace-setting New York Giants. The Giants, led by Mize, catcher Walker Cooper and outfielder Willard Marshall, were hitting homers at a record-breaking pace. They would eventually hit 221 that season, setting a National League record that was tied by the Milwaukee Braves in 1956. The Dodgers were in third place, two games back, but playing steady, if unspectacular, baseball.

Over the next five weeks the Dodgers gradually moved into first place. By July 4 they had a half-game lead over the Giants, whereas the Cardinals had moved out of the cellar, tied for fourth place, one game over .500 and four games behind the Dodgers. The Dodgers eventually reeled off a nine-game winning streak to secure a hold on first place. The Giants were still pounding the ball — Mize had 22 homers to match his 1946 total after just 65 games. The three top RBI leaders in the League were Giants: Cooper, Mize and Marshall. But the thinness of their pitching was beginning to tell. With the exception of rookie Larry Jansen and left-hander Dave Koslo, the Giants' staff was shaky. The Giants also suffered from a lack of team speed. They stole a grand total of 29 bases that year, the same total as Jackie Robinson. Over the next month they would fade from pennant contention.

The Dodgers played the best ball in the League because they had the most balanced team. Eddie Stanky had a solid year at second, Pee Wee Reese played his accustomed steady shortstop, and in the outfield Carl Furillo had his first good year, hitting .295 and driving in 88 runs in less than 500 times at bat.

Behind the plate Bruce Edwards led all National League catchers in putouts and hit solidly. Like Furillo he batted .295 and drove in 80 runs. The pitching staff was shaky, a perennial Dodger problem related to pitching half their games in the Ebbets Field bandbox. Ralph Branca, on his way to winning 21 games, and Hugh Casey, having his last great year in the bull pen, anchored the staff. Casey would win 10 games and save 18 others. Both figures led the League for relief pitchers. The rest of the Dodger pitchers, including Joe Hatten, Vic Lombardi and Harry Taylor, were suspect.

By Labor Day, as the season entered its last month, the Cardinals had moved into second place, but they were 6½ games behind the Dodgers. They staged a brief rally in September but only cut a game and a half off the Dodger lead. The Cardinals won nine fewer games than they had in 1946 and were never really in contention. Roger Kahn has argued that a healthy Stan Musial might have cost the Dodgers the pennant in 1947. He points out that Musial hit just .225 in 11 games in Ebbets Field that year; the next season he hit .535 there, with 23 hits, 6 homers and 19 runs scored. If Musial had a typical Ebbets Field season, Kahn says, you could color the pennant Cardinal Red (Kahn, *Era*, 94–95). I doubt it. With all the hitting that Musial did in 1948 in Brooklyn, the Cardinals finished just one game ahead of the Dodgers. Musial made the difference in one game, not five.

The Dodgers won because they were the best team in the League. A half dozen players had good seasons, and the team had just enough balance to win. They were second in team hitting, third in runs, second in fielding and third in ERA — just good enough to outlast the Cards and the Braves, who, led by two 20-game winners, Johnny Sain and Warren Spahn, were the closest thing to a surprise in the National League. Spahn beat the Cards and Giants five each that season to herald his arrival as a top competitor. The Braves also produced the League MVP in Bob Elliott, who batted .317, with 22 homers and 113 RBI, striking out just 50 times.

The American League race was less interesting than the National. When the season began, the Tigers and Red Sox started off quickly whereas the Yankees were sluggish. In late May the Yankees literally destroyed the Red Sox in a four-game series in the Stadium, outscoring them 40 to 5. Kahn refers to this as the "Birth of the Bombers" (Kahn, *Era*, 79–99). This series saw the beginning of Joe Page's career as a fireman. He was brought into a game against the Red Sox, with two men on base, no one out and the Yankees losing 3–1, to face Williams, Rudy York and Bobby Doerr. It was Page's last chance. He had worn out his welcome with the Yankees despite his great talent and was on his way back to the minors. Williams dribbled a grounder and was safe on an error. Page went 3-0 on York and then came back to strike him out. He then struck out Doerr and got the last batter Eddie Pellagrini to fly out. Page went on to have a great season, winning 14 games and saving 17 others at a time when saves were hard to come by.

By Memorial Day the Tigers held on to first place by 3½ games over the rapidly closing Yankees. Boston had dropped to .500 in fourth place. But the Yanks were on the threshold of their greatest team winning streak. They won 19 games in a row and 30 of 34. On June 20 they took over first place and never relinquished it. They had a six-game lead over the Tigers by July 4 and a 10½ game lead by Labor Day. The Yankees were never challenged. The Red Sox picked up and played better baseball the last half of the season, but by then the race was over. The Yanks finished in first by 12 games over the Tigers and 14 over the Red Sox.

The 1947 Yanks were a solid club. Bobby Brown said there never was a mentally tougher team than this club (Kahn, *Era*, 90). They also had a lot of talent. They were first in hitting, first in homers, first in team ERA and second in fielding, making only 109 errors all season. Joe DiMaggio recovered from his off year in 1946 to hit .315 and drive in 97 runs. Tommy Henrich hit .287 and led the team with 98 RBI. When Charley Keller went down with a bad back that eventually finished his career, Johnny Lindell filled in, hitting 11 homers and driving in 75 runs.

The infield of Bill Johnson, Rizzuto, Snuffy Stirnweiss and veteran George McQuinn hit solidly and fielded well. Catching was a problem, though. The young Yogi Berra was crude behind the plate, and Aaron Robinson, who did most of the catching, had a poor year. Aside from Page, the key figure on the pitching staff was Allie Reynolds, who in his first year as a Yankee won 19 and lost just 8. Rookie Spec Shea won 14 with a very good ERA of 3.07. Spud Chandler had started well, winning nine games early in the season but was then put on the disabled list with a sore arm. Aside from two innings in the 1947 World Series, he never pitched again. The young Vic Raschi replaced him, going 7-2 the rest of the year. The other Yankee starters were Bill Bevens and Bobo Newsome. Both had subpar seasons.

This was not a dominant Yankee team. They won because they played steady, if unspectacular, baseball. They also won because their two rivals, the Tigers and Red Sox, collapsed. Hal Newhouser, who had won 81 games in the previous three years, had a terrible season, losing 17 games. Manager Steve O'Neill fined him $250 for "indifferent performance" in August. Newhouser struggled the entire season, getting off to a ghastly start. After winning his first game over the lowly Browns, he lost four games in a row and was just 2-4 by the end of May. Many people in the baseball world thought that the loss of Paul Richards, who was Newhouser's favorite catcher, hurt him in 1947. Others blamed his decline on O'Neill's pitching him on a 40-degree day early in the season (*SN*, 5/21/47). It wasn't just Newhouser, however, who slumped badly. Virgil Trucks and Dizzy Trout were 20–23 after having won 31 and lost 22 games in 1946. The team had no first baseman, and shortstop Eddie Lake hit just .211 and made 43 errors. Dick Wakefield continued to decline offensively, and the rest of the outfield was either too young (Evers, Wertz) or finished, like Roy Cullenbine, who despite hitting 24 homers in 1947 never played another game in the Majors.

The Red Sox decline was easier to diagnose. The pitching staff collapsed. Dave Ferriss and Tex Hughson, who between them had won 47 games in 1946, were 24 and 22 one year later. Ferris at 26 was shot. He walked 92 against just 64 strikeouts and never again was a big winner. Those missing 22 games were the difference between the two seasons. The rest of the Red Sox team performed at the 1946 level. Doerr had something of an off year for him, hitting only .258, although he still drove in 95 runs, more than any other second baseman in the Majors.

The World Series of that fall is often regarded as one of the most exciting of all time. It was a close one, the Yankees winning four games to three, but its fame really rests on two games: Bill Bevens's near no-hitter and Al Gionfriddo's great catch of Joe DiMaggio's long drive. What made this series interesting was the fact that the two teams were such contrasts — the great Yankee dynasty against the upstarts from Brooklyn. This gave the New York press an angle to stress.

The games were not particularly well played, although there was only one blowout, a 10–3 Yankee win in game two. Team ERAs were high, over 4 runs per game for the Yankees and 5.55 for the Dodgers. The Yankees outhit the Dodgers by over 50 points. No one for the Dodgers really hit that well. Their best RBI man was Reese, with just four. On the Yankee side Johnny Lindell had a great series, hitting .500 with seven RBI. DiMaggio hit two homers but only batted .231. In the final analysis, the Yankees won because Harris clearly outmanaged Shotton and had the right person ready at the right time whether that was a pinch hitter like Bobby Brown, who went three for three, or the right pitcher for the right game.

Shotton was not much of a game manager; he always seemed a batter or two behind. But he had gotten the most out of his team during the season. It is hard to believe that Durocher could have done any better. But Shotton's handling of his pitching staff during the World Series is questionable.

His best starter by far was Ralph Branca, a 21 game winner. He started the first game and pitched brilliantly for four innings, striking out five, and the Dodgers had given him a lead by scoring a run in the first. Branca came apart in the fifth after DiMaggio beat out a hit to deep short. For some reason Branca began to unravel and hurry his pitches. "I was grabbing the ball and throwing it and not taking my time, pressing and I ended up wild," Branca later recounted (Golenbock, *Bums*, p. 174). Before the inning was over, he had walked one batter, hit another, gave up a bases-loaded double to Lindell and was out of the game. The Yankees behind Spec Shea won 5–3 despite getting only four hits. Where was Shotton when Branca began to press? He should have sent someone out to the mound to calm the 21 year old down. Instead he did nothing. Can one imagine Durocher getting caught off guard like that?

The Yankees easily won game two behind Allie Reynolds 10–3 with the Series now shifting to Brooklyn. The Dodgers were in trouble. To make matters worse, Shotton had lost faith in his best pitcher. Branca, having the honor of starting the first game of the Series, would not start again. A look at the list of Dodger starters from game two through seven is revealing: Lombardi, Hatten, Taylor, Barney, Lombardi and Gregg. Barney and Gregg, the latter starting the most crucial game of the Series, were marginal pitchers at best. Barney was a lifetime .500 pitcher who was 5-2 in 1947 with a 4.96 ERA. He also walked 59 batters that year and struck out 36. If anything Gregg was even worse. His ERA was 5.88, and he had a losing record that season, 4–5, yet he would start the crucial seventh game of the World Series.

The Dodgers won game three, an ugly 9–8 slugfest. Game four, Bill Bevens's near no-hitter, was one of the most dramatic in World Series history. Despite unusual wildness — he walked ten — Bevens carried a no-hitter into the bottom of the ninth, only to lose 3–2 on Cookie Lavagetto's two-out, two-run double. Bevens and Lavagetto were out of baseball by the next year.

The Yankees won game five behind the superb four-hit pitching of Shea and then failed to clinch the Series when Allie Reynolds was hit sharply and Al Gionfriddo, with the bases loaded, made his famous catch of Joe DiMaggio's 400–foot smash to the left-field bull pen. In the seventh game the Yankees won 5–3 when the Dodgers started Gregg and used four other pitchers to keep the game close. Page relieved in the fifth, with the Yankees clinging desperately to the lead. Harris was told by his bull-pen coach that Page had nothing, whereas Allie Reynolds was "knocking the glove off" the catcher's hand. Harris went with Page, the man who got the Yankees to the finals. Larry MacPhail later called the move "the most dramatic he had ever experienced in baseball" (Holland, 67). Page faced just 15 batters, striking out five to hold the Dodgers in check.

The fact that the Dodgers took the Yankees to seven games is a testament to the gritty way they played and the superb relief work of Hugh Casey, who won two games and had a glittering ERA of 0.87.

It was a surprisingly close series and a popular success with baseball fans around the country, who listened to it on the radio in huge numbers. It was also the first World Series to be televised, although only people in and around the New York area could see it. According to Dan Daniel in *The Sporting News*, Chandler had sold the rights to televise the series for $100,000 over the protests of McPhail (*SN*, 8/27/47, p. 1). Total attendance was high, 398,000, helped by four crowds averaging 70,000 in Yankee Stadium.

The series capped a wonderful year for baseball. Ted Williams won his second triple crown and walked a remarkable 162 times. Two men, Kiner and Mize, hit 50 homers, the first time this happened in the National League; and five men won 20 games in that league, including Spahn, who would add 12 more such seasons.

Attendance reached 19.9 million, topping the 1946 record by 7 percent. The Dodgers set their all-time attendance record in Brooklyn by drawing 1.8 million in a ballpark that barely held 33,000. From every standard, baseball seemed healthy. There was a good crop of rookies in both leagues — Jansen, Thomson, Robinson, Berra, Dale Mitchell, Shea among others — which seemed to herald a new golden age for baseball.

Boudreau's Magic Season

The 1948 season was something of a transition for baseball. The game remained immensely popular — for the third straight year a new attendance record was set. Integration continued slowly as Doby played his first full season in the Majors, Satchel Paige was purchased by Veeck, and in midseason Roy Campanella came up from the minors to take over as the Dodger catcher. Most dramatically, baseball's essential balance was demonstrated. For the fifth year in a row in the American League, fourth in a row for the National, a different team won the pennant.

There were some worrisome clouds on the horizon. The televising of games continued to grow as every team in the Majors joined the new medium. In some cases every home game was televised. Nobody really understood the potential of television. The lords of baseball began to go through the same painful process with television that they had with radio. Would it hurt attendance? Would it create new fans? Was the sport suitable to television? How to best make use of it? No one knew the answers, and everyone was afraid of television's growing power.

The 1948 season saw the first mad rush to pay huge sums to young, untested players, who would soon be called "bonus babies." The Phillies' Bob Carpenter took some of his du Pont millions and lavished it on his special love, hard-throwing pitchers. He had already paid $65,000 for an 18-year-old left-hander from Egypt, Pennsylvania, named Curt Simmons in 1947. In 1948 he would continue his largesse, handing out $25,000 to his wisest investment, Robin Roberts, out of the University of Michigan. Lou Perini of the Braves shocked the baseball world by paying a New York schoolboy, left-hander Johnny Antonelli, $75,000. The Pirates spent $130,000 of Frank McKinney's money on two players, Bob Chesnes and Ed Fitzgerald, neither of whom had distinguished careers. The race was on, and soon just about every team in the Majors tried to sign raw talent for big sums. Interesting enough, the most successful teams over the next decade in both leagues were those that used their money to develop their farm systems, like the Yankees and Dodgers, or those who cleverly exploited the talent of the Negro Leagues (e.g., the Dodgers and to a lesser extent the Braves). From the end of the World War II the Dodgers had 26 farm teams in operation pouring forth the young talent that Rickey so loved. The Yankees under their new general manager, George Weiss, were not far behind.

Baseball was on the cusp of a crucial era in its history that would forever transform the sport. The explosion of television broadcasting, the growth of the suburbs, the emergence of a new, vast automobile public, the gradual shriveling of the minors all took place over the next decade and found the lords of baseball at a loss to clearly understand what was happening. The baseball leadership, whether it was the commissioners or the owners, were mostly older men nurtured on baseball before World War II, and they lacked the foresight to deal with the rapid changes that would transform the sport.

Most of these problems were overlooked in 1948 as baseball experienced another successful season. Predictions by the so-called baseball experts were close but off the mark. J. Taylor Spink of *The Sporting News* picked the Red Sox to win the American League pennant because of the key additions of shortstop Vern Stephens and pitcher Jack Kramer. The Sox would be followed closely by the Yanks, Cleveland and Detroit. Others picked the Yanks to repeat, although the only significant addition the organization made was to trade catcher Aaron Robinson for left-hander Ed Lopat of the White Sox. It did not seem important at the time, but it gave the Yankees a solid left-handed starter, something they had lacked since the decline of Lefty Gomez. Over the next seven seasons Lopat would win 113 games for the Yanks and lose only 59. He was a powerful force on the Yankee staff because his slow stuff, what he called his "junk," was a perfect counterbalance to the hard fastballs of Raschi and, particularly, Allie Reynolds. Lopat was also effective in Yankee Stadium, with its deep left-field power alley, as he induced right-handed power hitters to hit long, useless fly balls. Along with the continued development of Raschi and the solid contribution of Reynolds, Lopat gave the Yankees three reliable starters.

In the American League a great race quickly developed, one of the best in its history, among four teams: Cleveland, Boston, New York and a surprising Philadelphia club. The A's astounded everyone by leaping off to a quick start. Building on the moderate success of 1947, Mack had constructed a balanced team. Relying on four good pitchers — Dick Fowler, Carl Scheib, Joe Coleman and rookie Lou Brissie — the A's sprinted into first place early in the season. If Phil Marchildon had maintained his 1947 form, when he had won 19 games, the A's might have proven unbeatable. But Marchildon struggled all season, eventually ending with a losing record. He was never an effective pitcher again. Some people blamed his collapse on a belated reaction to the war, when he had been a prisoner of war. He was essentially finished after the 1948 season.

The A's remained in contention until mid-August, when they lost their spark plug, shortstop Eddie Joost, to an ankle injury. They eventually collapsed because the team hitting was weak, finishing sixth overall in the League.

The starting lineup featured some quality players besides Joost. Barney McCoskey had his last great year, hitting .326, although it was a soft .326 with only 26 extra-base hits among his 168 safeties. Hank Majeski played a great third base and hit .310, driving in 120 runs. Elmer Valo was a reckless and daring right fielder who hit over .300 also. Ferris Fain avoided the sophomore jinx, hitting .281 and fielding his position brilliantly. In fact, the A's infield was on its way to establishing a reputation as one of the soundest in baseball, turning 180 double plays and making just 57 errors. What hurt the A's in 1948 as much as Marchildon's collapse was Sam Chapman's having an off year. He hit just 13 homers and drove in 70 runs out of the cleanup slot.

Even so the A's surprised everyone in baseball and stayed near the top most of the season. At the Memorial Day break, they led the Indians by two games, with the Yankees in third, whereas the heavily favored Red Sox languished in seventh place, 11½ games back.

Cleveland proved a better club than anyone had expected. Their pitching was superb, the best in the League if not the Majors. Feller, who would win 19 games that season, was not the overpowering pitcher of the past. He had hurt his arm pitching against the A's early in the 1947 season and never again had that combination of great fastball and unhittable curve. He was joined by two underrated starters: Bob Lemon, in his second full year as a pitcher, and rookie sensation Gene Bearden. Both would go on to win 20 games and have ERAs under 3.00, with Lemon pitching a no-hitter. For a fourth starter Veeck got lefty Sam Zoldak from the cash-poor Browns for $100,000. Boudreau paired Zoldak with righty Steve Gomek. Between them they went 18-9 for the Indians.

The Indians also benefited from career years by aging veterans Ken Keltner and Joe Gordon. Both men hit over 30 homers and between them drove in 240 runs. Doby had a fine rookie year, hitting .301, and he was joined in the outfield by second-year man, Dale Mitchell, who hit over .330 and led the League in hits and triples. In effect, the Indians had everything: good hitting, great pitching and solid defense. Boudreau had his best year not only as manager but at the plate, challenging Ted Williams for the batting title all season. He eventually hit .355, the highest average any shortstop had reached since Luke Appling hit .388 in 1936.

Between Memorial Day and July 4 the Indians forged into first place, leading the A's by 1½ games, the Yankees by 2½ and the rapidly closing Red Sox, who had wiped five games from their deficit, by only six games.

The Yankees seemed like a better team than the 1947 world champions, but something was missing. Joe DiMaggio and Tommy Henrich had great years, with DiMaggio either leading the League or challenging for the lead in homers and RBI all season. Yogi Berra, who split his time behind the plate and in the outfield, continued to develop as a hitter, batting over .300. But Charley Keller was through — he never recovered from his back problems and

Ferris Fain. One of the most aggressive defensive first basemen of his era. A fine hitter who won two batting titles for the A's, Fain led American League first basemen in assists for four seasons. No first sacker in his era took part in as many double plays in a single season as Fain did in 1949, 194. (Brace Photo.)

had lost his power at the plate. The double-play combination of Stirnweiss and Rizzuto had an off year. Both men hit .252 and never got going during the season. The Yankees had no first baseman. George McQuinn, who had given them a quality year at first in 1947, struggled all year and wound up hitting almost 60 points lower in 1948. Billy Johnson at third also had an off year offensively and defensively. He made 20 errors in just 118 games and drove in only 64 runs. In effect, the entire Yankee infield had an off year.

The Yankee pitching staff featured three dominating starters in newcomer Ed Lopat, second-year man Vic Raschi and Allie Reynolds. All had a good year, winning a total of 52 games. The club's problem was that it lacked a fourth starter to compete with the Indians. Spec Shea never recaptured his rookie-year form and stumbled around .500 all season. Lefty Tommy Byrne pitched well at times but was wild, walking more than he struck out.

Part of the Yankee problem revolved around Bucky Harris, a laid-back player's manager who had few rules. Harris believed the Yankees were professionals who would eventually pull together and win the pennant. This was dangerous thinking for him because Harris had been MacPhail's choice as manager, and new general manager George Weiss had no faith in him. Weiss wanted Harris to put pressure on the players and even hired a private detective to follow the players around. He ordered Harris to read the detective's reports to the team, which he did, making it clear that he thought the whole idea was absurd. If the Yankees didn't win in 1948, Harris was in trouble.

The magic of 1947 was gone particularly for Joe Page. Page had celebrated his fame in the off season and reported to spring training overweight and then developed a throat infection (Henrich, 201). He continued to save games at close to the 1947 level, but his ERA ballooned over 4.00 and he lost more games than he won.

With all their problems the Yankees played great baseball after July 4, going 37-22, .626 baseball, so that by Labor Day they were only a game from first. Unfortunately for them, the Red Sox were even hotter.

In July and August the Red Sox won 43 games and lost just 19, a .694 pace, to forge into first place a game ahead of the Yanks, 1½ over the Indians and 3½ over the fading A's. After a terrible start under their new manager, Joe McCarthy, the Red Sox started to mount a consistent team effort in mid-summer. The pitching staff was relatively untested now that it was clear that Ferris and Tex Hughson were just about finished. Jack Kramer, finally playing for a good club, became a big winner. Steady Joe Dobson had another good year, and he, along with Kramer and rookie lefty Mel Parnell, gave the Red Sox three quality starters. A fourth starter was a constant problem. McCarthy used Ellis Kinder and Denny Galehouse off and on, switching them from the bull pen to starting positions throughout the season. Even more important than the lack of a consistent fourth starter, though, was Boston's failure to develop a bull pen.

Boston's hitting was as good as usual but not up to past seasons in power. They finished well behind the Indians and Yankees in homers, with Ted Williams hitting just 25, his lowest total since 1940. Otherwise Williams had a great year, winning the batting title for the second straight season with a .369 average and again leading the League in walks with 126. Vern Stephens took over shortstop and hit well: 29 homers and 137 RBI. Doerr bounced back from a subpar 1947, banging 27 homers and 111 RBI. Johnny Pesky, who moved to third to make room for Stephens, had a poor year for him, hitting just .281. His fielding at third was adequate. Dom DiMaggio had a typical quality season, batting .285, driving in 85 runs and making 503 putouts in center field.

Cleveland won the pennant by playing the best baseball of the top three teams during September, going 22 and 8 to overcome a Boston lead. With just nine games remaining the Indians, Red Sox and Yankees were in a virtual tie for first. Williams got hot and went 11 for 27 in the last eight games of the season to help keep Boston in the race. In the last weekend of the season the Red Sox eliminated the Yankees, and Cleveland had a chance to clinch the pennant by beating the Tigers on the last day of the season. But Hal Newhouser, who had rebounded from a poor 1947, outdueled Bob Feller 7–1, winning his twenty-first game. Cleveland and Boston were forced into a one-game play-off, the first in the history of the American League.

The whole season came down to one game in Fenway Park, where the Red Sox were just about unbeatable. Their record, 55-22, was the best in the Majors. Lou Boudreau clearly outmanaged the great McCarthy. As his starter, Boudreau chose rookie Gene Bearden with his tantalizing knuckleball, despite Bearden's having had only one day's rest. Some Indian players were upset by the choice. John Berardino complained that it was dangerous to pitch a lefty in Fenway with its short left-field fence. But Boudreau stuck with his choice (Boudreau, *Boudreau*, 121). McCarthy turned to 36-year-old veteran Denny Galehouse, a mediocre pitcher having a .500 year for a team that played .619 baseball.

McCarthy's choice was incredible. He had used his aces Dobson, Kramer and Parnell in his last three games, and he was gambling that Galehouse could give him a quality performance. In naming Galehouse he passed over Kinder, who had gone 4-1 against first-division teams and had the eighth-lowest ERA in the League. Originally McCarthy picked Parnell to start but changed his mind when he saw the wind blowing out to left field. Parnell had volunteered to pitch and was not reluctant to start again (as some rumors held) (*SN*, 3/26/52, p. 6). In fact, Galehouse himself was surprised that he was named (Golenbock, *Fenway*, 176). Boudreau thought that McCarthy was trying to put something over on him by announcing Galehouse as the starter. He sent the traveling secretary to look around the stadium to see if the Red Sox were secretly having someone else warm up (Boudreau, *Boudreau*, 123).

The game was tied 1–1 after three innings. In the fourth the Indians put the game away and knocked out Galehouse. After singles by Boudreau and Gordon, Ken Keltner hit his thirty-first homer over the Green Monster. Larry Doby then doubled and scored on a sacrifice and an infield out, giving the Indians a 5–1 lead. Boudreau's second homer of the game in the fifth made it 6–1, and the Indians cruised to victory. Bearden gave the Red Sox just five hits over nine innings. Interestingly, Galehouse would pitch just two more innings in his career and then retire early in the 1949 season. McCarthy, it seemed, had lost his magic touch.

Cleveland's pennant was a team effort, featuring great pitching, superb defense and solid hitting. Boudreau did a great job of managing in 1948, which is interesting considering that before the season began Veeck had wanted to fire him and replace him with Jimmy Dykes, an old warhorse who had never won anything. Although Boudreau was only 32, he would never again approach the level of baseball play or managing he displayed in 1948. He was an easy choice for American League MVP and manager of the year.

The National League in 1948 did not produce a pennant race as exciting as the record-breaking one in the junior circuit. Attendance figures told the story. Whereas the American League alone drew more fans than the entire Majors in 1945, the National League actually saw a drop-off of 600,000 over the record-breaking 1947 season.

In a preseason poll of BWAA, Billy Southworth's Boston Braves were a clear favorite over the Cardinals, with the Dodgers and Giants finishing third and fourth. *The Sporting News* expressed surprise at the showing of the Braves among the writers, although the Braves had played impressively throughout the 1947 season (*SN*, 4/21/47, p. 1). There was a lot of talk that the Dodgers would have troubles with Durocher back as manager after serving his suspension, and the Cardinals looked unchanged from the previous season when they had fallen just short.

In fact, all the favorites started slowly. The Giants set the pace for the first month and a half of the season behind the long-ball hitting of Johnny Mize and Sid Gordon. The rest of the Giant long-ball threats — Willard Marshall, second-year man Bobby Thomson and catcher Walker Cooper — struggled most of the year. But the Giant pitchers were surprisingly effective. The staff leaders were veteran Ray Poat, who was 7-1 by the All-Star break, rookie Sheldon Jones and second-year man, Larry Jansen. The team's lack of depth and mediocre fielding eventually took its toll, however, and the Giants dropped out of the pennant race in June.

The Braves started slowly and then got hot in June to pull into a 1½ game lead over the Cardinals by the All-Star break, July 13. The Braves seemed unspectacular, but they had the best overall team depth. Tommy Holmes was his usual capable self, third in the League in hitting at .357. The double-play combination of Ed Stanky, who had come over to the Braves in the off season, and rookie shortstop Alvin Dark was giving the Braves good defense and hitting over .300. Bob Elliott at third slipped from his MVP form in 1947 but continued to drive in runs and field his position well. The Braves had added a long-ball threat in outfielder Jeff Heath. But the real strength of the team was its pitching. Johnny Sain picked up where he had left off in 1947 and was 10-5 by the All-Star break. He would eventually win 24 games, all of which he completed except for his twenty-fourth victory. Rookie Vern Bickford was

4-3, and vet Bill Voiselle, old "96," was 8-5. Only Warren Spahn had a hard time recapturing his 20-victory form. In effect, the Braves had a three-man rotation: it wasn't "Spahn and Sain and pray for rain"; it was Spahn and Sain and Voiselle and Bickford and then begin praying. In a weak National League year it would prove enough.

The Cardinals were in second largely because of the hitting of Stan Musial and the brilliant pitching of Harry Brecheen. After a slow start Enos Slaughter came on strong the second half of the season, and rookie first sacker Nippy Jones drove in 81 runs but could not get his batting average over the .260 mark. The Cardinals were plagued by pitching problems all season. Howie Pollet struggled for the second straight season, and George "Red" Munger and Murray Dickson were below .500 all year. Whitey Kurowski suffered a total collapse and dropped to .214, with only two homers and 33 RBI for the season. In effect, he was finished at age 30. Aside from Musial, Brecheen and Slaughter, the Cards looked like an aging, tired team. Even so, they had enough to stay in contention all season and almost steal a pennant.

Other than the Braves the closest thing to a surprise in the National League in 1948 was the enormous improvement of the Pirates. Tied for last in 1947, under new manager Billy Meyer they stayed in contention most of the 1948 year. At the All-Star break they were in third place, a half game behind the Cards and three ahead of the sagging Giants. They had another big home-run year from Ralph Kiner, although he slipped sharply from his great 1947 season. He still tied with Mize for the home run lead and managed to drive in 123 runs, hitting just .265. The double play combination of young Stan Rojek at short and veteran Danny Murtaugh at second was solid defensively, and both men hit .290 for the year. The Pirates got a good year from ancient hurlers like Elmer Riddle, Rip Sewell and rookie Bob Chesnes who were 39-19. Meyer did a good job keeping a weak team in contention, but after a great August (19-9) the team finished the last month one game over .500 to fall from the pennant race.

In a different sense the Dodgers were also a surprise. With Durocher back and feuding with Jackie Robinson because of his poor conditioning in spring training, the team got off to a very slow start. Durocher and Robinson could not get along. Both had huge egos. Robinson remembered every slight, and Durocher couldn't abide anyone who didn't fawn over him (Eskenazi, 224). The two men feuded all season. Durocher made his last contribution to the Dodgers by moving Billy Cox from shortstop, where he had played with the Pirates, to third base. For a half dozen years Cox was one of the best defensive third basemen in the National League.

At the All-Star break the Dodgers were in sixth place, 7½ games behind the front-running Braves. Durocher sensed he was in trouble. He no longer felt that he had a close relationship with Rickey and that in some way the old man blamed him for Chandler's suspension. The two men had been at loggerheads since the beginning of the season because Durocher wanted to make Campanella his regular catcher because Bruce Edwards had come down with a sore arm. Rickey wanted Campanella to integrate the American Association. Durocher didn't give a damn about the American Association or integration, but he believed Campanella was already as good as any catcher in the National League.

Durocher had also run into a streak of injuries, as well as players who were having off years. At the All-Star break, only one Dodger, Furillo, was hitting over .300 and only one pitcher, Ralph Branca, who was 9-6, was ranked among the top 20. The Dodgers suddenly got hot and forced their way into contention, but it was too late for Durocher. In mid-July Rickey, who believed that the Dodgers had a real chance for another pennant if Shotton returned, pushed Durocher out as manager. Durocher landed on his feet and in the headlines when he was named manager of the New York Giants in one of the most shocking sports turnabouts in baseball history.

Horace Stoneham, the owner of the Giants, wanted to change managers and get rid of his beloved Mel Ott, only the third man to manage the team in its history. He thought that Shotton might be available and approached Rickey, not knowing that Rickey also wanted to make a change. When Rickey told Stoneham he could have his choice, Stoneham picked Durocher. The change in managers took the Giants-Dodgers rivalry to a new level of intensity for the next decade.

Under Shotton the Dodgers did rally and forced their way into contention in August behind the solid play of Campanella, new first baseman Gil Hodges, who was switched from catching by Durocher in one of his last acts as Dodger manager, and the sudden effectiveness of the wild Rex Barney. The Dodgers swept a doubleheader from the Cards on August 29 to take first place from the Braves, who lost two to the Pirates and dropped from the lead for the first time since June 12.

At the beginning of September the Dodgers and Braves were tied for first, and the Cards and Pirates were just two games back. Yet what looked like another breakneck National League race turned into a Braves rout when they went 21-7 in the last month. The Dodgers faded to 16-17, and the Cards played good ball, 17-12, but couldn't keep up with the Braves, who won the pennant by 6½ games, the biggest margin in the National League until the Dodgers ran away from the rest of the League in 1953.

Neither the Cards nor the Dodgers had enough to challenge the Braves. Dodger pitching was terrible. The club's leading pitcher, Branca, won just five games after the All-Star break, and the bull pen collapsed entirely. Branca was on his way to becoming an enigma. He would pitch brilliantly, even overwhelmingly, and then something disastrous would happen. Some writers and players believed he lacked heart. The Cards stayed in contention largely because of Brecheen and Musial. The latter had the greatest season of his distinguished career. He not only hit .376 and led the League in RBI but missed the triple crown by one homer. His 230 hits were the most in the National League since 1937. His slugging percentage of .702 was the highest since Hack Wilson in 1930. He also led the League in doubles, triples, total bases, and runs scored. In fact, of the 12 offensive categories listed in the *Baseball Encyclopedia*, Musial led the National League in eight and was second in one other. It wasn't enough to save the Cards.

The Braves, under Billy Southworth, had been a good club since 1946 and had played some of the best baseball in the National League in 1947. They had developed new talent — players like Dark and Earl Torgeson — made some good trades for established stars like Stanky and Heath and blended them with vets like Holmes and Sain into a solid, if underrated, club. When the club suffered any setbacks, such as Stanky's breaking his ankle in mid-season, Southworth adjusted and kept the team on track. Southworth was a good, possibly even great, manager who is all but forgotten today, but for almost a decade in the 1940s, first with the Cards and then with the Braves, he established an impressive record. He won three pennants in a row with the Cards, 1942–1944, won two World Series and then turned the Braves into a contender, helping them to their first pennant since 1914. He had lost a beloved son after World War II, never really recovered and started drinking heavily. By the end of the 1940s he had lost his interest in baseball and retired in 1951. During his 13 years as a manager he won 1815 and lost 1054 for .593, the fifth highest win record in baseball history, higher than Casey Stengel, John McGraw, Connie Mack, Miller Huggins, Bucky Harris or Leo Durocher, all of whom are in the Hall of Fame. Southworth belongs there also.

The 1948 World Series was the last one in which at least one New York team didn't play until 1965. Cleveland was favored because they had beaten two better teams than the Braves had. Cleveland looked stronger in all three categories: hitting, pitching and fielding.

The Series was the first one to be seen widely on television. It was estimated that 7.7 million people watched the games, foreshadowing the rise of a new giant sports media. *The Sporting News* believed that the television audience the next year would be double that of 1948 (*SN*, 10/27/48, p. 7).

The Series itself was somewhat anticlimactic. The Indians won in six games. The games were close: three were determined by one run, one by two runs and another by three runs. There was only one blowout, an 11–5 Braves rout of Bob Feller, which featured two homers by Bob Elliott. Pitching dominated and neither team did much offensively. Bob Lemon won two games and Gene Bearden pitched 10⅔ innings without allowing an earned run. For the Braves Sain pitched brilliantly, splitting two games but with an ERA of 1.06.

The Indians just had too much pitching depth. They were able to start their big three — Feller, Lemon and Bearden — in five of the six games. Their fourth starter, Steve Gromek, beat Sain in game four, 2–1, which just about guaranteed the Indians a victory because it put them up 3–1 in the Series with Feller, Lemon and Bearden rested. On the other hand, the Braves had to go to veteran Nelson Potter in game five and Voiselle in game six when time ran out.

The Series wasn't much aesthetically, but it was a huge financial success. Because the Indians played in massive Municipal Stadium, the crowds were enormous. The Series saw records for a single game (86,300), as well as for a six-game series (358,000). As a result the winning players share also set a record: $6,772, an enormous figure for a time when many players were only making around $10,000 for the season.

Baseball could be satisfied with itself in 1948. For the third year in a row a new attendance record, 20.9 million, was set, a figure that Major League baseball would not match until 1962, when there were four new teams added to the Majors. The sport was booming, reflecting the prosperity and optimism of the late 1940s in the United States. America seemed all powerful behind its atomic monopoly and with no economic rivals to fear. But there were problems on the way.

3

The Yankees Return
to Power, 1949–1950

Baseball's Problems Begin

Following three successful and prosperous years Major League baseball was optimistic about the future as the national pastime approached the mid-century mark. The doubts that plagued the game in the depression era and during World War II were forgotten in a rush of profits. But baseball was about to enter a decade and a half when it was beset by problems over what direction to take. Attendance would begin a slow, steady decline in 1949 for five straight years, dropping from 20.9 to 14.4 million in 1953, reflecting manifold problems confronting the sport. The 6.5 million decline was greater than the attendance of either league in any year before 1945.

If you take baseball attendance as a percentage of the population, the sport was losing its audience throughout the 1950s. At its peak in 1948 baseball attendance was around 14 percent of the population. It dropped by the end of the decade to just over 11 percent despite a net population growth of 28 million during the 1950s.

Television viewing was taking hold in the nation. After slow growth in the late 1940s, sales of television sets exploded in the first half of the 1950s as prices dropped to reasonable levels. In 1950 12 percent of American homes had television. Five years later the figure had grown to 67 percent. Never before in our history has there been a comparable explosion of a technology.

The televising of baseball grew accordingly. By the mid-1950s some teams televised all their home games as well as some road games. Three New York teams, for example, provided saturation coverage. This led some baseball people to attribute the decline of game attendance to baseball viewing at home.

Walter O'Malley believed that the public was "T-V sated" by the middle of the decade (Rader, *In Its Own Image*, 170). This didn't stop him from investigating the possibilities of pay television. Unfortunately for him the technology wasn't perfected as yet. There is little doubt that the public got into the habit of sitting at home and watching games, especially once coverage became more sophisticated and picture quality improved.

The baseball owners were in a quandary. They saw attendance declining — by 31 percent between 1948 and 1953 — and yet they were making more money than ever from television. The Dodgers, for example, by 1955 took in almost $800,000 from local television and radio rights at a time when the team payroll was around $500,000 (Kahn, *Era*, 285). This meant that the team had a guaranteed profit before the first game of the season was played. Revenue from broadcasting had risen by 800 percent since 1946. At the same time ticket prices stayed around the same or even dropped slightly. Average ticket price for a baseball game was $1.60, the equivalent of $8.23 in 1990 dollars (Peter Gammons, *SI*, 4/16/90, p. 42).

Televising of the World Series proved a huge success, with the Gillette Razor Company keeping its monopoly as sponsor and successfully promoting its new products. What Gillette began in 1939, first on radio and then on television, would last for 32 years and embed its product in the male mind as synonymous with shaving. An entire generation of men grew up with the jingle ringing in their ears: "To look sharp and feel sharp use Gillette razor blades."

Baseball was making money from television and radio, but it didn't grasp the connection between declining attendance and the clear popularity of the game over the air waves. The owners had belatedly recognized that radio had created new fans, especially women, but television confused them. Branch Rickey believed that there was a significant difference between the two media and their impact on baseball. Radio created a desire to see baseball in person, whereas television fulfilled that need (Miller, 6). In the 1950s Rickey seemed correct. Rickey's insight was, as the English say, "too clever by half." Later it would become clear that correctly handled with good announcers television could dramatically increase audience enthusiasm and interest in a baseball team.

One thing was clear: television was destroying the minor leagues. Attendance had jumped from 15 million fans in 1946 to 42 million in 1949. Eight years later that figure dropped back to 15 million and then shrunk five million more by 1960. The people in minor league cities turned away from their teams and were watching the Major Leagues on television (Rader, *American Sports*, 255).

Among the first to realize the change taking place in American habits in the 1950s were the beer companies. By the mid-1950s they were willing to pay high advertising rates to reach the virtually all-male audience watching baseball on television (Miller, 63). The bar-stool potato gradually gave way to the couch potato with his new treat, the six pack in nice, cold aluminum cans, as television was adopted in more and more homes. Another interesting aspect of the role that the beer industry played in baseball history was the change in sponsorship. For a while local brewers sponsored their area teams but they were eventually ousted by the more powerful national beers, Miller and especially Budweiser, as they saw the size of the potential audience.

Combined with the growing popularity of television, baseball confronted another complex problem in the 1950s. The Major League ballparks, all of which had been built between 1909 and 1932, were located in crowded urban areas, where they had been placed to take advantage of public transportation.

Suddenly the cities were beginning to change. Postwar prosperity had led to a huge home-building boom in the suburbs and a population transfer out of the cities. The automobile revolution of the 1950s gave the public more mobility and got people out of the habit of using public transportation. Most of the ballparks were not only in declining neighborhoods but had virtually no provision for parking. Shibe Park in congested North Philadelphia, for example, had parking for about 1000 cars, and the area around Ebbets Field could provide parking for 700 cars. These figures could be duplicated throughout the Majors. The new baseball fan preferred to stay home and watch the game on television to battling for a parking space or using public transportation. A revolution in American social habits was taking place and the lords of baseball were at a loss to understand its consequences.

By 1949 baseball was at its balanced best in years. A different team had won the pennant in the American League for five straight years, in the National for four years in a row. This helps to explain why six NL and every AL team established attendance records in those years. Good pennant races, joined with a built-up enthusiasm for the sport, gave Major League baseball an enormous sense of optimism in 1949. Part of that optimism was about to be washed away in the overwhelming domination of the game by the New York area teams for over a generation. Between 1949 and 1966 a team from New York (or derived from New York, like the Los Angeles Dodgers and San Francisco Giants) would play in every World Series and win 15 of 18 world titles. (Exceptions were the 1957 Milwaukee Braves, the 1960 Pirates and the 1964 Cardinals.) Not until the Cardinals defeated the miracle Red Sox in 1967 did two non–New York teams reach the World Series, 20 years after the Braves and Indians had last done it. This New York domination was disastrous for baseball competition.

The domination of the New York teams was built on superior organization, especially the careful nurturing of homegrown talent in their farm systems and, in the case of the Dodgers and Giants, the exploitation of the Negro Leagues for new talent. As the 1949 season opened the Dodgers had 25 farm teams, the Yankees 21 and the Giants 19. Among them these three teams also had seven Triple-A teams. Only the Tigers and Cardinals had more than one Triple-A team. Teams like the Senators, with just nine farm clubs and none at the Triple-A level, or the White Sox and Cincinnati, with 11 teams, could not compete with the New York–area teams. They lacked the money to develop new talent, as well as the organizational skills to compete with the most successful franchises.

Rickey, as Dodger general manager, had carefully constructed the farm system just as he did before with the Cardinals. During the late 1940s and early 1950s talent passed throughout the Dodgers organization: Gil Hodges, Duke Snider, Don Newcombe, Jim Gilliam, Carl Erskine and others. In 1947, against the wishes of other Dodger owners, Rickey purchased a former naval station in Vero Beach, Florida, and developed a new concept: the Major League–minor league complex where the Dodger brand of baseball could be taught and systematized. Players would learn baseball fundamentals the same way at every level taught by experts: George Sisler on hitting, Pepper Martin on baserunning, Clyde Sukeforth on catching, Durocher on infield play (Polner, 134). It was expensive, but it paid large dividends. Eventually the Dodgers were able to produce Rickey's "quality from quantity." It also meant that Rickey could sell off or trade excess Dodger talent and fill the team's coffers, as well as his pockets because he received a percentage of all player sales (Parrott, 230). In 1954 there were 43 Dodger products on Major League rosters, more than any other team in baseball.

George Weiss, who ran the Yankees after MacPhail sold out his interest in 1947, was not as shrewd a judge of talent as Rickey, but he put together a superb group of scouts and then didn't interfere with them. Weiss and the Yankees were notoriously cheap, but they skimmed off some of the best baseball players in the nation. As a result, from 1949 to the early 1960s, when Yankee owners began to cut back on expenses to maximize profits before selling the team, the Yankee farm system bailed the team out at crucial moments: Mantle when DiMaggio was finished; Elston Howard in 1955, when Berra needed relief behind the plate; Bill Skowron, Whitey Ford, Bobby Richardson, Tony Kubek to fill gaps in the lineup. With the advice of Stengel, Weiss also proved adept at rescuing players deemed finished: John Mize, Johnny Sain, Enos Slaughter. Weiss used his excess talent to negotiate some great trades — such as the swaps for Roger Maris, Bob Turley, Don Larsen — to help the team continue winning pennants.

Enter Casey Stengel

When the Yankees hired Casey Stengel after the 1948 World Series, they didn't know what to expect. Weiss believed Stengel was a good teacher with a solid baseball background, but his managerial record was unimpressive. In nine seasons he had one winning record and his highest finish had been fifth place. Stengel understood what was expected of him. "I didn't get the job through friendship," he told the press after his appointment. "The Yankees represent an investment of millions of dollars. ... I got the job because the people here think I can produce for them" (Golenbock, *Dynasty*, 5).

Baseball experts tended to regard Stengel as something of a clown. But Stengel had never managed in a first-class organization before. He had learned his baseball from some good teachers, especially John McGraw. Stengel knew the game intimately, and he applied many of McGraw's techniques, modified by the condition of the Yankee team of 1949. Stengel was a believer in teaching fundamentals and stressed team morale and versatility (Koppett, 154–155). The writers showed their confidence in Stengel by picking the Yankees to finish a distant third behind the Red Sox and Indians. Out of 206 members of the Baseball Writers Association of America, exactly six named the Yankees as pennant winners (Kahn, *Era*, 172). Even Dan Daniel of the *New York World Telegram*, a notorious Yankee booster, believed that Boston was too strong for the rest of the American League. He believed that the pitching shortage that plagued the Red Sox in 1948 would be relieved by comebacks by Dave Ferris and Tex Hughson, as well as by the development of sensational rookie Mickey McDermott. The BWAA was influenced by other factors, particularly the injury problems facing the Yankees. Joe DiMaggio, at 34, was showing signs of being injury prone despite his great 1948 season, Tommy Henrich was hobbled by bad knees, and Charley Keller's career was threatened by continued back problems. As it turned out none of these injuries mattered.

The Yankees held first place for all but four days in 1949, a remarkable performance given the health of the team. Red Patterson, the Yankee public relations man, made much of the injuries the Yankees suffered during the season. He published a list of 72 major and minor injuries for the 1949 campaign. In fact, the Yankees were hard hit. Stengel was forced to platoon. DiMaggio was out until mid-June with a painful bone spur in his heel, Billy Johnson and Bobby Brown alternated at third, and Henrich was at first for 46 games and in the outfield for 102. Platooning was rare in the late 1940s, but it is a technique that McGraw had used successfully in the past. Stengel borrowed and adapted the concept masterfully. In a short time Stengel's success with platooning led other managers to adopt the practice. By the mid-1950s platooning had become widespread.

Too much can be made of the Yankee injuries and Stengel's platooning. The team won because it had superb pitching, excellent defense and Joe Page in the bull pen. Page's return to form after his off year in 1948 was probably the key to the Yankees winning. Until that time no relief pitcher ever had the kind of season that Page tore off in 1949. He not only won 13 games, but he saved 27 others, meaning that he played a part in 40 of the Yankees' 97 wins, a 41 percent ratio. Some idea of what his save total means can be derived from the fact that the next-highest number in the American League was 10 and that Ted Wilks led the National League with nine. Page defined the role of the bull pen ace for the future — ideally a hard thrower who came into the game late and fired bullets. Just as platooning took hold because of Stengel's success in 1949, so did the idea that a contender needed a dominating presence in the bull pen. No longer would the bull pen be dominated by over-the-hill types. It didn't happen all at once but emerged gradually over the next decade or so. Page gave way to Jim Konstanty, Joe Black, Hoyt Wilhelm, Don Mossi and Ray Narleski. By the end of the next decade every team, even the poor ones, had a big gun in the bull pen.

It is difficult to understand how the Yankees won. The Red Sox outhit them in almost every category. No Yankee hitter made the top five offensively except for Tommy Henrich, who was a distant third in homers and slugging percentage behind Ted Williams and Vern Stephens. Cleveland's pitching was better than the Yankees.' Still the Yankees won.

Their big four starters — Raschi, Lopat, Reynolds and Tommy Byrne — plus Page won 91 games versus just 42 losses. The four aces started 128 of the Yankees 154 games. Aside from a brief midseason slump by Raschi, the starters never faltered. Stengel kept them fresh by not overworking them. Raschi hurled the most innings, 275; the others averaged slightly over 200 innings. This was a pattern Stengel did not deviate from in his years as Yankee manager. No Yankee starter threw 300 innings between 1949 and 1960 at a time when 300 innings wasn't uncommon (Kahn, *Era*, 182). Robin Roberts, for example, did it six straight times, Warren Spahn twice, Bob Lemon, Bob Friend and Vern Bickford of the Braves once. Stengel preferred to blend in starters with long and short relievers as a way of extending the life of his staff. Interestingly, in 1949 a Yankee pitcher ranked in the top five in every pitching department.

The Yankees broke away from the rest of the League early. Even without Joe DiMaggio the Yankees played .630 baseball. Tommy Henrich, whom Mel Allen had nicknamed "Old Reliable," lived up to his title by driving in the winning run in 18 games, despite being hobbled by a bad knee (Henrich, 229). Pitching and defense were the keys. At the July 4 point of the season, the big three of Raschi, Reynolds and Lopat were 26-7.

The only other team that showed any life in the first half of the season was Connie Mack's A's. The A's used brilliant pitching from rookie Alex Kellner, veterans Lou Brissie and Dick Fowler plus the solid hitting of leadoff man, Eddie Joost, to close to within 4½ games of the Yankees by July 4. The highly favored Red Sox languished in fifth place, 12 full games out of first. Aside from Mel Parnell, who was 10-4, and their usual fine hitting, the Red Sox were struggling. From early July on the Red Sox got hot.

Between July 4 and Labor Day Boston played the best baseball in the Majors. Parnell was now joined by Ellis Kinder as the best back-to-back starters. Kinder reeled off 15 wins in a row to move the Red Sox into contention. Boston had four regulars hitting .300 or better and one, Bobby Doerr, at .299. In August the Red Sox starters, Parnell, Kinder, Stobbs and Jack

Kramer, were 18-0 (Halberstam, 212). Boston made up ten games by going 44-16, and the Yankees were a steady 31-22. Raschi was just 5-7 in July and August. Tommy Byrne picked up some of the slack, winning seven of ten games. The A's sagged badly, largely the result of bad hitting, and were passed by Detroit and Cleveland. In September the American League pennant race boiled down to a head-to-head battle between the Red Sox and the Yankees.

The Yankees won essentially by playing the more balanced baseball in the crucial last month of contention. The Red Sox's lack of pitching depth betrayed them. McCarthy largely turned the race over to Parnell and Kinder. Between them they started ten games and relieved in seven in September and threw 121 innings (Halberstam, 223). The other starters hurled just 48 innings. In contrast, the Yankee big four averaged 40 innings, whereas Page pitched 29 innings in 13 games.

The Red Sox were exhausted by the end of the season. All eight regulars had played in virtually every game. When Boston came to New York for the last two games of the season with a one-game lead, two tired teams faced each other, but the Yankees were fresher. Reynolds and Raschi backed up by Page would face Parnell and Kinder with no bull pen to speak of. Parnell later admitted he was exhausted, as was Kinder (Golenbock, *Fenway*, 180).

The Yankees won both games. In the first Page's relief and a homer by reserve outfielder Johnny Lindell allowed the Yankees to overcome a 4–0 Red Sox lead. In the final game Raschi outdueled Kinder, holding a 1–0 lead for eight innings. When McCarthy removed Kinder for a pinch hitter, the Yanks broke through for four runs in the bottom of the eighth. Although the Red Sox rallied in the ninth, Raschi held them off.

For the second year in a row McCarthy was blamed for losing the pennant. He removed Kinder, who was pitching brilliantly, for a pinch hitter, Tom Wright, who had three at bats in 1949. Kinder was furious. He confronted McCarthy after the game calling him a "gutless old clown" who "couldn't manage my dick" (Kahn, *Era*, 224). Kinder believed that if McCarthy had let him hit the Red Sox would have won the pennant. Other Red Sox players also blamed McCarthy, some wondering if he really didn't want to see his old team win after all (Golenbock, *Fenway*, 182–183). McCarthy was a tired old man and his two failures in the final games of the 1948 and 1949 seasons wore out his welcome in Boston. He was gone before the next season was half over.

In the final analysis the Yankees won for two reasons: the inability of the Red Sox to win on the road and Joe Page. Page's relief work gave the other Yankee pitchers an opportunity to pace themselves. He was the crucial difference between the two teams. Most of the Red Sox understood Page's significance. Parnell said that the lack of a bull pen killed the Red Sox. Williams put it more succinctly: if we had some like Page we would have won the pennant by ten games (Halberstam, 200). The next-to-last game gave a clear illustration of the Red Sox's lack of a stopper. With a 4–0 lead they had to stay with

Parnell because McCarthy didn't have a reliable bull pen ace. Although Page held the Red Sox in check, the Yankees gradually overcame this deficit and won the game.

The Red Sox record in Fenway was 61-16, but they were under .500 on the road. The Yankees were more consistent. They won at home and on the road. In fact, the Yankees were one of two teams (the other was Cleveland) with a better than .500 percentage on the road.

Stengel also deserves credit for keeping his team fresh. He maneuvered cleverly all season. He only had one regular who played in 150 games, Phil Rizzuto. A rookie, Jerry Coleman, played the next-highest number of games, just 128. In contrast, the Red Sox had six men who played more games than that. The Yankee bench was stronger throughout the season, as reflected in Lindell, a reserve player who won the next-to-last game of the season. Boston had no one of Lindell's ability coming off the bench. Their reserves consisted of weak hitters like Matt Batts, Billy Hitchcock, Lou Stringer and Tom O'Brien.

When it counted the Yankees found a way to beat Boston. Their record against them was 13-9. Vic Raschi was 4-1, Reynolds 3-2, which was matched by Parnell and Kinder against the Yankees. The Yankees' second-line pitchers beat Boston six times, whereas the only Red Sox pitchers other than Kinder and Parnell to beat the Yankees were Mickey McDermott and Jack Kramer, who each won one game. On the other hand, the Yankees beat Kramer, Ernie Johnson and Joe Dobson twice, Tex Hughson and Walt Masterson once.

In 1949 Stengel established the pattern of Yankee success for the next decade and a half—good starting pitching, a talented bull pen, a strong bench, first-class defense mixed in with a half dozen quality hitters. It was a formula that proved unbeatable when combined with Weiss's shrewd trades and the constant flow of talent from the Yankee farm system.

The National League race was as close as the American League's, even if it lacked the excitement of the junior circuit. Before the season began the baseball writers split about evenly between the Dodgers and Braves for the pennant. Bob Broeg of the *St. Louis Post Dispatch* predicted a very tight race, with the Dodgers and Braves vying for first and the Cardinals a close third. He noted that in 1948 the National League had been balanced—only 30 games separated the first- from the last-place team. He also believed that the Dodgers would benefit from what he described as a "full soothing" season of Burt Shotton after the turmoil of the last two years in Brooklyn. He correctly spotted the Cardinals' weakness: too many injuries in the infield, no center fielder to replace Terry Moore and the need for Howie Pollet to recover his past form. Broeg overrated the Braves off their 1948 performance (*Pic Baseball*, spring 1949, p. 19–20). In retrospect it can be seen that 1948 was a freak year for the Braves: a number of players had career years, and the team just jelled, whereas the rest of the National League sagged badly.

The pennant race panned out just about the way Broeg and others had predicted. Brooklyn — behind the superb hitting of Jackie Robinson, who came into his prime in 1949, and the pitching of Ralph Branca, who won 10 of his first 11 decisions — broke on top. By July 4 they led the Cardinals by two games, and the surprising Phillies were tied for third with the Braves, 5½ games back.

Robinson's hitting was sensational. He led the National League by 19 points at midseason and was even setting the pace in RBI with 60. He was happy playing for Shotton, whom he genuinely admired, and Rickey had taken the wraps off him to answer any racial taunts. Robinson played with unmatched drive in 1949. He was determined to prove to all doubters that he was a great ballplayer. Gil Hodges also came into his own in 1949. He hit 11 homers to match his 1948 totals by the All-Star break. Preacher Roe and rookie Don Newcombe backed Branca in the starting rotation. Roy Campanella, Duke Snider, Pee Wee Reese and Carl Furillo joined with Robinson and Hodges to give the Dodgers six tough outs in the lineup.

What made the Phillies such a surprise was the power hitting of Del Ennis and catcher Andy Seminick. Ennis was fourth in the National League in homers at the midseason mark and tied for second in RBI. Seminick led all catchers with 12 homers and 40 RBI, and provided steady defense behind the plate. The Phillies' starting pitching was even more impressive. Led by veteran Ken Heintzleman, 9-3, the four Phillies starters, who also included Russ Meyer, Robin Roberts and Hank Borowy, combined for a 30-19 record.

The Braves were on a downward spiral. Only one regular, Alvin Dark, was hitting, the team was riddled with injuries, and even steady Tommy Holmes was down at .239, the lowest average of his career at the midway mark. Warren Spahn and Vern Bickford pitched well, but Johnny Sain was in the midst of his worst season in the Majors, suffering from arm miseries. He blamed his problems on barnstorming after the 1948 World Series and not getting in shape for spring training (Cairns, 62–63). The team was also in turmoil. Dark and Eddie Stanky were feuding with manager Southworth, who was drinking heavily again. Southworth eventually lost control of the team and took a month's leave of absence toward the end of the season. Johnny Sain said he never felt the same about Southworth after he heard him say that the Braves had not had a good team in 1948. "They didn't win the pennant. I won it" (Peary, 87).

The race between the Dodgers and Cards stayed close all season. By Labor Day the Cards had inched ahead of the Dodgers by two games. They did it essentially on the mound. The Cardinals were getting solid pitching from Ted Wilks, Al Brazle, George Munger and Pollet, who had bounced back from injuries. Among them they were 53-22, easily the best pitching staff in the League. The traditional solid hitting of the Cardinals was a little off form — Red Schoendienst, Slaughter and Musial were having typical seasons, but the remaining regulars were unimpressive. First base, where Nippy Jones held forth, and third, played by Eddie Kazack, were weak spots in the infield.

The Dodgers eventually won the pennant because they put together a superb September/October, going 19-6, whereas the Cardinals were a steady 17-10. The Dodgers won in the area where they were weaker than the Cardinals, pitching. Roe, Newcombe, Erskine and even Rex Barney, who had been a flop all season, combined for a 13-4 record. The Dodgers' hitting in this month was unimpressive, but Furillo carried the team, hitting .430 and raising his batting average 33 points.

The Cardinals' pitching slumped just when it was needed most. Wilks didn't win a game all month. Munger and Brazle were 3-5, and only Pollet and Harry Brecheen came through. Musial hit well, as usual, cracking nine homers and almost overtaking Robinson for the batting title. He finished at .338, four points behind the Dodger second baseman.

In reality this was the 1940s' death gasp of the great Cardinal dynasty. The Red Birds slipped out of contention after the 1949 season because they suffered from a lack of talent in the farm system. Between 1948 and 1953 the best the Cardinal system could produce were some marginal players like Solly Hemus, Ray Jablonski and Vinegar Bend Mizell. Not until Wally Moon came up in 1954 did the Cardinals produce a first-class rookie. As a result they dropped into fifth place in 1950 and then gradually slid into the second division, landing in seventh place in 1955, 18 games out of first place, for their worst showing since 1938, when they finished that many games behind the pennant-winning Cubs.

With two games left the Dodgers had a one-game lead over the Cardinals, but unlike the Red Sox–Yankee contest, the two teams in contention were not playing each other. With Branca on the mound the Dodgers couldn't hold a 3–0 lead and lost the first of a two-game series in Philadelphia against the surging Phillies, who had won 16 of their last 26 games. Fortunately for the Dodgers, the Cardinals also lost to the seventh-place Cubs in Chicago.

On the final day of the season a clearly tired Dodger team was forced to start a weary Don Newcombe against Russ Meyer, who had won his last eight games in a row. Newcombe and Rex Barney allowed the Phillies to overcome a five-run deficit. Then Jack Banta took over in the sixth inning and shut the Phillies down on two hits the rest of the way as the Dodgers won the game in the tenth. This was a satisfying victory for Banta because he had lost a key game to the Phillies one week earlier when he served up a homer to Andy Seminick. This time he had faced Seminick in an almost identical situation and struck him out (Banta to author, April 1995).

The Cardinals also won that final Sunday, but the Dodgers' one-game lead held up.

Rickey was intensely proud of this Dodger team because it was truly his, unlike the 1947 squad, which had been put together by Larry MacPhail (Golenbock, *Bums*, 230). Even so, the Dodgers had staggered to the pennant and the race with the Cardinals had left the team physically and emotionally exhausted.

The same was true for the Yankees, and as a result the World Series was a letdown.

The Yankees won in five unexciting games in which neither team played up to its true abilities. Reynolds outpitched Newcombe in the opener, winning 1–0 on Tommy Henrich's leadoff ninth-inning homer. Preacher Roe duplicated Reynolds's feat the next day, also winning a 1–0 game. This was a sure sign that both teams were tired and flat.

Games three and four were close contests that the Yankees won because of superior pitching and a stronger bench. Johnny Mize won the third game with a pinch single in the ninth inning, and Joe Page closed down the Dodgers with 5⅔ innings of relief. Shotton brought Newcombe back on two days rest in game four and he lasted only 2⅔ innings. This time after the Yankees had built a lead, Stengel turned to Reynolds who shut the Dodgers down with 3⅓ shutout innings.

The fifth and final game was a Yankee blowout as they won 10–6. The Yankees built up a 10–2 lead before the Dodgers scored four in the seventh, but then again Page choked off another Dodger comeback.

The Yankees won because they had superior depth in pitching, they had a solid bench, and they had learned to deal with adversity during their season-long struggle with injuries. Stengel clearly outmanaged Shotton. The Yankee skipper always had the right man ready for the right situation, whether a pinch hitter or a reliever like Page or Reynolds. The best epitaph for the series was written by Rud Rennie of the *New York Herald Tribune*: neither team was at its best, "but the fair conclusion is that the Yankees outplayed the Dodgers and outgamed them as well" (Kahn, *Era*, 239).

The Year of the Whiz Kids

Although attendance had dipped slightly in 1949, Major League baseball was optimistic about the new decade. The country had recovered nicely from the war, banishing fears of a new depression or runaway inflation. To be sure the cold war was growing more menacing, and anticommunism was on the rise. In the fall of 1949 President Truman announced that the Soviet Union had exploded an atomic bomb years before it was expected, and almost at the same time the communist forces of Mao won the Chinese civil war. None of this boded well for the future, but baseball was oblivious to these problems. In fact, baseball served as a soothing diversion from them.

Before the season the BWAA picked the Red Sox to win in the American League, well ahead of the World Champion Yankees, with Detroit, Cleveland and the A's drawing a handful of votes. Of 194 writers, 116 picked Boston to win, and only 38 favored the Yankees. In the National League the Dodgers were an even more overwhelming choice to repeat, drawing 145 first-place votes against 17 for the Braves and 15 for the Cardinals. The eventual champs, the Phillies, got exactly nine votes (*SNG*, 1951, pp. 9, 51).

These seemed like reasonable choices. The Red Sox were an awesome assembly of hitters, and there was no doubt that a full season of Kinder, Parnell, and a maturing Mickey McDermott, as well as the return to form of Jack Kramer, would mean a better team than the one that just missed the pennant. There was little sense that the Yankees were a better squad than in 1949. Too many players were getting old and injured. Would Joe DiMaggio be able to play a full season at 35? Was Charley Keller finally finished by his chronic back problems? Most disturbing of all was the fact that Tommy Henrich, who had carried the team for the first half of 1949, had an injured back to go with his bad knees.

In the National League, the Dodgers would only get better. Leo Durocher, for example, thought they were unbeatable in the National League. The Phillies he dismissed as having only two decent starters, Roberts and Russ Meyer. The Dodgers were essentially a young team with few flaws, as they had proved in 1949. Rickey's farm system had paid major dividends since 1947. The Braves and Cards were professional teams, but despite their competitive play in recent years they were not in the same category as the Dodgers. The Cards were still relying on what the farm system had produced in the early 1940s. As for the Phillies, although they had played great baseball in the last two months of the 1949 season, it was easy to discount a franchise that had been down for so long. Their manager, the calm and professional Eddie Sawyer, thought they had a real chance to win because they had finished third in 1949 and had good players at almost every key position. The only real question was whether Eddie Waitkus could recover from the near-fatal gunshot wound by a deranged admirer in June 1949. The Phillies had four fine starters in Roberts, Curt Simmons, Kenny Heintzleman and Russ Meyer; a couple of solid rookie pitchers in Bubba Church and Bob Miller; and quality players at key positions; Granny Hamner at short; Mike Goliat, good glove but no hit, at second; Ashburn in center and Andy Seminick, the best catcher in the National League in 1949. "Frankly," Sawyer said, he "would have been surprised if we hadn't won in 1950" (Honig, *50s*, 1).

As usual, the BWAA was looking backward when it made its choices. Every season there are surprises, but in some years it is easier to see patterns. The Braves, for example, were a team in decline, who had lost their manager from stress for a key part of the 1949 season. After the 1949 season they had also traded away the double-play combination of Dark and Stanky, which had helped them in their pennant-winning year. When Durocher found out that they were available, he implored Giants owner Horace Stoneham to get them. They were his kind of players: hard-nosed, aggressive, thinking ballplayers. Durocher knew that Dark and Stanky had feuded with Southworth and that the Giants could get them for the right package of players. He also knew that they could be the keys to turning around a sluggish Giant franchise that he was already beginning to transform from a slow, home run–hitting bunch to a team based on pitching, defense and speed. He believed that the new double play combination would improve Giant pitching by 100 percent. The deal eventually made was Dark and Stanky for long-ball hitters Willard Marshall, Sid Gordon and shortstop, Buddy Kerr. To Durocher the deal meant that the team's complexion had changed. "We won't need any bulldozers," he joked, "to push our men around the bases" (Eskenazi, 241). Of the players traded away, Durocher only regretted giving up Gordon, whom he always regarded as a winning player (Durocher, 294–295).

If the Braves and Cardinals were slowly slipping while the Phillies and Giants were being transformed, a similar process was taking place in the American League. The Tigers, under their new manager, former Yankee third baseman, Red Rolfe, were a team on the rise. On the other hand, Cleveland was a team remaking itself and trying to stay in competition.

The Tigers had finished impressively in 1949 behind young talent that seemed to have a glowing future: hitters like Hoot Evers and Vic Wertz; third baseman George Kell; and a solid pitching staff anchored by veterans Hal Newhouser and Virgil Trucks, that included young arms like lefty Ted Gray and right-hander Art Houtteman. Evers was an enigma. After four seasons, 1947–1950, in which he averaged better than .300 and twice drove in 100 runs, he suddenly went into a tailspin. In 1951 his batting average dropped by 99 points, and he never again was much of a player. Kell attributed Evers's decline to a fear of being in the spotlight (Peary, 132). The Tigers had a few holes to fill, such as first base, and they were weak behind the plate, but their pitching was among the best in the American League.

Cleveland, which won 89 games in 1949, had too many older players in key positions: shortstop, third, second and even on the mound, where Bob Feller was no longer the anchor. Boudreau had slowed down, and Ken Keltner and Joe Gordon were just about finished. Bill Veeck shrewdly sold out in 1949 to a syndicate headed by businessman Ellis Ryan for $2.2 million. The Indians looked like a bargain because they had drawn 2,334,000 fans in 1949, but in fact, they were a team in need of redefining. Fortunately for the new owners, Veeck's farm system had talent to spare: 1950 rookies included Al Rosen and Luke Easter, and the season would also see the blossoming of Bobby Avila and Ray Boone as key figures in the infield.

The A's had won 81 games in 1949, leading Connie Mack to stay on for one last effort to win a pennant. The A's were coming off three straight winning seasons, but they lacked the depth to compete with the Yankees, Red Sox, Indians or Tigers. Whereas the Yankees and Indians were drawing over two million fans a year and the Tigers and Red Sox were setting yearly attendance records, the A's could never break the one million mark. The problem intensified in 1950 when a poor start for the A's, combined with the success of the pennant-bound Phillies, sucked more fans away. This season would provide the first indication that Philadelphia could not support two baseball teams.

The National League pennant race was a close four-team affair among Brooklyn, St. Louis, Boston and the Phillies for the first four months. The Dodgers broke on top in April and May but then sputtered in June. Their hitting — led by Jackie Robinson, having another superb season, leading the League at .371 and Duke Snider, Carl Furillo, Gil Hodges and Roy Campanella — was the best in the National League. But the pitching was another matter. Preacher Roe and Don Newcombe got off to good starts and were among the League leaders in victories. But behind them the staff consisted of nothing but question marks: Jack Banta, Bud Podbielan and Ralph Branca, who again was failing to live up to his reputation, struggling along with just two victories by July 4.

The Cards set the pace for most of the first half of the year, led by Musial and Slaughter at bat and a surprisingly effective pitching staff. By July 4 the Cards had four pitchers — Max Lanier, Gerry Staley, Al Brazle and Howie Pollett — with a combined record of 30-16. But the lack of stickwork was putting a strain on the pitchers. The Cards had too many holes in their lineup once you got past Musial, Slaughter and Red Schoendienst. Young players like Eddie Kazak, Nippy Jones and Bill Howerton were always getting hurt and could not match the caliber of the Dodgers, Phillies or Giants. The second half of the season would wipe out the Cardinals' fast start. Country Slaughter symbolized what happened to the Cardinals in 1950. He was hitting .333 with 81 RBI on August 6. The rest of the season he hit .181 and drove in exactly 16 runs.

The Phillies played solid baseball in the first half of the new season picking up where they left off in 1949. In fact, they were in and out of first place a half dozen times by early July. On July 4 they were in second place, just 1½ games behind the Cardinals. The Phillies did it with great starting pitching from Roberts, Simmons and rookie Bob Miller, who began the year winning eight games in a row. These three were 28-8 at this point, and they were supported by bull-pen ace, Jim Konstanty, whom Sawyer had rescued from the minors. He was saving games at a record pace with his assortment of junk, featuring a devastating palm ball that hitters flailed at and missed. The Phillies' hitting, 1-8, was better than the Dodgers. Led by Del Ennis, Willie Jones at third, Hamner at short, a steady Ashburn in center and a surprising Dick Sisler, hitting at .331, in left, the Phillies were an aggressive, hard-nosed team that didn't beat itself. They were young and beginning to realize how good they were. Eddie Waitkus recovered nicely from his gunshot wound and played virtually every game at first base. If the Phillies seemed to have a problem, it was their bench. Sawyer stayed with his eight regulars and made virtually no use of his reserves. Eventually this would take its toll on the team.

The Braves stayed competitive most of the season before dropping out in September. They got a big comeback year from Johnny Sain, who eventually won 20 games, another 21-victory season from Spahn and 19 wins from young Vern Bickford. But behind this big three they had next to nothing. The Braves' hitting was led by Bob Elliott, who was getting old, newly acquired Sid Gordon and the first black to play on a Boston team, rookie Sam Jethroe, who had come over to them in one of Branch Rickey bargain basement sales. Jethroe scored 100 runs and led the National League in stolen bases with 35.

The Korean War, which broke out in June, began to cause problems for baseball almost immediately. Some players were subject to the draft, and others who were part of the military reserves began to miss time. The war came as a surprise to Major League baseball, as well as to the rest of the nation. There was no time to prepare as there had been in the months after Pearl Harbor, and as a result baseball scrambled to meet the crisis. Eventually the Korean War had less impact on baseball than had World War II because a full-scale national mobilization wasn't proclaimed. Still the impact of the crisis was felt over the next three years. Curt Simmons had to go on reserve duty for two weeks in mid-July. At that point he was 14-5 and probably the best pitcher in the National League. He would go 3-3 the rest of the year until his reserve unit was called up on September 10, just when the Phillies could ill afford to lose him. It almost cost the Phillies a pennant. In subsequent years the Korean conflict caused Willie Mays to miss two full seasons, probably hurt the career of pitcher Chet Nichols and took another couple of years away from Ted Williams when he was reactivated.

In another sense the Korean War, combined with the sagging attendance problems that first became noticeable in 1950, began to cast a sense of gloom over baseball in the early 1950s. The war, which the American public found difficult to understand, intensified the anticommunist search for scapegoats and embittered American society. Senator Joseph McCarthy had his career as the nation's premier anticommunist enhanced by the war. Without the confusion sowed by the conflict, it is doubtful that he would have been able to ride this issue as long as he did. As usual, baseball reflected the sense of confusion in the nation. Soon the Cincinnati Reds would change their name to the less-controversial "Redlegs."

The Phillies won the pennant in July and August, when they pulled away from the rest of the League by going 42-21. On July 25 they moved into first place and stayed there for the rest of the season. Del Ennis led the team in July by driving in a Phillies' record 41 runs. Rookie Bubba Church began to take up the slack when pitchers Ken Heintzleman and Russ Meyer slumped. The Phillies stayed hot in August, at one point going 12-4 during a long homestand. By the beginning of September they led the Dodgers by 7½ games and the Braves by nine.

Then the team hit its first streak of bad luck. On September 3, after a very successful road trip where they went 11-4, Sawyer warned the celebrating Phillies fans that with 27 games remaining, "We don't have this pennant won" (Westcott and Bilovsky, 98). How right he was.

Bob Miller hurt his arm, Church was hit in the face by a line drive off the bat of Ted Kluszewski, and Andy Seminick chipped a bone in his ankle. The Dodgers suddenly got hot and went 20-15 for the last month of the season. Meanwhile the Phillies, without Simmons, Miller and Church, depended on Roberts, Konstanty and a team that stopped hitting. Sawyer's reluctance to rest his starters showed through at this point. The Phillies were a young team in the heat of a pennant race, and they were both physically and mentally exhausted. Five of the regulars had played just about every game in the schedule. This included Waitkus, who looked like a concentration-camp victim by the end of the season. The other regulars averaged 139 games among them.

With two games left in the season the Phillies, with a two-game lead, had to finish the season in Brooklyn. They were easily beaten in the next-to-last game of the season and entered the final day with a one-game lead. Roberts started for the Phillies, making his sixth attempt to be the first Phillies pitcher to win 20 games since Grover Cleveland Alexander. It was also his third start in five days. He was opposed by Don Newcombe, who also was going for his twentieth victory.

In a tight, well-played game the Phillies won because the Dodgers made an uncharacteristic mistake. Tied 1–1 in the bottom of the ninth, Cal Abrams walked and was singled to second by Pee Wee Reese. With Duke Snider up and no outs the Phillies infield and outfield shortened up, looking for a bunt. Snider swung away and lined a sharp single to center. Ashburn caught the ball on the hop and fired a perfect strike to catcher Stan Lopata. Third-base coach Milt Stock sent Abrams home, and he was out by 12 feet. The runners moved up a base.

It was a senseless play with Robinson, Furillo and Hodges coming up next and would cost Stock his job. He was fired at the end of the season. Years later, when being teased about his weak throwing arm, Ashburn would answer, I only had to make one throw that counted in my career, and I did.

Sawyer ordered the dangerous Robinson walked. Furillo, an overly aggressive hitter, swung at the first pitch and popped up. Hodges hit a long twisting fly to right, and the Phillies were out of the inning. In the top of the tenth, the Phillies staged their only rally of the game. Roberts and Waitkus led off the inning with singles, but Ashburn couldn't bunt them over. With runners on first and second Dick Sisler, having the best year of his career, came to bat against Newcombe. Sisler already had three hits and usually hit the big Dodger right-hander. Sisler swung at the first two pitches. With the count 0-2 Newcombe, instead of pushing Sisler off the plate, went outside, and Sisler pounded the ball into the left-field bleachers. After the game Sisler remarked, "How I love to hit in this park."

Roberts set the Dodgers down easily in the bottom of the tenth, and the Phillies had their first pennant in 35 years. The Phillies staggered to victory. Willie Jones did not hit a home run in September, Hamner's batting average dropped ten points, and Seminick drove in eight runs for the month. But it was the pitching that let the Phillies down. Roberts was 2-5, and Church and Miller were 0-7 for the last month. Konstanty kept the Phillies in game after game, and Ennis, Ashburn and Sisler did enough hitting to make the Phillies competitive.

Fortunately for the Phillies, the Dodgers played only good ball in September and October. A 20-15 record was not a pennant-winning pace. Dodger hitting was solid throughout the last month as their big five — Robinson, Snider, Hodges, Furillo and Campanella — hit 24 homers among them. But the pitching was not up to pennant–winning form. The team ERA of 4.24 was three-quarters of a run higher than the Phillies and eventually doomed them. Their big two of Roe and Newcombe went only 6-5 for the month. The Phillies were fortunate that their main competitor was the Dodgers and not the Giants, who were the hottest team in the League, winning 50 of their last 72 and going 21-11 in September. In the last two months of the 1950 season, Durocher finally had his kind of team in place. Over the next five years a scrappy Giant club would average 89 wins and be in the middle of every pennant race except 1953, when the Dodgers ran away with the League.

The Yankees Again

The American League race in 1950 was also a four-team struggle and even closer than the National League contest. Only six games separated the top team, the Yankees, from the fourth-place club, Cleveland. Each of the top four clubs won at least 92 games. The fifth-place Washington Senators were 31 games out of first place, a clear indication that the American League was divided into the haves and the have nots.

The Tigers were the surprise team of the League, spending 119 days in first place, compared to just 51 for the Yankees. The Tigers had finished third in 1949, winning 87 games in the process and showing signs of promise. They had demonstrated a nice blend of youth and age plus a healthy balance between the offense and the pitching. They continued to progress in 1950. After battling the Yankees for first place in April and May, the Tigers sprinted into first place with a four-game lead by July 4 by going 21-9 in the month of June.

Despite the fact that their ace, Hal Newhouser, didn't win his first game until five weeks into the season, the Tigers were playing some of the best baseball in the League by the July 4 dividing line. Newhouser wasn't particularly concerned. After his first victory in late May, he talked of winning 20 games again (*SN*, 05/31/50, p. 9). George Kell set the pace in batting at .371, with Hoot Evers in fourth place at .349. Other solid hitting came from Vic Wertz, who was among the League leaders in RBI, shortstop Johnny Lipon, hitting .308, and outfielder Johnny Groth at .300 even. The pitching staff was paced by youngsters Art Houtteman, who was tied with Bob Lemon for the lead in wins with 11, and Ted Gray with 10. Meanwhile veterans Fred Hutchinson and Newhouser had 16 wins between them. The top four Tiger starters were 38-18 at the halfway point.

The Yankees kept pace with the Tigers for the first two months of the season only to slump badly in June, going 15-17. Joe DiMaggio looked terrible, hardly justifying the record breaking $100,000 salary the Yankees were paying him. Stengel had dropped him out of the cleanup spot for the first time in years, hitting Berra there instead. DiMaggio was worried. "I haven't got that feeling…," he said, "that I can walk up there and hit any pitcher who ever lived" (Golenbock, *Dynasty*, 37). At the July 4 point he was hitting .266, although he had 17 homers and was fifth in the League in RBI with 67.

The Yankees were staying in the race because Rizzuto was having a career year at bat and in the field and Stengel once again was platooning brilliantly in the outfield and at third. Henrich, although hitting over .300, was just about finished by his knee and back problems, and Stengel brought Johnny Mize back on July 16 from a brief trip to the minors and had installed him at first base. Mize hit 23 homers and drove in 60 runs in the second half of the 1950 season.

What saved the Yankees from total collapse was their usual first–class pitching and their remarkable bench. Their starters, Raschi, Lopat, Reynolds and the surprisingly effective Tommy Byrne, who won 8 games in a row, were a combined 36-19 by the season's midpoint. Stengel could bring people like Bobby Brown, Cliff Mapes, Gene Woodling or Hank Bauer off the bench in key situations. No other team in the League could match the Yankees' depth.

Aside from DiMaggio's slump, the Yankees were most hurt by the near total collapse of Joe Page, who had almost single-handedly kept them in the pennant chase in 1949. He had celebrated too much after his great 1949 year and arrived at spring training in poor condition. His drinking had never affected him before, but now he no longer had the great fastball that had made him the most effective relief pitcher in the League. He was finished at 32.

Cleveland and Boston vied for third place 5 and 6½ games behind the Tigers. Cleveland counted on its usual good pitching to keep it in contention. The staff, led by Bob Lemon and Early Wynn in his second year with the Indians, backed up by Mike Garcia and Bob Feller, were a solid 33-20 by the middle of the season. The good pitchers were backed by some new hitters: rookie Al Rosen was hitting over .300 and leading the League in homers with 25, and big Luke Easter, the Negro League slugger, had 16 homers, 45 RBI and a .293 batting average. Larry Doby was off to his best start ever, second in batting at .356, and Ray Boone took over at shortstop from Boudreau and batted over .300. In some ways the Indians were comparable to the 1948 world champs; they just had the misfortune to have to face stiff competition. Their eventual victory total, 92, was the fourth highest in Cleveland's history. Despite this victory total Cleveland never mounted a run at the top. They were a consistent club, but they were one solid winning streak from getting into the pennant chase.

Boston's problem revolved around a slow start complicated by manager McCarthy's worsening drinking problems. He had apparently lost his taste for baseball after the dual disasters in 1948 and 1949 (Golenbock, *Fenway*, 185–186). In late June, just as the team was beginning to hit its stride, he quit. He was replaced by third-base coach Steve O'Neill. O'Neill was a laid-back, old-fashioned manager who let the players alone. If you look at his record as manager, he usually had a quick positive effect on a disenchanted team. It worked in Detroit and later with the Phillies in 1952, but O'Neill soon wore out his welcome because he wasn't much of a baseball presence.

The Red Sox certainly took off under his light rein. They were in fourth place at the end of June, 6½ games back. From the time O'Neill took over they went 56-25 to play some of the best baseball in the Majors. They did this despite losing their best hitter, Ted Williams, to a broken elbow while playing in the All-Star game. At the time, Williams was tied for the League lead in homers with 25 and RBI with 83 although hitting .323, a low for him. Despite losing him until September the Red Sox stayed in the race because of the hitting of rookie giant, Walt Dropo, who, after being called up from Louisville a week into the season, tore the American League apart. At midseason he was not only hitting .350 with 19 homers, but he was tied with Williams for the RBI lead. Along with Junior Stephens and Bobby Doerr, Dropo gave the Red Sox the most awesome hitting ensemble in the American League in years. Eventually, the Red Sox would hit .302 as a team and lead the League in runs, hits, total bases, RBI and doubles and would finish a close second in homers.

As usual the Red Sox problem was related to pitching. By midseason their two aces of 1949, Parnell and Kinder, were a combined 12-16. Boston's best pitchers were Joe Dobson and two youngsters, Mickey McDermott and Chuck Stobbs. Parnell and Kinder would eventually straighten out during the second half of the season, but their record of 32-22 was a far cry from the 48-13 of the previous year. Anything close to those figures and the Red Sox would have waltzed away with the pennant.

Once again, the Red Sox also struggled to win on the road. Their home record, 55-22, was the best in the American League, but they were just one game above .500 on the road. This was the third year in a row that Boston had the best home record in the American League and the fourth year out of five. Although murdering the second-division teams, they could not beat their rivals. Their overall record against the Yankees, Tigers and Indians was 29-37 compared to 65-23 against the teams finishing fifth through eighth. The Red Sox were 38 and 6 against the Browns and A's.

The Red Sox got back into pennant contention by September. With Williams due back for the last month of the season, Boston felt it had a real chance to win. It never panned out because the Yankees once again played some of their best baseball while the pressure was on. New York went 18-10 in September/October, fending off the Tigers, who stayed close at 18-12, and the Red Sox slipped past Cleveland into third place by two games.

Unlike 1948 and 1949 the pennant race this time didn't go down to the last day of the season. The Yankees staved off the Tigers by beating them two out of three games in a mid-September series in Detroit. After the teams split the first two games, Stengel took one of his patented gambles and started rookie Ed "Whitey" Ford in the third game. Ford, who joined the club in mid-season when the Yankees had a pitching letdown, won his seventh game in a row. The Tigers were tenacious, but the Yankees wouldn't crack. Detroit had a superb starting eight, but its bench was terrible and could not match the Yankees in depth.

New York won again in 1950 because of their pitching strength and an MVP year from Phil Rizzuto plus great second halves by Joe DiMaggio and Johnny Mize. Along with Yogi Berra, who had his first great power year, hitting .322 with 28 homers and 124 RBI, Mize and DiMaggio carried the Yankees at the plate. After staggering around .260–.270 all season, DiMaggio got hot the last two months of the season. He hit around .370, drove in a ton of runs and boosted his average over .300. Mize was a devastating fill-in first baseman. He hit 25 homers and drove in 72 runs on just 76 hits, despite playing only 72 games at first.

The Yankees' pitching, without a great season from Page out of the bull pen, was not up to past performances, but it was good enough. Raschi had his second 21-victory season. He and Lopat, who won 18, and Reynolds, who won 16, gave the Yankees three good starters. When Byrne slacked off the second half of the season, Ford came up from the minors and went 9-1, with a low 2.81 ERA. Byrne and Ford combined for 24 victories against 10 defeats.

For the Yankees the 1950 pennant was unexpected but easier than the season before. The rest of the American League couldn't rest with the thought that age was finally catching up to the Yankees. In 1950 their 18 farm teams produced 64 All-Stars or one for every four minor leaguers under contract to them (Golenbock, *Dynasty*, 54).

The World Series was anticlimactic. The Phillies had staggered to the pennant and were incapable of playing at the level they had through most of the 1950 season. Del Ennis believed that they could have given the Yankees a battle if they had clinched earlier and had had time to regroup (Peary, 140). Winning had taken everything out of them. The Yankees were in much better shape, even though winning the Series proved more difficult than expected.

The Yankees' four-game sweep, however, is deceptive. They won because their pitching was masterful. The ERA of their four starters Raschi, Reynolds,

Lopat and Ford was 0.00, 0.87, 2.25 and 0.08. The Yankee team ERA was an incredible 0.73.

The Phillies' pitching was also impressive. They got wonderful efforts from Konstanty and a clearly exhausted Roberts. But the Phillie hitting was terrible. Key players just stopped hitting: Ennis batted .143, Ashburn .176, Seminick .183 and Sisler, who had performed so well in September, a woeful .059.

The biggest surprise of the Series was Sawyer's decision in game one to pitch Konstanty, who had not started a game since he came to the Phillies in 1948. As an unorthodox move it ranked with Connie Mack's choice of Howard Ehmke to open the 1929 World Series. Unfortunately for the Phillies, the final result was not the same.

Sawyer, normally a conservative by-the-book manager, had no choice. Roberts was in desperate need of a rest, and Church and Miller had been useless the last month. Konstanty did a masterful job before losing 1–0 to Raschi. Konstanty went on to pitch effectively in three games of the Series.

The Series was a huge hit on television, which reached from the East Coast as far into the Midwest as Omaha, Nebraska. Thirty-eight million people watched it, and another 70 million listened in on the radio (*SNG*, 1951, p. 117).

By most standards 1950 was a successful season. Two good, if not great, pennant races with a new team winning in the National League seemed to bode well for the future. But the sag of 13 percent in attendance was disturbing. For the second year in a row baseball at the Major League level had dropped off. Moreover, if you looked closer at these figures there was an even more disturbing trend apparent. Home attendance of the top four teams in the American League accounted for an incredible 77.8 percent of the total figure for the League. In the National League the imbalance was not as noticeable. There four teams — the Phils, Dodgers, Cubs and Pirates — accounted for 57 percent of the League total.

Baseball writers and owners gave a number of explanations for these trends, but none seemed very convincing. Some blamed the Korean War for distracting attention from baseball, but this was impossible to document. Others blamed the spread of television watching. Set ownership was growing with incredible rapidity, and baseball executives were arguing that people were now staying home and watching the games. Finally, some writers blamed the weather — too many rainouts and too many hot days in August. In reality, by 1950 baseball was entering a time of great crisis.

4

A New Yankee Dynasty, 1951–1953

Unhappy Chandler

Late 1950 to early 1951 saw the United States sink to the grimmest moment in the postwar world. In November 1950 the Chinese massively intervened in the Korean War, turning an American victory into what *Time* magazine called "the worst defeat the United States has ever suffered" (Manchester, 547–548). Christmas 1950 found the United States in the worst mood since the Battle of the Bulge six years before. Nothing seemed to be going right. U.S. troops were in retreat, Russia was threatening to enter the war, and President Truman hinted that he might use nuclear weapons to stop the Chinese. World War III seemed in the offing. In the United States anticommunism was sweeping all before it, in the process turning an obscure senator from Wisconsin, Joseph McCarthy, into one of the most powerful forces in the nation.

For baseball the situation seemed almost as grim. Commissioner Chandler was pessimistic about the upcoming season. In late December he told reporters that he believed that the military manpower shortage would require total U.S. mobilization, thus wiping out the baseball season ("Surprise," *Time,* 12/25/50, p. 42). Chandler's timing could not have been worse. He made these remarks just a few days before the owners winter meeting.

Chandler did not realize it, but he was in trouble. The owners had lost confidence in him. They found his constant interventions in their affairs tiresome. And what was worse for him, they no longer believed that they needed him. He had been hired in 1945 because he had solid political connections in Washington, and they wanted someone who knew his way around the corridors of power. But when World War II ended suddenly, Chandler discovered that his position had been weakened. By seeming at a loss over what to do in the face of a growing crisis in Korea Chandler had further undermined his position.

Toward the end of the 1950 season stories surfaced that certain baseball owners were angry at Happy Chandler for taking an activist role as commissioner. This wasn't a surprise. As far back as the Durocher incident some owners believed that Chandler had overstepped his position. Larry MacPhail predicted in 1947 that baseball "would have to redefine the powers of the commissioner" (Warfield, 194).

In 1950 Del Webb, Lou Perini and Fred Saigh of the Cardinals were among those most upset by some of Chandler's actions and his interpretation of the commissioner's role. At the winter meetings in December 1950 in St. Petersburg, Florida, Chandler's contract was up for renewal. Although he still had 16 months remaining on his old contract, he expected to be given an extension. But Chandler had made too many enemies.

Some of his clashes with ownership were minor, such as a refusal to allow the Cardinals to make up a game on a Sunday night, as well as warnings not to sign high school or college players before they graduated. But Chandler also followed in Judge Landis's footsteps by freeing farmhands he believed were not treated fairly and by investigating some owners, particularly Webb, for possible gambling infractions. Webb claimed that he had nothing personal against Chandler. "I don't dislike Chandler," he told *The Sporting News.* "I simply think we could get a better commissioner"(*SN*, 3/21/51, p. 14). This bland remark belies the vigor with which Webb orchestrated Chandler's removal.

Chandler also had irritated the owners by a pet project that he pushed to hire the politically well-connected Steve Hannagan for $50,000 plus $150,000 in expense money to publicize baseball's golden jubilee in 1951 ("Surprise," *Time*, 12/25/50, p. 43). This had the look of a cozy payoff to an old political chum and raised questions about Chandler's judgment.

Unlike Landis, who was backed by the sportswriting fraternity, Chandler had few supporters in the press. The New York contingent, which was influential in those days, of five large major papers treated him as a southern cornball. They referred to him as "Sappy" and "Playboy" Chandler. Chandler was surprised, then, in St. Petersburg to find that a preliminary vote showed that contract renewal passed by a narrow 9–7 vote. Because he needed three quarters' approval Chandler decided to postpone any decision until he had time to get his case together.

In the three months before the spring meeting of the owners in Miami Chandler believed he had lined up enough support for renewal. He was wrong. Webb proved a better politician than the former governor and senator. The vote in Miami was the same, 9–7. Chandler resigned the $50,000-a-year job effective in July.

Chandler's failure to survive had many causes. First, the owners did not want another Landis. They believed that they could run baseball better without a commissioner butting into their affairs. Chandler had taken his responsibilities too seriously. They wanted a laissez-faire commissioner.

The owners were not upset by some of Chandler's major accomplishments, such as setting up a new baseball contract or negotiating a radio-TV deal for the All-Star game and World Series. But they were concerned at his tendency to interfere in the day-to-day running of the game, the velvet glove that hid an iron fist, as *The Sporting News* put it. Chandler believed that his ouster was brought about when he antagonized the Yankee ownership. But it went deeper than that. Most owners were tired of him and his constant interference. They wanted no more high commissioner or dictator in the commissioner's office.

Chandler's failure to secure renewal in December 1950 set off speculation about a replacement. Among those mentioned prominently were national figures such as Judge Medina, who had presided at the trial of major communist leaders; Senator Frank Lausche of Ohio; Governor Earl Warren of California; Jim Farley, former postmaster general of the United States; and even J. Edgar Hoover of the FBI. None of these men expressed any interest. Hoover told the owners that after the way they had treated Chandler, he wouldn't touch the job. It is difficult to believe that Hoover would leave his post in the FBI, then at the peak of its power and influence, to take over as a water boy for the baseball owners. Warren Giles of the Cincinnati Reds in April 1951 suggested General MacArthur, who had just been removed from his command in Korea by President Truman.

None of these individuals, with the possible exception of Farley, were really interested in the job. The owners' behavior since naming Chandler in 1945 made it clear that they, and not any commissioner, would run baseball.

By midsummer the list of effective candidates was reduced to two: Giles and National League president Ford Frick. The influential *Sporting News* all but endorsed Frick in a July 4 editorial. Frick, they argued, was "well liked by club owners in the American League as well as the National. He has the confidence of the fans and players. He is an experienced administrator, familiar with baseball's tremendous problems in television and radio contracts, the functioning of the pension system and the game's position in respect to antitrust legislation.... It would seem to the *Sporting News* [Frick] is the man to lead [baseball] out of the existing wilderness" (*SN*, 7/4/51, p. 12). More important, Frick had won the support of the powerful Walter O'Malley. Saying that he had no candidate of his own, the Great Oom went on to argue that Frick would be a good choice. "He has done a great job for our league and I am sure he would do as well for our sport" (*ibid.*, p. 30). O'Malley knew a pigeon when he saw one.

In late September, just as the pennant races reached a furious climax, the 16 owners met in New York to choose a new commissioner. Giles was a slight favorite because it was believed that he was the candidate of the nine owners who had supported Chandler (*NYT*, 9/21/51). After numerous votes, Webb said at least 50, neither man could command the three quarter majority necessary.

Baseball had no logical third candidate who could step in. At this point Giles withdrew his name in favor of Frick.

Frick's election was then made unanimous. He was a popular choice, the first time that the sport named a baseball man to its highest position. He had been serving as president of the National League since 1934 and had been a strong candidate to succeed Landis when Chandler was picked. A former teacher and sportswriter who covered the Yankees, he ghostwrote columns for Babe Ruth. That might explain his effort to protect Ruth's record of 60 homers when that record was challenged by Roger Maris in 1961. As the only commissioner to come from the ranks of the working press he was popular with the baseball writers at the time (Rosenthal, 20). Chandler's reaction was sour but probably right on the mark: There was a vacancy in the Commissioner's office and the owners decided to continue with it.

The Shot Heard 'Round the World

The 1951 season is one of the most famous in baseball history: It was the year the Giants came from 13 games back to win the pennant on Bobby Thomson's "Shot Heard 'Round the World." But it was more important as a transitional year for baseball. Joe DiMaggio played out the string, and Mickey Mantle and Willie Mays, two of the stars who would dominate baseball for the next decade and a half, made their initial appearances. Nineteen fifty-one also saw a continuing problem with attendance, with an overall drop of 1.3 million. In the National League five teams experienced a decline, led by the Braves, whose drop was almost 50 percent, foreshadowing the eventual collapse of the franchise. Even the Giants, with their great come-from-behind victory, only showed a modest gain of 50,000. The situation in the American League was similar: five clubs saw attendance drop, with the Tigers leading the group with a decline of over 800,000. Even the Yankees, on their way to their third-straight pennant, slipped under the two-million mark for the first time since 1945. The Korean War and the growth of television were singled out as culprits.

Fortunately for the owners baseball was still profitable because the biggest costs, salaries, remained low. Inflation inspired by the Korean War was a concern. It ran at a very high 7.9 percent for 1951, a figure that could have caused serious problems if it had continued for any appreciable period. The entire American League payroll was approximately $2.75 million. The Yankees' share added up to 20 percent of the total figure. In the National League the figure was around $2.5 million, with the Cardinals carrying the biggest payroll, $385,000. The average salary was $12,500, with Joe DiMaggio and Ted Williams making in the $90,000–$100,000 class (Honig, '50s, 35). Money was flowing in from television and radio. The average revenue from both local and national broadcasting was in excess of $210,000, enough for a profit if the club drew adequately (Markham and Teplitz, 287, Table 1). Some idea of what was needed to show a profit can be gained from a declining franchise, the Athletics. In the early 1950s, they needed to draw 550,000 to show financial solvency (Kuklick, 120). In fact, after the 1949 season the A's did so only once before they moved from Philadelphia — in 1952 when Bobby Shantz had a phenomenal year and won 24 games.

America was beginning to change from an urban to a suburban society. The first Levittowns had shown the direction of the future — out of the cities to the open spaces. Baseball was trapped in the inner cities, which were beginning to die as they slowly changed over racially from lower-middle-class white to working-class white to minority domination. Major League baseball had not undergone a structural reformation since the building of the great ball parks between 1909 and 1923. The 1950s would see the beginning of the game's transition as franchises moved out of those 11 cities that had constituted the Major Leagues since the founding of the American League.

In 1951 none of this was clear. Events on the field took precedence. It was *not* an exciting year for baseball. There was a difference of opinion among sportswriters responding to UP and AP polls over who would win the National League pennant, with UP favoring the Giants and AP picking the Dodgers. The Red Sox were yet again the perennial favorite to win in the American League according to both UP and AP, with the Yankees picked to finish second. Cleveland was a distant third in both polls, and in the National League the Phils were an equally distant third, followed by a few scattered votes for the Braves.

John Drebinger of the *New York Times* predicted tight races in both leagues, but he too thought the Red Sox would win. They had added a talented pitcher in Ray Scarborough and Lou Boudreau had come over from the Indians to provide depth and leadership. Drebinger also thought that the "calm and sagacious" Steve O'Neill was a perfect choice to direct the talented, but underachieving, Red Sox.

In the National League Drebinger thought the Giants had the proper mix of "hustling, fine-spirited" players to edge out the Dodgers. He believed that the Dodgers' lack of pitching depth might be their biggest weakness, although the new manager, Chuck Dressen, was a plus (Drebinger, *NYT*, 4/15/51, pp. 1–2).

Overall, despite the Giants great comeback it was a pretty dull season. In the National League the Giants made a race only for the last month and a half. Before that the Dodgers set the pace to such an extent it looked as if they would run away with the pennant. The Giants began by falling flat on their face. They lost 12 of their first 14 games, 11 in a row.

The Phillies, fat and complacent after winning in 1950, matched them for ineptitude. They quickly earned the nickname "Fizz Kids" for their early season performance, and they slipped into the lower reaches of the second division. Some key performers reported to spring training out of shape but with hugely inflated egos. Second baseman Mike Goliat reported at 198 pounds and then proceeded to play himself out of the lineup. He wound up being waived to baseball's graveyard, the St. Louis Browns, in September (Westcott and Bilovsky, 241). Other Phillies had disastrous years. Clutch-hitting catcher Andy Seminick dropped from 24 homers to 11 and drove in just 37 runs. Seminick got beaned early in the season and never really recovered his stroke (Clayton, 16–17). Jim Konstanty, the best one-season reliever in National League history at that point, went from 16 wins to 4, and his ERA almost doubled.

According to Seminick, Konstanty altered his motion in 1951 and thus was no longer deceiving the hitters. "Batters swung at his motion in 1950, not at the ball," according to the Phillies backstop. In 1951 Konstanty tried desperately to regain the form that had made him a big winner, but he became more confused and was hit around as a result (*SN*, 2/20/52, p. 13).

Manager Sawyer tried everything to get Konstanty untracked during the year but eventually came to the conclusion that some relievers have to have bad years after a couple of solid seasons (Interview, 12/18/94). Despite another 20-win season from Robin Roberts and Richie Ashburn, hitting .344 and leading the League in hits, the Phillies were never a factor in the pennant race.

The Dodgers streaked off to a quick lead, winning 28 of their first 36, and held the lead through most of the season. At one point after hitting 40 homers in 31 games, Warren Giles of the Reds remarked that if they didn't win the pennant, "the Kefauver Committee may have to schedule an extra session" (*SN*, 5/30/51, p. 4). By the July 4 midpoint they led the Giants by 6½ games with the Cardinals lagging eight games back. They were the only National League teams over .500. The Dodgers were winning mainly because of their hitting. They led the Giants by almost 20 points at this time and had the leading home-run hitter in the League in Gil Hodges, with 26; the second-leading hitter in Jackie Robinson, hitting a robust .364; and the second-leading RBI man, Duke Snider, with 55, just four behind Wally Westlake of the Cardinals. The Dodgers' pitching was a little shaky. Preacher Roe and Don Newcombe were 24-5, the rest of the staff 22-21.

After their disastrous start, the Giants began to right themselves. In May, when they reached into the minors and brought up Willie Mays, they were in fifth place. This enabled them to move Bobby Thomson from center, where he was struggling, to third base. From that point they played solid baseball and reached the midpoint seven games over .500. The Giants were hitting a lot of homers and scoring runs, but essentially they were being carried by their pitching depth, which was much greater than the Dodgers'. In the long run this depth enabled them to win the pennant. Their top three, Maglie, Jansen and Hearn, were 29-16, but they had rookie George Spencer, plus veterans

Robin Roberts. The greatest right-handed pitcher of the postwar generation won 20 or more games for six straight seasons, 1950–1955. In the same period he averaged over 300 innings pitched. He averaged 24 complete games between 1950 and 1958, including an incredible 33 complete games in 1953. Roberts was also the first bonus baby to make good. (Brace Photo.)

Dave Koslo and Sheldon Jones in reserve. Durocher was doing a good job getting the maximum performance from his staff. He was a surprisingly good judge of pitchers, more conservative in handling them than the way he manipulated his offense.

The Dodgers appeared to have sewed up the pennant with a scorching pace in July and early August. After beating the Giants in a doubleheader,

Dressen told *The Sporting News* that the Giants could be counted out as a pennant threat. "They're through," he said in words that would come back to haunt him. "They'll never recover. They'll never bother us again" (*SN*, 7/18/51, p. 7).

On August 11 the Dodgers were 70-36 and held a 13-game lead over the Giants. But from that point the Giants got hot by reeling off 16 wins in a row, eventually closing the gap to a difficult but manageable six games by Labor Day. The Giants won the pennant because they went 37-7 over the last month and a half of the season. At the same time the Dodgers staggered along at a slightly better than .500 pace, 26-22. In normal times with a 13-game lead in August that would have been enough. But 1951 wasn't normal. It seemed that every time the Dodgers lost the Giants won. From Labor Day on, the Dodgers went 14-12 whereas the Giants were 19-5 to finish in a tie. In the final two weeks of the season, as the Giants developed momentum, Durocher decided to gamble: He would go with Maglie, Jansen and Hearn the rest of the way. When asked who would pitch tomorrow if one of the three had problems, Durocher gave a characteristic answer: "I want to win today. Tomorrow? It might rain" (Eskenazi, 254). He was going against the book, but one thing about Durocher: He was never afraid to take a chance. He was also willing to take the credit.

Dodger hitting held up although Snider had a terrible September and October, hitting just one homer, driving in nine runs and batting .187. Still their pitching did them in. Their big hitters, Snider, Robinson, Campanella, Furillo and Hodges had great years. The team hit a league-leading 184 homers and scored almost 75 more runs than the Giants. But pitching told the story.

Over the last month plus the playoffs the Dodger big four — Roe, Newcombe, Clyde King and Erskine — went just 9-6. Meanwhile, the Giant big three were 16-6, and lefty Dave Koslo got hot and won four games without a loss.

Everyone focuses on the third game of the play-offs, when Bobby Thomson hit his dramatic homer but over the past season and a third the Giants had been a better team than the Dodgers. Since August 1950 when Durocher's team began to jell, the Giants played a more consistent brand of baseball. Durocher was always a brilliant tactician when he had a good club, and he had his kind of team now: fast, solid defense, enough hitting and great pitching. There were a lot of reasons for the Giant victory in 1951 but Durocher was one of the keys. Monte Irvin attributed six to seven victories that season to Durocher's strategy (Honig, *Between the Lines*, 189).

The American League race proved close but lacked the dramatic ending of the National League. The favored Red Sox were never a factor. The team didn't collapse but it lacked the offensive talent of the previous two seasons. For the first time since 1948 Boston did not lead the League in hitting. They scored 225 fewer runs than in 1950, and the team batting average dropped by 36 points. Their 87 victories marked their poorest showing since 1947. In fact, the team was going through a decline. A couple of key players were getting old, and others were injured. Bobby Doerr was suffering from back problems and only played in 106 games. He would retire at the end of the year. Vern Stephens missed thirty-five games and hit just 17 homers and drove in 78 runs after three straight years averaging 33 homers and 146 RBI. He would never be a regular again and was essentially finished at 31. Even Ted Williams had a poor year — for him. Still suffering from the aftereffects of his broken elbow in 1950, he hit just .318, with 30 homers and 126 RBI — great totals for some players but not for Williams.

A special case was Walt Dropo, who had an extraordinary year in 1950. He started slowly in 1951 and found himself benched and then back in the minors before finishing the year with pathetic numbers: 11 homers, 57 RBI and a .237 batting average. The pitchers discovered the big first baseman couldn't hit a curve and gave him a steady diet of breaking balls. Dropo attributed his poor showing to a combination of bad luck and injuries (Golenbock, Fenway, 193). He stubbornly refused to adapt to the way the pitchers were now approaching him. But whatever the reason, he was never the player he seemed on his way to becoming in his rookie year. Early the next season he was traded to the Tigers and began a journey around the Majors from Detroit to the Chicago Americans to Cincinnati to Baltimore, one more example of unfulfilled talent.

Boston's pitching was mediocre. The team ERA was 4.14, slightly higher than the League average and a half a run per game below the pennant-winning Yankees. Mel Parnell and Ellis Kinder were still top-notch hurlers, but the second-line pitching didn't develop. Mickey McDermott won only eight games, and young Chuck Stobbs won ten. Pitching which had plagued the Red Sox in the past was their biggest flaw once again.

Boston's drop in 1951 from 94 victories in the previous season to 87 was the beginning of a decline that would last until the miracle year of 1967. They would not be a serious factor in the American League for another generation.

The two surprise teams of the American League were Cleveland and, especially, the White Sox. Al Lopez had replaced Boudreau as Cleveland's manager, and Lopez began his career of building contenders by reshaping the Indians. Over the next decade, first with the Indians and then the White Sox, his teams would never finish lower than third. He was a quiet, unassuming man who got the most out of a team. With the Indians it was a blend of pitching and good hitting but practically no team speed. When he moved over to the White Sox it was great pitching combined with speed but very little hitting (Koppett, 181–182). He won with both types of teams and earned his way into the Hall of Fame in 1977.

The Indians of 1951 were a fine team with good balance between power and pitching. They eventually produced only one .300 hitter, second baseman Bobby Avila, but they had six hitters who reached double figures in homers including three — Luke Easter, Al Rosen and Larry Doby — who hit over 20. They tied for the League lead in homers with the Red Sox, with 140. But it was Lopez's staff that made Cleveland a success. Led by Bob Feller, who had his last great year, winning 22 games, Lopez had four top starters: Mike Garcia and Early Wynn, who each finished with 20-13 records, and Bob Lemon, who went 17-14. No one in the American League could match that. These men enabled Cleveland to stay in contention all season as they set the pace in league ERA at 3.38. The Indians won 93 games, their most since the pennant season of 1948. Lopez was in the process of molding a team that would give the Yankees their only challenge in the first half of the 1950s.

The great surprise in 1951 was the emergence of the White Sox as a winning team. They had been a losing franchise since 1943, a team with little money, marginal fan support and only a few talented players. Improvement began with the arrival of Frank Lane as general manager in 1949. Nicknamed "Trader Frank" for his love of dealing, he made some key acquisitions for the White Sox, including Nelson Fox and Billy Pierce. In 1951 he hired Paul Richards as manager and the team finally clicked, winning 81 games. In subsequent years they won 81, 89, and 94 games to become one of the premier franchises in the American League. They also set attendance records at a time when the figure for the Majors was declining. Between 1952 and 1958 the White Sox averaged 1.2 million fans.

Richards was a shrewd judge of baseball talent and understood how to put a team together. He had a gift for teaching pitching, and under him the White Sox in the age of the long ball emphasized pitching and team speed (Koppett, 201).

Lane traded away Gus Zernial, the first White Sox long-ball threat since Al Simmons, in a complicated three-way trade with Cleveland and the A's and got back Minnie Minoso who better fit Richards's stress on speed. Along with Jim Busby, whom Richards installed in center field, Chico Carresquel at short and Nelson Fox at second, the White Sox fielded one of the better defensive teams in the American League. The team ERA was lower than the Yankees', even though aside from Pierce the White Sox lacked a topflight pitcher. Under Richards's tutelage, Saul Rogovin, a journeyman right-hander Lane stole from the Tigers, won the League ERA title at 2.78. Rogovin was one of two pitchers in the American League with an ERA under 3.00; Ed Lopat was the other.

The American League started with a four-team race among the surprising White Sox, who set much of the pace early in the season, the Yankees, the Indians and the Red Sox. By July 4 only 4½ games separated the first-place White Sox from the fourth-place Indians. The White Sox were winning with a combination of good pitching, high-average hitting, and a commanding lead in team speed. They had 21 more stolen bases than their nearest competitor. Minoso was second in hitting, and little Nelson Fox was fourth.

The other big surprise of the 1951 season was the collapse of the Tigers

Al Lopez. After a 19-year career as a catcher in the majors with four teams, Lopez became, after Casey Stengel, the most successful manager of the generation after World War II. His teams won two pennants and finished second seven times between 1951 and 1960. His winning percentage of .581 is the ninth highest in baseball history. (Brace Photo.)

after a wonderful second-place finish in 1950. The Tigers dropped 21 games in the standings to finish a sad fifth, 25 games behind the Yankees. It was a team effort. Other than George Kell, who hit .319, and Vic Wertz, who smashed 27 homers and drove in 94 runs, practically everyone had a poor year. The pitching staff was hurt by the loss of Art Houttemann, a 19-game winner, to the military. The rest of the pitchers were getting on in years. Dizzy Trout would be 36 during the year and was about at the end of the string. Much was expected from Hal Newhouser, who had a good 1950, going 15-13. In spring training manager Red Rolfe talked of the return to form of Virgil Trucks and continued top performance from Newhouser to make up for the loss of Houttemann (*SN*, 3/7/51, p. 21). The Tigers cut Newhouser's salary, even after his fine 1950 year, from $53,000 to $42,000, almost the maximum allowed at that time (Jordan, 219). It didn't matter in the long run, as Newhouser hurt his arm and was finished by midseason with just a 6-6 record. His performance was symptomatic of what went wrong for the Tigers.

The Yankees played a steady brand of baseball all season even though they did not have a very impressive team compared with the 1950 squad. DiMaggio was clearly at the end of the line. He could no longer get around on a good fastball, and he was seeing nothing but hard stuff. At midpoint in the season he was struggling at .261 with just 6 homers and 31 RBI, the worst figures in his career. Unlike 1950 there were no signs that he would break out of his slump in the second half of the season. The Yankees did not have a hitter in the top ten. In fact, at the end of the year only Yogi Berra would put up any offensive numbers. He would tie for fourth place in homers with 27. But no Yankee would drive in 100 runs for the first time since 1947. The best Yankee hitter was a rookie, Gil McDougald, who was filling in at third base.

The Yankees were able to stay in contention because of pitching and the shrewd handling of the squad by Stengel. At the midpoint, Lopat, Raschi and Reynolds were 32-13, and Stengel was juggling his regulars even more impressively than in 1949. Seven Yankees hit homers in double figures, although only two, Rizzuto and Berra, got to bat over 500 times. Three others barely made 400 plate appearances. Stengel platooned Joe Collins and Johnny Mize at first and got 19 homers and 97 RBI out of them. He used Coleman and McDougald at second, McDougald and Bobby Brown at third, Bauer and rookie Mickey Mantle in right, Woodling and Jackie Jensen in left and got the maximum out of them all.

The Yankees were gradually playing younger players at crucial positions — Coleman in 1949, Ford in 1950, Mantle and McDougald in 1951 — and in the process were transforming the team. No one had their depth or their devotion to Stengel's managerial philosophy, which Stengel absorbed from John McGraw: "Most games are lost, not won." The Yankees rarely beat themselves.

The pennant race stayed a four-team one through July, with the White Sox wilting first. In July and August the Indians won 44 of 63 games to forge into first place. But the Yankees stayed close. On September 1, it was down to a three-way race as the Yankees led Cleveland by one game and the Red Sox by five. From that point the Yankees pulled away by winning 17 of 26, whereas Cleveland split 24 games and the Red Sox slipped under .500 at 12-16. At one point late in September, with the Indians closing in on the Yankees, Hank Greenberg, Cleveland's general manager, predicted his team would win. "The Yankees have too many games left with Boston and we have five left with the Tigers who have been a easy mark" (*SN*, 1/2/52, p. 9) The Yankees won seven of eight, and the easy mark beat the Indians four out of five games.

During that September streak the Yankee big three, Raschi, Lopat and Reynolds, went 12-5. The Yankees won essentially on the strength of their arms. They averaged just four runs a game in September/October, but combined with strong pitching, this was enough.

Following the Giants' dramatic victory in the play-offs, the World Series was something of a letdown. The two teams matched up rather evenly statistically in runs scored, home runs and team ERA, but the Giants couldn't maintain the spirit of their successful overtaking of the Dodgers. Their enthusiasm carried over to the first game of the Series, where Dave Koslo outpitched Allie Reynolds and Monte Irvin went on a tear with four hits. If they could have won game two behind Larry Jansen the Giants might have won the Series. But "steady Eddie" Lopat cooled off the Giants on five hits and one run. Jansen pitched well himself, allowing just six hits and three runs.

The Giants had a chance when game three moved to the Polo Grounds, and Jim Hearn easily beat the Yankees with the help of Whitey Lockman's three-run homer. But the Giants had shot their bolt. After a day off because of rain, the Yankees swept three games in a row. Joe DiMaggio hit the last homer of his career to help win game four and the Yankees erupted for 13 runs, including McDougald's grand slam in game five. The Giants behind Koslo, Hearn and Jansen made game six close, but the Yankees got great relief from Bob Kuzava to win a squeaker, 4–3. It was typical of the Yankees that a key role in their victory was played by a player they traded for during the season. They had gotten Kuzava from Washington in exchange for three players — Tom Ferrick, Fred Sanford and Bob Porterfield — who were superfluous, although Porterfield turned out to be an effective pitcher.

What lost the Series for the Giants was the collapse of the fine pitching that had enabled them to overtake the Dodgers. Maglie and Jansen were hit hard and lost three games between them. They lost half as many games in four days as they had throughout the month of September. Yankee pitching was superb. Lopat's ERA was 0.50, and Raschi's was slightly higher at 0.87. Combined with just enough hitting and their usual tight defense — the Yankees made four errors, Giants fourteen — this was just enough for the Bombers to win.

The Series lacked the drama of the play-offs and produced little excitement. It had its significance, though. It saw Joe DiMaggio's last appearance as a player and Mickey Mantle's first in a Series. Mantle also seriously injured his knee making a catch in the Series, the first of a long series of ailments that would rob him of at least part of his career. Most importantly, it was the first World Series to be televised across the country and was watched by a huge audience.

No More Miracles for the Giants

The year 1952 was another grim one for the United States. The Korean War dragged on, and the stalemated peace talks frayed the nation's temper. At least, inflation eased to just 2.2 percent, a sustainable figure after 1951's high rate. Senator McCarthy's anticommunist campaign grew in popularity, partly as a result of frustration over the war. The fact that 1952 would be a presidential election year didn't bode well. As it turned out the two candidates, Adlai Stevenson for the Democrats and Gen. Dwight Eisenhower for the Republicans, conducted a civil campaign that calmed the nation down considerably. But the tensions that plagued the nation were largely hidden by the enormous prosperity of the postwar period that continued to sweep across the country. The unemployment rate for 1952 was just 2.7 percent, which statistically is tantamount to full employment.

Baseball continued to be hurt by the Korean War in a very direct way. At least 26 players or 6.5 percent of the Major League rosters were in the military during 1952. Among these were such future Hall of Famers as Willie Mays, Whitey Ford and Ted Williams who was called back into the Marines early in the 1952 season. The figures didn't approach those for World War II, but virtually every team suffered from military requirements.

Baseball had escaped political interference in 1952. Emmanuel Celler, a powerful Democratic congressman from New York, had conducted an extensive investigation into the monopolistic nature of baseball. The Major League owners held their breath, hoping that the committee's report would not interfere with baseball's antitrust exemption. When the committee reported on May 23, 1952, it recommended no legislation. Instead, it called for the reserve clause, which was being challenged in a number of lawsuits to be tested in the courts. In effect, the report was giving baseball, rather than have Congress, an opportunity to modify the reserve clause and put its house in order. Baseball had dodged the political bullet once again.

In his first state of baseball address as commissioner, Ford Frick noted that over 1800 players were in the military. Where he got that figure, whether it included minor leagues and semiprofessional players, he didn't explain. But overall he was encouraged about baseball's future. He predicted that attendance would not vary much in the future from past seasons. He even had nice things to say about the possibility of the Pacific Coast League taking the first step toward becoming a third Major League (*NYT*, 4/13/52, V, p. 3). Frick was whistling in the dark. Baseball was not sharing equally in the nation's prosperity. Its popularity was down, and it now had competitors — tennis, golf, even basketball and college football — competing aggressively for the sports dollar.

For the fourth straight year Major League attendance declined, this time by 9 percent to the lowest level since 1945. The problem was serious throughout both leagues. In the National League only Chicago and Cincinnati experienced slight increases. The rest had sharp drops from almost 300,000 in Pittsburgh to around 200,000 for both Boston and Brooklyn. The situation was especially serious for the Braves, who had seen a decline of almost 1.2 million since the pennant–winning year of 1948. The next-lowest attendance (Cincinnati's 604,000) was 325,000 more than the Braves had drawn. Combined with the fact that the Red Sox were still drawing in excess of one million fans even though their caliber of play had declined, this spelled doom for the Braves' franchise.

In the American League the situation was only marginally better. There three teams showed net increases, but one was tiny, only 4000, and another, in Philadelphia, was largely attributable to one person, Bobby Shantz and the phenomenal season he had.

The usual excuses were trotted out by baseball. The change in the cities, the growth of the new suburbs, television watching, the unstable international situation. But no one could hide the fact that baseball was in trouble. One of the many popular baseball journals, Dell's *Major League Baseball: Facts and Figures*, sought to explain the sport's problems from a variety of directions. The publication traced the problem to too many diversions. In the past, it said baseball had no competition for the attention of young men. Now it had to compete with other sports, such as football, basketball and even golf. It also argued that too many automobiles and too many movies distracted the attention of the public from baseball (Salsinger & Black, p. 6). The point about the movies was off the mark. Average weekly attendance at the movies had suffered a catastrophic decline from its peak year, 1948 (the year baseball's attendance hit a peak also), dropping from 90 million to 51 million in 1952 (Steinberg, 46). The motion picture industry was in worse shape than baseball. The cause was the same, the growing popularity of television, but unlike baseball, which eventually gained new fans from television, the movies were being slowly strangled by the new medium.

Nineteen fifty-two also saw an ugly squabble develop over radio and broadcasting rights. Since 1948 the Liberty Broadcasting Network had been successfully doing a "Game of the Day." By 1952 the game was heard on 435 stations in 33 states. Despite the existence of a contract with four Major League teams, baseball owners that year decided to take control of every aspect of broadcasting. Liberty filed a $12 million lawsuit against 13 of the 16 Major

League teams, the commissioner of baseball and both league presidents, charging them with conspiracy to monopolize and restrain competition in baseball broadcasting. Liberty argued that it was being frozen out of broadcasting rights. Judge John D. Barnes of Chicago's Federal Court ruled against Liberty on April 14, 1952, on the grounds that baseball teams had a right to control and profit from broadcasts of their games (Ira Horowitz, "Sports Broadcasting," in Noll, 280). Liberty Broadcasting went out of business in May 1952 (*SNG*, 1953, p. 95).

Baseball was making huge sums from radio and television, and each team wanted to control every aspect of its broadcast. Some teams, including Bill Veeck's poverty-stricken St. Louis Browns, wanted money for games they played on the road that were televised by the home team. The Yankees, Red Sox and Indians dropped any Browns games from their television schedule in retaliation. Veeck's demand helped sow the seeds for his eventual ouster from baseball.

The pennant races in both leagues in 1952 lacked the flair and drama of the National League race in 1951. The BWAA made Cleveland and the Dodgers favorites to win the pennant in 1952. The contest in the American League was expected to be close. Cleveland was the choice of 114 writers, and the Yankees were a close second with 91 votes. In the National League, the Dodgers were a prohibitive choice, 134 votes to 41 for the Giants. The relatively low support for the Giants resulted from two factors: the possible drafting of Willie Mays and Monte Irvin's breaking his ankle shortly before the season started (*SN*, 4/16/52, pp. 1, 4). For Durocher the injury to Irvin was key. When it happened he remarked, "They're carrying our pennant chances off the field" (*ibid.*, 4/9/52, p. 3).

Although both eventual pennant winners won by small margins, there wasn't much tension in either league. In the National League, the Giants streaked off to a quick lead, winning 26 of their first 34 games. Then Willie Mays was called into the Army in late May. The Giants had tried to get a deferment for him, but he didn't qualify under any of the existing rules. Once they lost Mays something went out of the team. The Giants proceeded to lose six of their next eight games. More importantly, the Dodgers had not panicked when the Giants started quickly. They were just a half game behind at the Memorial Day break. The Cubs, who had been in the doldrums since winning the pennant in 1945, were in third, just five games back. No other National League team was playing .500 baseball. At this point the Giants' quick start was traceable to their fine starters: Maglie was 9-0, and Jansen and Hearn were 4-1 each. The team wasn't hitting much, just .253, largely because they missed Monte Irvin who broke his ankle just before the season began. The 1952 team would come close to approximating the statistical levels of the 1951 squad, although their total runs scored, home runs and batting average would be slightly lower. But the Giants couldn't overcome injuries, the loss of Mays and steady level of play that the Dodgers maintained. The 1952 Dodgers didn't crack.

What hurt the Giants as much as the loss of Mays and Irvin was a plague of injuries to the pitching staff. From June on Maglie was just 9-8, the result of a sore back, and Jansen also hurt his back and went 7-10. Jansen was worthless the second half of the season, not winning a game after July 26. Hearn pitched steady baseball, eventually winning 14 games and leading the team in innings pitched with 224, compared to the 298 and 278 innings that Maglie and Jansen had hurled in 1951. Other than the pitching of Hearn, what kept the Giants alive in 1952 was the work of a 28-year-old rookie, Hoyt Wilhelm. Wilhelm came out of nowhere to give the Giants the kind of bull pen that Konstanty and Page had provided their teams in the past. Wilhelm won 15 games and lost just 3 while saving 11 others. He pitched in 71 games and threw 153 innings, unusually high figures for a relief pitcher. In spite of this, Durocher was unusually quiet in 1952, as though he sensed that there would be no repeat of 1951's miracle.

The Dodgers began to pull away from the Giants and the rest of the League in June. By July 4 they had a three-game lead over the Giants in second place. The Dodgers were playing .700 baseball, a pace that was wearing down the competition. After reaching a point, 60-22, the Dodgers just played .500 ball the rest of the season. They were doing it with their usual fine hitting. Robinson and Billy Cox were hitting over .300, whereas Reese, Snider, and Andy Pafko were around the .290 mark. Gil Hodges, although hitting just .235, was second in the League in homers with 16 and third in RBI with 53. What was remarkable about the 1952 Dodgers was their pitching. Unlike past Dodger teams, which had depended on two or perhaps three arms, this team did not have a dominant pitcher. Instead, the victories and innings were spread among four starters and one great reliever. Roe, at 37, was finally showing his age, and he became just a once-a-week pitcher. He was still tough to beat. The other Dodger starters were Erskine and rookies Billy Loes and Ben Wade.

The key to Dodger success in 1952 was Joe Black, who wasn't even on the team roster in spring training. Black was to the Dodgers what Wilhelm was to the Giants — the single, dependable arm. He only started two games going 1 and 1 but pitched 54 times out of the bull pen, winning 14 games and losing just three in relief while saving 15 others. When Dizzy Dean saw him pitch for the first time, he told manager Dressen: "Hey, that big colored guy throws as hard as me" (Golenbock, *Bums*, 318).

Dressen deserves much of the credit for keeping the pitching in line. He had lost his dominant pitcher, Don Newcombe, to the military, and he depended on three rookies plus Erskine. Dressen had a tendency to talk too much, especially about himself. Someone observed that Dressen won 96 games while the Dodgers lost 57. In the middle of September with the Giants threatening to repeat the miracle of 1951 an article under his byline appeared in

Colliers entitled: "The Dodgers Won't Blow It Again." Fortunately for him, they didn't. His job guiding this flawed club may have been the best managing job of his career, even better than the 1953 squad that would win 105 games.

No other National League team was a serious contender. The Cubs after their fast start wilted, although they finished at .500 for the first time since 1946. They got great years from Bob Rush, who won 17 games, and Warren Hacker, who came out of nowhere to win 15. But the reason for their success in 1952 rested on the large shoulders of Hank Sauer, who had a career year. The 35-year-old outfielder tied for the homer title with Ralph Kiner, each hitting 37, led the League in RBI with 121, and came in second to Musial in total bases and slugging percentage. For this he was voted league MVP.

The Cardinals, under their new manager, former second baseman Eddie Stanky, started slowly and came on to finish with 88 wins, a return to their past form that proved short-lived. After enforcing a series of fines and fighting with everyone including his own players, Stanky settled down and the Cardinals were a good second-half club. The Cardinals, behind the hitting of Musial who won another batting championship (his sixth), Enos Slaughter and Red Schoendienst, led the National League in hitting. The pitching staff was surprisingly effective, especially Gerry Staley who won 17 games. One of the most remarkable performances was put on by rookie Eddie Yuhas. Pitching almost totally in relief, the 27-year-old rookie won 11 and lost just one game. He also saved six others. At one point he won ten games in a row, the longest winning streak in the National League. He looked like a great find for the Cardinals but he hurt his arm, and the following season, after pitching just one inning, he was out of baseball permanently. His career is an extreme version of what happened to one of the other rookie pitchers, Joe Black. After his incredible 1952 year, Black hurt his shoulder and lost his great fastball. He held on in baseball for five more years, during which time he won 15 games to match his 1952 single-season total.

Eddie Sawyer believed the Phillies' problems were related to a lack of dedication. He instituted stern rules in spring training, no swimming, no golf, no wives and no cars. His plan didn't work (*SN*, 1/30/52, p. 1). The players were outraged, and Sawyer lost control. On June 26, with the Phillies stuck in sixth place, Sawyer was relieved as manager and replaced by Steve O'Neill. The Phillies immediately came alive under the light hand of O'Neill. He ended all the restrictions that Sawyer had put into effect, such as banning all card playing and establishing a rigid curfew, and left the players alone to play baseball. "Stout" Steve dozed on the bench while the remnants of the Whiz Kids put together a fine second half. Led by Robin Roberts, who had the greatest year of any National League pitcher since Dizzy Dean won 30 games, the Phillies' staff dominated the League. At the July 4 point Roberts was 11-5; he went 17-2 in the second half of the season to lift the Phillies almost single-handedly into fourth place. He was supported by Curt Simmons, who got out of the Army just before the season began and who slowly rounded into form. He won 14 games, as did Karl Drews, who the Phillies salvaged from the minors. Eddie Sawyer believed that the military had taken something out of Simmons. He was a good pitcher in 1952; Sawyer thought he had the ability to be a great pitcher on a par with Roberts when he went into military service in 1950. Russ Meyer made a comeback and won 13 games, and Jim Konstanty recovered from his disastrous 1951 season to win five games and save six others.

The Phillies, although they lacked a .300 hitter, got solid hitting from Del Ennis, who drove in 100 runs after failing miserably in 1951, and from catcher Smokey Burgess, who replaced the traded Andy Seminick behind the plate. Burgess hit a sharp .296. Richie Ashburn saw his average drop 55 points, but he still hit a commendable .282 and led all National League center fielders in putouts and assists.

Under O'Neill the Phillies went 59-32, a .647 level that was .020 higher than the Dodgers' final record. Like Stanky O'Neill was credited with reviving a sagging, demoralized team. But also like Stanky he would discover that the rot went deeper. The Phillies' 1952 success rested on the broad shoulders of one man, Robin Roberts. His final figures should have won him the MVP Award: He finished at 28-7, including six wins over the Dodgers, while leading the League in innings, complete games, finishing second in winning percentage, third in strikeouts and ERA. In one of the worst decisions in National League history, the voters placed him ten points behind Hank Sauer. Apparently, Stan Baumgartner, a local Philadelphia sportswriter, left him off the ballot because of personal animosity (Rosenthal, 67).

By the beginning of September the Dodgers had a seemingly safe nine-game lead over the Giants, when Durocher's team suddenly made a run at them. Irvin returned from the disabled list, and the Giants, with Wilhelm pitching almost every day, went 11-3 at one stretch. Maglie won four games and Wilhelm went 3-0 during the last three weeks of the season, but it wasn't enough. In mid-September, with the Giants just 3 out and 11 games to go, Durocher made one of his typical gambles; he started rookie Jack Harschman against the Cubs in order to give his pitching staff a breather. It didn't work. The Cubs clobbered the Giants, and Durocher was sharply criticized. Ken Smith of the *New York Daily Mirror* said that in using an untried rookie, Durocher had demoralized the team (*SN*, 9/24/52, p. 9).

The Giants' hitting wasn't enough to compensate for the lackluster performance of the pitching staff, other than Maglie and Wilhelm. People talked of another "Miracle of Coogan's Bluff," but this time there was no lighting. The Dodgers played steady ball with solid hitting right through the lineup and held the Giants off to win by a comfortable 4½ games, with the Cardinals in third at 8½ games back, one game ahead of the fourth-place Phillies. A major reason for the Dodgers' success this time was the way they handled the weak teams in the League. They were 54-11 versus Cincinnati, Boston and

Pittsburgh whereas the Giants went 45-21 against them. The Giants handled the Dodgers easily during the season, going 14-8 but they couldn't beat the weaker teams.

The "Perfesser" Does It Again

In the American League the Yankees made it four in a row in what was essentially a dull two-team race with the Indians. Stengel and general manager George Weiss were gradually transforming the team from the one that Stengel took over in 1949, and they were doing it while winning. Since 1949 they had lost Tommy Henrich, Charley Keller, Joe DiMaggio and Joe Page but brought in such replacements as Mickey Mantle, Whitey Ford, Billy Martin and Gil MacDougald. Part of the reason for the Yankee success was constant turnover from their highly rated farm system and from shrewd trades by Weiss. Stengel also liked versatile players whom he could move about. MacDougald, during his career, for example, would lead third basemen, shortstops and second basemen in double plays at different times (Golenbock, Dynasty, p. 81).

The year 1952 was a major year in this Yankee transformation. It saw the first blossoming of Mantle as a potential superstar, and it was also Billy Martin's first full time season. The Yankees had a solid, steady club, although they were beginning to show age in the pitching staff. Their key men that season — Raschi, Lopat, Reynolds and Johnny Sain — were either 33 or 34. All of them had one good season left. The rest of the staff was unspectacular but steady. The Yankees wound up the 1952 season with a team ERA of 3.12, one of the lowest in their history.

Cleveland was their major competition, with the White Sox regarded as a long shot. Lopez had a handful of powerful hitters and three great starters in Wynn, Lemon and Garcia. Feller began to slip that season, winning only 9 games and losing 13, the first time he was under .500 in his career. The power was supplied by Al Rosen, Larry Doby, and Luke Easter, while Bobby Avila and Dale Mitchell both were .300 hitters. Avila was in the process of showing why he was the best second baseman in the American League. The Indians would chase the Yankees all season but never completely overhaul them.

Paul Richards's White Sox started off impressively and gave the Yankees fits in the early going, but they eventually wilted. Richards, as usual, produced an effective pitching staff, led by Billy Pierce and Saul Rogovin. He also revived the career of Joe Dobson, who at 35 won 14 games with a low 2.51 ERA. Even more spectacularly, Richards took a 34-year-old journeyman, Marv Grissom, and got 12 wins out of him. The White Sox's team ERA was second only to the Yankees', and Richards's ability to develop pitchers was confirmed. However, the White Sox were weak at bat. Only three teams scored fewer runs. Minoso had a bad year for him, hitting only .281, with just 13 homers and 61

Minnie Minoso. The first of the great black Latin players, Minoso hit .300 or better seven times. Despite not reaching the majors full-time until he was 27, he played for seventeen years in the majors. The White Sox brought him back to DH at age 53, and he got a single. He also appeared in two games at age 56. (Brace Photo.)

RBI. The team's big hitter was first baseman Eddie Robinson, who drove in 104 runs, but he clogged up the bases for the speedy White Sox. After the season Richards would unload the lumbering left-handed hitter to the A's in return for batting champ Ferris Fain and a young outfielder, Bob Wilson, who would fail to live up to his potential.

When the season started the Yankees were plagued with assorted injuries to key players: Mantle, Berra, Coleman and, most significantly, Vic Raschi. Raschi's knee problems, which dated back to 1950, were beginning to take a toll. By Memorial Day Cleveland was in first place by a game and a half over the Red Sox, with Washington, the White Sox and the Yankees struggling for third place. Five teams were over .500 at this point, compared to two in the National League. Stengel was worried because the team seemed to lack power. At this point in the season the Yankees' leading home-run hitter was Hank Bauer, with just six, whereas Mantle and Berra each had three homers. The pitching of Raschi, Reynolds and Sain was keeping them in the race. Lopat had a sore arm and was struggling with just one win versus three defeats at this point. He would not be much help in 1952.

The Yankees began to pull things together in June. Mantle and Berra recovered from their injuries and started hitting. Berra hit ten homers in June to put the Yankees back in contention. Stengel was platooning frantically. During the season he would use over 100 different lineups. MacDougald batted in eight different slots, Bauer in seven, Irv Noren in seven, and Berra batted in every position from second through seventh (Koppett, 156). The vaunted Yankee versatility paid off. On June 14 they were in first place, where they stayed except for one day in August.

By the July 4 midpoint the Yankees were beginning to click. Mantle was hitting over .300 and showing occasional awesome power. Berra was leading the League in homers, and Woodling and Bauer were sharing outfield duties and hitting. Woodling was hitting .320, Bauer .292. Together they had 14 homers and 57 RBI. The big three of Raschi, Reynolds and Sain were 25-9. Raschi would eventually win 11 games in a row. Lopat was making some progress at 5-5, and Bob Kuzava was proving a pleasant surprise both starting and relieving at 4-3. The Yankees were unstoppable. They were not an awesome team who beat you decisively. They just outpitched you, outfielded you and had enough hitting especially in the clutch to outlast you.

The White Sox were still in contention, but they began to wilt in July, as did Boston and Washington, who had been early-season surprises. Cleveland was coming on — they were three games back in third place, and they would present the only challenge to the Yankees the rest of the way. They stayed close to the Yankees, never more than a handful of games behind, but they couldn't close the gap. They were 2½ games out when September started and at one point even got as close as ½ game. But although they played brilliantly in September, going 19-5, the Yankees duplicated that record. Their winning margin was two games, although they won the fewest games for them since 1948.

The Yankees won once again because they had good pitching, combined with a tight solid defense. They didn't overpower anyone as past Yankee teams had, but they still came in second in homers behind Cleveland. They scored the second-highest number of runs again behind Cleveland, but their pitching staff gave up the fewest runs. Defensively they were second in the League but made the most double plays. Cleveland's defense was terrible. They were tied for the most errors and made the fewest double plays in the League. First sacker Easter, second baseman Avila and shortstop Boone came in last in fielding at their positions.

For the second year in a row the White Sox came in third with the same record, 81-73, and the A's finished fourth, two games behind them. The A's record was largely the work of four players. Ferris Fain, whose salary for 1952 was $25,000, the highest of any Athletic since Jimmy Foxx's $36,000 in 1933, won his second straight batting title with a .327 average and led the League in doubles. Gus Zernial hit 29 homers and drove in 100 runs, and rookie pitcher Harry Byrd won 15 games with a low 3.31 ERA. But the most dramatic reason for the A's success was the work of Bobby Shantz. He hurled 280 innings and went 24-7 with a 2.48 ERA. The little southpaw would have won even more, but he suffered a broken wrist in mid-September. He caught the attention of Philadelphia fans as few athletes have. He was the biggest drawing card in Philadelphia since Connie Mack's great teams of the late 1920s and early 1930s. When he pitched, the A's averaged 18,000 fans; without him the average was 8,000. His 16 Shibe Park starts accounted for almost 44 percent of the A's home gate (Kuklick, 119).

The Red Sox without Ted Williams continued their decline under their new manager, Lou Boudreau. They finished in sixth place, 19 games off the pace. The team was a patchwork quilt with a few veterans like George Kell and a fading Dom DiMaggio blending in with new faces like Jimmy Piersall and catcher Sammy White plus an assortment of untalented outfielders. Vern Stephens, who had suffered a deep tear in his thigh in 1951, never recovered the power he had shown in the 1948–1950 period. The pitching staff was a disaster zone with Mel Parnell leading an old, worn-out staff with 12 wins.

Bill Veeck's pathetic St. Louis Browns were kept out of the cellar only by the total collapse of the Tigers, who lost 104 games, a decline of 45 games since they almost won the pennant in 1950. This collapse cost Red Rolfe his job, and he was replaced on July 5 by Fred Hutchinson. The Tigers performed just as poorly under their new skipper, going 27-55. The outstanding performance for the Tigers was two no-hitters by Virgil Trucks. What made it so impressive was the fact that he won just 3 other games that season and lost 19 games. Trucks, Art Houtteman and Ted Gray went a combined 25-56 to sink the Tigers into the basement. The Tigers suffered a major blow when Ned

Garver, a former 20-game winner whom they got from the last-place Browns in 1951, developed arm problems and won exactly one game for them. Fortunately, they hadn't given up much to get him, although Vic Wertz, the key player in the deal as far as the Browns were concerned, was still a quality player with good years ahead. In 35 games with the Browns, Wertz hit .346. Newhouser made a mild comeback, splitting 18 decisions. Not bad for someone making around $31,000 per year (SN, 3/12/52, p. 5).

For once the World Series lived up to its image. It was a seven-game bloodbath between two good, evenly matched Yankee-Dodger teams. Neither club hit for much of an average, a testament to good pitching on both sides, but between the two they clubbed 16 homers, for a World Series record. The Yankees' batting average of .216 was the lowest for any winning team.

The Yankees won because of superior pitching, which held the Dodger big hitters in check. Gil Hodges did not get a hit, taking the collar in 21 times at bat, and Campanella and Robinson had exactly one extra-base hit between them. Duke Snider was the hitting star for the Dodgers, smashing four homers, to tie the record set by Babe Ruth, and hitting .345. For the Yankees, it was a study in contrast, the youngest Yankee, Mantle, and the oldest, Mize, shared honors. Mantle hit two homers and batted .345, whereas Mize smashed three homers and hit .400.

Both teams were in decent shape for the Series, unlike some past years. Dressen surprised everyone by picking Joe Black to start game one, only the third start of his Major League career. It was a gutsy but sensible choice; Black was the best Dodger pitcher by far. As Erskine noted, nobody questioned Dressen's choice (Golenbock, *Bums*, 320). Black came through, pitching a six-hitter, and the Dodgers hit three homers to beat Allie Reynolds. In game two, Raschi evened things with a three-hitter, beating Erskine.

When the Series moved to Yankee Stadium for the weekend, Preacher Roe out-dueled Ed Lopat, 5–3. Game four was a reprise of the opener only this time Reynolds was better on two days' rest than Black. The "Superchief," as he was known because of his Indian heritage, had one of his best World Series outings. He shut out the Dodgers, gave up just four hits and struck out ten batters. Black pitched well, he gave up just three hits in seven innings but he was wild and walked five batters. The Dodger offense had gone into the doldrums after the first game. They had gotten just one extra-base hit since then, a double by Furillo. It looked like the Yankee jinx on the Dodgers was going to work once again.

Game five was one of the greatest World Series games in history. Erskine started against Ewell Blackwell, whom Weiss had plucked out of the National League late in the season, hoping for another Mize or Sain. But Blackwell was shot. He had hurt his shoulder after his fabulous 1947 season and then had a serious kidney operation. After the 1952 season he would pitch just 23 innings in the rest of his career. The Dodgers jumped off to a 4–0 lead, largely because of Snider's three-run homer, when the Yankees came to bat in the fifth. They scored five runs off Erskine with Mize's three-run homer the big hit. Dressen left Erskine in to the surprise of most people. Dressen like Durocher was a hunch player, and he didn't want to go to his bull pen. The Dodgers tied the game in the seventh, and despite a couple of scares on long drives caught against the low railing in right field, Erskine shut the Yankees down the rest of the way. The Dodgers won the game in the eleventh on Snider's clutch double off Sain. The Dodgers were back to a 3–2 edge with the Series due to return to Brooklyn.

The odds shifted to the Dodgers' favor because they were unusually tough at home. Interestingly, this year was quirky. The Dodgers played .680 ball on the road and only .577 at home. Game six featured Raschi's second start, this time against Billy Loes. It was another close game, with Raschi striking out nine Dodgers before leaving in the eighth inning leading 3–2. Stengel brought in Reynolds, who struck out Campanella with the tying run on second and then retired the side easily in the ninth inning. In relief Reynolds could be overpowering, firing nothing but fastballs, and Stengel would often use him in that capacity. In 1952 Stengel used him six times in relief, and Reynolds got a save every time.

Game six's other claim to fame was Billy Loes's comment that he lost a ground ball in the sun. Raschi hit a grounder back at him, which glanced off his leg. Loes told the reporters that the late-afternoon sun shining through the opening in the grandstand had temporarily blinded him. The press played it up as typical Dodger nuttiness but Erskine confirmed that it was reality to anyone pitching in Ebbets Field (Golenbock, *Bums*, 323).

The seventh game the Dodgers went back to Black for the third time, whereas Stengel defied odds by starting a left-hander, Lopat, against the right-handed power of the Dodgers. Black pitched well, giving up just three runs in a little over five innings. When Lopat loaded the bases in the fourth inning, Stengel went back to Reynolds, who stymied the Dodgers for three more innings. With the Yankees leading 4–2 in the bottom of the seventh, the Dodgers loaded the bases with one out against Raschi, who had relieved Reynolds. They had Snider and Robinson due up.

Stengel was desperate. He had used Lopat, Reynolds and Raschi and was left with two choices: Sain or lefty Bob Kuzava. He brought in the left-hander, who had had success facing Snider in the minors. Snider turned out to be easy. He popped up. Kuzava believed that he would be taken out and Sain brought in to face the clutch-hitting Robinson (Kahn, *Era*, p. 309). He believed that Stengel didn't want to let Robinson beat the Yankees.

There was real animosity between Stengel and Robinson. They had exchanged derogatory comments in the press, with Robinson arguing that the Yankee manager was overrated and the Yankees prejudiced against blacks. Earlier after Reynolds had struck Robinson out in a key situation, Stengel got off a zinger: "Before that black son of a bitch accuses us of being prejudiced, he should learn how to hit an Indian" (Golenbock, *Dynasty*, 93).

Kuzava was surprised. Stengel left him in. After Robinson hit two hard fouls to left, Kuzava slowed up with a curve, which he got too high. Kuzava says he got away with a bad pitch partly because it was so high that Robinson couldn't drive the ball (Kuzava to author, 3/22/95). Robinson hit another high pop-up, which caused trouble because first baseman Joe Collins lost the ball in the sun. With two out Billy Martin made a desperate knee-high catch on the dead run to save three runs. Kuzava breezed through the last two innings as the Dodgers went quietly. For the second World Series in a row, he got the last out for the world champion Yankees. Kuzava was typical of the kind of player that Stengel got the most out of. Kuzava was considered a marginal pitcher, but Stengel used him wisely and milked two good seasons from him.

Baseball didn't have a great year in 1952, but no one could have asked for a better, more exciting World Series. As the Series ended there were enormous problems confronting the national game, of which the most pressing was the possibility that for the first time since the organization of the American League, there would be franchise moves. In the December 1952 meeting of baseball owners in Phoenix the rules for moving a team were modified. No longer would a unanimous vote of both leagues be necessary to move a team. Indemnities would have to be paid to other teams in the area, that is minor league teams, but the way was cleared for a long-overdue restructuring of Major League baseball.

On to Milwaukee

Nineteen fifty-three was an important year in baseball and in America's history. For the first time since the Baltimore Orioles moved to New York in 1903, a Major League team changed cities as the Boston Braves pulled up stakes for the untapped, rich territory of the upper Midwest, the beer capital of America, Milwaukee. For the United States, 1953 saw a new Republican administration, led by Dwight Eisenhower, end 20 years of Democratic rule. In July 1953, in his first success as president, Eisenhower helped put an end to the war in Korea, which had cost 45,000 American lives. For the first time in over three years no American soldier died in battle. The economy continued to boom, and unemployment even dropped .2 percent from its incredible low of 2.7 percent the year before. Inflation became irrelevant, dropping to less than 1 percent. The Eisenhower prosperity had begun, and what the country would remember as the solid, stable fifties was launched.

Even with all its problems baseball seemed ideally suited to the decade of the 1950s. Just as Eisenhower had a calming effect on the nation's nerves so did baseball play a similar role. As David Voigt has pointed out, baseball symbolized the American dream, with its emphasis on pure ability to succeed (Voigt, *Baseball*, 220). The myth was never stronger than in the 1950s, especially once the color barrier was removed and more and more black players made their presence felt in the Majors. Integration continued slowly, with 24 blacks on a Major League roster in 1953 (Roth, *Who's Who in Baseball*, 1954 edition).

Attendance continued its downward trend, reaching its postwar low of 14.4 million, a decline of 6.6 million fans since the 1948 peak year. No team in the American League experienced an increase in attendance, with two weak franchises, the Browns and A's, losing over 225,000 fans each. What saved the National League from a similar collapse was the immense popularity of the new Milwaukee franchise, which outdrew the Boston Brave team of 1952 by almost 1.6 million fans. Two other teams, the Phillies and Dodgers, also experienced small gains. The rest of the National League saw attendance drop. The Cubs, always a good draw in the Windy City, declined by over 260,000 fans and lost $500,000 in 1953 (Langford, 75).

Just as baseball seemed most stable, the beginning of its great transformation into a truly continental game was about to begin. The two men who personified this change were profoundly different types: Bill Veeck, the game's greatest self-proclaimed hustler, and Lou Perini, owner of the Boston Braves, a quiet nondescript businessman.

The Braves and Browns were in terrible shape in 1952. Since the end of the war, the Browns had been a pathetic second-division team whose highest finish was sixth place and who attracted over 500,000 fans in just two years, 1946 and 1952. Despite one of the lowest payrolls in the Majors, a little over $190,000 in 1950, the Browns constantly lost money (*SN*, 2/20/52, p. 12). Veeck had purchased the team in July 1951 but had little excess capital to develop the franchise properly. He was running the team on a shoestring, resorting to various gimmicks, including sending a midget to bat and having the fans manage a game to attract a crowd. He started new promotions, such as "Bat Day," to lure fans to the park. But the Browns had to resort to selling off their best players to pay the bills. Veeck had his eyes on richer areas: either Milwaukee, which he knew from his minor league days, or perhaps California, although the West Coast was still impractical until jet service reduced flying to a reasonable time.

Perini was in better shape. He had money — he was a successful builder — and his team had a perennial contender in the National League since World War II, winning a pennant in 1948. The Braves had averaged over 1.2 million fans between 1946 and 1950. Even in 1950, when they drew 944,000 fans, the Braves suffered a loss of $257,000. The last year Perini made a profit was 1949 and then it was only $70,000 (*SN*, 2/6/52, p. 2).

The Braves fell on hard times. The team slipped out of contention and lost the support of its fan base in Boston to the Red Sox, who outdrew them by 2.4 million fans in 1951 and 1952. For the Braves the bottom dropped out in 1952. They drew just 281,000 fans and finished in seventh place, with only the pathetic Pirates keeping them from the cellar. Perini's loss that year was $700,000, the greatest in baseball history until that point (Allen, "Unthinkable," *Diamond*, July 1993, p. 23). Perini saw no future in Boston and hinted in the fall of 1952 that unless he was assured of fan support he would consider moving. Unlike Veeck he had a place to go, and he was popular with his fellow owners.

Perini struck first. With new rules in effect for a franchise move, Perini rejected an offer of $750,000 from Veeck to buy the rights to the Braves' minor league franchise in Milwaukee. Although he had promised the people of Boston after the 1952 season that he would give them two years to support his team, Perini announced in March 1953 that he wanted to move his team to Milwaukee. A new stadium with parking for 14,000 cars awaited him along with a baseball-starved public. Commissioner Frick had argued that no move was possible so close to the beginning of a new season, but the National League owners, led by Walter O'Malley, paid no attention to him and gave Perini a unanimous vote of support for this action.

No one could have foreseen the love affair — more Brooklyn than Brooklyn — that Milwaukee would have with its new team which played a much-improved brand of baseball in 1953. Milwaukee adopted the players literally by giving them free food and housing. The first year in Milwaukee the Braves drew 1.8 million fans, almost 700,000 more than their nearest rivals, the Dodgers. In two years Perini had made a huge profit (Lowenfish, 76). Interestingly, the city of Milwaukee did well in getting the Braves. According to one analysis, one third of the fans attending Braves games were from out of town, and they spent an average of $11 dollars in the city, which added up to between seven and eight million dollars in revenue for the city (Powell, 113).

The lesson of Perini's coup was not lost on other owners, in particular Walter O'Malley of the Dodgers.

In the meantime, the baseball establishment closed ranks against Veeck. Perini's move to Milwaukee ended that possibility, and when Veeck sought to take the Browns to Baltimore, he found that he had too many enemies. At the December 1952 meeting of baseball owners Veeck had offered some new ideas on the game's future including the unrestricted drafting of minor leaguers. This was regarded by the more successful teams with large farm systems as a way to harness talent without paying for it. Veeck also called for sharing all television revenue equally among the Major League teams (Veeck, 224–230). These actions, coming at a time when he was considering uprooting the Browns, bordered on suicide. The main excuse used to thwart Veeck was that a team in Baltimore would threaten the Philadelphia fan base north of the city and the Senators' base south of the city. Bob Carpenter of the Phillies labeled Veeck's plan "asinine" (Miller, 30). The opposition to Veeck was orchestrated by the Yankee owners, especially Dan Topping, who despised Veeck. Veeck was isolated, losing money in St. Louis, and his only out was to sell the team because the American League owners would not approve a move while he was in charge.

On the field 1953 lacked excitement. Neither league experienced a pennant race. The Giants and Phillies who had played exciting baseball in the last half of the 1952 season, were flops. The Giants experienced almost a total collapse of their pitching staff and within a matter of weeks were bogged down in seventh place. The Giants still fielded a quality batting order: seven of their regulars hit .288 or better and as a team they finished second to the Dodgers in homers with 176. But the rotation was a disaster. Their biggest winner was a 26-year-old rookie, Ruben Gomez, who won just 13 games. The big three of Maglie, Hearn and Jansen all suffered a variety of ailments and finished the year, 28-37, a net decline of 15 games over the 1952 season. Even Wilhelm flirted with the sophomore jinx. He still led the League in appearances and saved 15 games, but his record went from 15-3 to 7-8. Durocher lost interest in the team and toward the end of the season he was allowing Dark, Westrum, Rigney and Lockman to manage the team (Eskenazi, 268). All three became successful Major League managers.

The Phillies started off well under the light rein of Steve O'Neill, winning 9 of their first 11 games. The team was optimistic. They would have Curt Simmons from spring training on; a new pitcher, Steve Ridzik, had shown promise in 1952; and the team had filled the hole at first base by getting Earl Torgeson from the Braves for Russ Meyer. Eddie Waitkus had never been the same since his shooting in June 1949. Torgeson had a bad year with the Braves in 1952, but he was only 29 and had shown signs of speed and power with the Braves.

In May Simmons cut off the tip of his big toe with a powermower and missed a month of the season. The team never really rebounded. They finished tied for third with a poorer record than the fourth-place 1952 team and, what is more revealing, 23 games behind the first-place Dodgers. Roberts won 23 games, Simmons 16 and Jim Konstanty 14. Ridzik was a letdown. The hitting was good. Ashburn hit .330 and led the League in hits. Ennis drove in 125 runs, and Granny Hamner, splitting his time between short and second, hit 21 homers and drove in 92 runs. Torgeson was lackluster and seemed out of place. He hit a soft .274, but the high right-field fence in Shibe Park robbed him of his long-ball power. He hit just 11 homers and drove in 64 runs.

The surprise team of the League was the new Milwaukee Braves. Although they had played poorly for a couple of seasons, the Braves had the nucleus of a solid club. They had the best left-hander in the National League in Warren Spahn, and general manager John Quinn made a brilliant trade with the Yankees when he got Lew Burdette for an aging Johnny Sain. Burdette won 15 games in 1953. Bob Buhl came out of the military in time for the 1953 campaign and won 13 games. Bonus baby Johnny Antonelli had his first big year, splitting 24 decisions.

The starting lineup was impressive. Quinn had gotten Joe Adcock from Cincinnati, and he anchored first place, easily outperforming Torgeson in all offensive categories. Johnny Logan had his first good year at 26, hitting .273 and driving in 73 runs. Andy Pafko came over from Brooklyn, where he had never really fit in and became a folk hero to the Polish population of the Milwaukee area. He hit .297 and played left field effectively. Rookie Bill Bruton was a tremendous defensive center fielder with great speed and range. He led the League in stolen bases with 26. But the real shock to baseball was the emergence of Eddie Mathews as baseball's premier long-ball threat. Mathews, who had shown signs of power in his rookie year of 1952 by hitting 25 homers, came into his own in Milwaukee. He hit 47 homers, dethroned Ralph Kiner as homer king and hit over .300, driving in 135 runs. He was an adequate third baseman but showed signs of getting better. Milwaukee never really challenged the Dodgers, but they wound up in second place and won 92 games, one more than the 1948 pennant-winning team.

The Dodger team of 1953 won 105 games, the most in its history, and may have been the best club Brooklyn ever fielded. They certainly were the best offensive Dodger team. They hit 208 homers, including 40 or more by Snider and Campanella. Eight Dodger players were in double figures in homers. The team scored 955 runs almost 200 more than their nearest rival. Three men — Snider, Campanella and Hodges — drove in over 120 runs, and two others — Furillo and Robinson — were in the 90s. Furillo won the batting title with a .344 average, although it was something of a fluke. He broke his hand in a brawl with Leo Durocher in a September game and sat out the rest of the season while Red Schoendienst and Stan Musial closed in on him. He won by 2 points.

What made the Dodgers human was their pitching. It was good but ranked third behind the Braves and the Phillies in ERA. Erskine won 20 games for the only time in his career, and Russ Meyer, who came over in a complicated three-way trade among the Dodgers, Braves and Phillies, contributed 14. Loes won 14, and Preacher Roe in his last winning season won 11. No Dodger pitcher had a losing record. The biggest letdown was Joe Black who failed to match his 1952 year.

The National League race was mildly competitive until June, when the Dodgers forged into the lead. After the All-Star break they reeled off 41 wins versus just 9 defeats to seal up the pennant. Their clinching of the pennant on September 12 was the earliest in National League history, and their margin of victory over the Braves, 13 games, the largest in the League since the Cards won by 14 games in 1944.

"One More Time"

When spring training began in 1953 Eddie Lopat said that a bunch of the veteran Yankees got together and agreed to try and win "one more time." Lopat realized that the key pitchers did not have much time left. They were all in their mid-30s, and it was clear that the Yankee transformation, already far advanced offensively, was about to reach the pitching staff. Lopat didn't need to worry. The Yankees ran away with the American League race much as the Dodgers did the National League. They held first place for all but nine days of the season. Their eventual winning margin, 8½ games was the biggest of Stengel's career as a Yankee manager so far.

The Yankees effectively won the pennant in late May/early June when they reeled off 18 wins in a row, including 14 on the road. At this point they led the second-place Indians by 10½ games. Ford and Lopat had a total of 14 wins and no defeats. The rest of the American League never recovered.

The Yankee team of 1953 was a fine, balanced, highly professional squad that hardly ever beat itself. It had solid performers, if not super-talents like the Dodgers, at almost every position. By 1953 Stengel had fine-tuned the concept of platooning. He had hoped to have a fairly stable lineup built around Mickey Mantle, but that didn't work out. Mantle missed 24 games with a badly swollen knee. As a result Stengel had to wheel and deal. He used over 80 different lineups. As the baseball writer Ed Linn noted Stengel learned how to protect even good hitters from top pitchers and what is even more important how to choose the best spot to capitalize on a weak hitter's strength. Stengel showed how to use your best pinch hitter when you needed him, not to just wait until late in the game (quoted in Creamer, 252).

The Yankees led the League in hitting, tied for second in lowest fielding average and had the lowest ERA in the League. Seven players hit homers in double figures; five pitchers won ten more games, and another won nine. Only one Yankee, Berra, was among the League leaders in any hitting department but five regulars hit better than .285; and two, Woodling and Bauer, hit .300.

The Yankee starters (Lopat, Raschi, Sain and Reynolds), now joined by Whitey Ford back from the military and an 18-game winner, went 61-23. Reynolds alternated starting and relieving, winning 13 games and saving another 13. The team only allowed 557 runs all season, an average of 3.6 runs per game.

Cleveland finished with 92 wins, one less than in 1951 and 1952, and the White Sox rose to 89 victories for their best showing in years. The Red Sox were a distant fourth, and the Senators played slightly better than .500 baseball. The last three teams in the League — Detroit, the A's, and the pathetic Browns — were more than 40 games out of first place.

Cleveland fielded a good hitting team again, led by Al Rosen, who just missed winning the Triple Crown by .001 as Mickey Vernon edged him out for the batting title. Rosen hit 43 homers and drove in 145 runs. Larry Doby hit 29 homers and also drove in over 100 runs, and Dale Mitchell hit .300 in his last regular season in the Majors. At $28,000, Doby was now the highest paid Cleveland regular other than the pitchers (Moore, 103). Luke Easter broke his foot and was released, and Ray Boone was traded to the Tigers. His shortstop position was taken by the weak-hitting, George Strickland.

The Indians' pitching was among the best in the American League, but although their starters, Wynn, Lemon, Garcia and Feller, won 66 games, they also lost 43 for a much poorer ratio than the Yankees' staff.

Paul Richards's White Sox had a superb year even though team hitting was poor. Only Minoso was over .300, and they had no power. But the pitching staff was excellent with the second-lowest ERA in the League, just 3.41. Once again Richards did a magnificent rescue job, this time with Virgil Trucks, who won 15 games in a comeback year from his five wins of 1952. Billy Pierce was establishing himself as one of the best left-handers in the League. He won 18 games, hurled 270 innings, led the League in strikeouts and had the second lowest ERA in the League, 2.72. Harry Dorish came out of the bullpen to save 18 games. Like the Yankees the White Sox didn't beat themselves. Their defense was tight, and they had the best double-play combination in the League in Chico Carresquel at short and Nelson Fox at second.

In early August Richards got his team to within five games of the Yankees. But the Yankees took the first three games of a four-game series, including a doubleheader shutout by Ford and Kuzava, to finish the White Sox off for the year.

The Red Sox won 84 games largely because of pitching and not hitting as had been their tradition. The pitching staff, led by 21-game winner Mel Parnell and 18-game winner Mickey McDermott benefited from Ellis Kinder's brilliant relief. In 69 games he recorded 27 saves with an incredible ERA of 1.85. The vaunted Red Sox hitting had disappeared with the retirement or trading of Vern Stephens, Bobby Doerr and Dom DiMaggio. Ted Williams, who was away most of the year in the Marines, returned with typical explosive impact. In less than 100 at bats he hit 13 homers and batted .407.

The Tigers and A's were terrible teams, losing over 90 games each and only kept out of the basement by the Browns, who went 54-100. The A's got a good year from Gus Zernial, who hit 42 homers, the most for any A's player since the halcyon days of Jimmy Foxx. The A's pitching staff never got over the loss of Bobby Shantz, who hurt his arm in spring training and only pitched 16 games, winning just five of them. The A's were in a freefall, with attendance plummeting and the team in desperate financial shape.

The World Series should have been as exciting as 1952 because both teams were so talented. But once again the Dodgers folded. Something was always missing it seemed in the Dodger makeup. The intensity wasn't there in the Fall Classic. Of the big five Dodger hitters — Campanella, Furillo, Hodges,

Robinson and Snider — only the latter rose to the occasion in the World Series. Robinson, one of the greatest competitors of his generation, played inconsistently in the World Series. In 38 games he batted just .234, driving in 12 runs. Invariably when the Dodgers played the Yankees, their stars would have a poor Series, whereas the Yankees would find a hero in the strangest places: Bobby Brown hitting .500 in the 1949 Series, Woodling .429 in 1950, Kuzava coming out of the bull pen in 1951 and 1952. The 1953 Series was no exception. This time Billy Martin, a .257 hitter during the regular campaign, did the Dodgers in by hitting .500.

The Yankees won the first two games in the Stadium despite a very well-pitched game two from Roe in which he allowed just two hits. The Dodgers took game three in Brooklyn when Erskine struck out 14 for a then World Series record. They also handily won game four behind Billy Loes, 7–3. The Yankees came back to win the crucial fifth game and go up one game by hitting four homers and getting fine pitching from a relative unknown, Jim MacDonald. This was the sole highlight of MacDonald's career as a journeyman pitcher. He went 7-9 the rest of his career but Stengel had gotten seven plus innings out of him in a crucial game. The last game was a closely fought battle marked by good pitching from both teams. But after seven clutch innings from Ford, Stengel turned the ball over to Reynolds, who got the victory when Billy Martin got his twelfth hit of the Series to drive in the winning run in the bottom of the ninth.

Dodger fans were disconsolate. They really believed that this was their year and that they had the better team. The Dodgers actually outhit the Yankees in the Series, but once again they came up short in the pitching department. The Yankees always seemed to have the right arm to turn to, whereas the Dodgers were a man short. Behind Erskine they had to rely on Loes and Meyer, both flakes of a grandiose order. Roe was just about finished at 35. The Yankees meanwhile could start Reynolds, Lopat, Raschi, Ford, in the first four games and still have resiliency in the staff. In game six, a must-win contest for the Dodgers, Ford and Reynolds were a more reliable choice than Erskine, Bob Milliken and Labine.

5

Baseball in Stagnation,
1954–1956

Back to Baltimore

The middle years of the 1950s witnessed a growing stability as the postwar transformation of American society continued. The decline of the cities, suburbanization, and the growth of what later would be called the Sun Belt progressed. Inflation remained low, reaching an almost unheard-of 0.5 percent in 1954. Unfortunately, 1954 saw a recession as the economy cooled off from the Korean War–induced levels of spending. Eisenhower in his first two years in office ordered a 20 percent reduction in spending for the military. Unemployment in 1954, 5 percent, was double the 1953 figure.

Internationally, the United States remained at peace, and Eisenhower avoided involvement in Vietnam when the French Empire collapsed. He would send financial aid but refused American troops. A balance of international terror prevailed. The United States had exploded the H bomb in 1952, and it took the Soviet Union just a little over a year to end the U.S. monopoly of that horrible weapon. The cold war took on a less-ugly tone in 1954 as Nikita Khruschev won the power struggle in the Soviet Union after Stalin's death and called for peaceful coexistence. In the U.S., McCarthyism peaked early in 1954 and then dissipated in the face of exposure on television during the Army-McCarthy hearings in the spring of 1954. By the end of the year, Senator McCarthy had been censured by his colleagues and was a spent force. The worst excesses of anticommunism were over.

In professional baseball the stability that took hold in the United States in 1954 turned into a form of stagnation. The internal game was flat and lifeless — homers rose as did strikeouts. Beginning in 1953 in the American League and 1954 in the National League, the number of strikeouts increased every year for the rest of the decade. It appeared that batters were swinging for the fences even if that meant an increase in strikeouts. There was little hit-and-running, and base stealing remained rare. Until Luis Aparicio stole 56 bases in 1956 only one player, Willie Mays, stole more than 30 in a season. Mays pilfered 40 in 1956, a figure not reached in the senior circuit since 1929.

Baseball's attendance rose in 1954 for the first time since 1948. It continued a slow but steady increase for nine straight years save for a slight dip in 1956. Major League baseball breathed a sigh of relief that the puzzling decline had stopped, but temporary external factors explained much of this growth. In 1954 a new franchise in Baltimore drew 764,000 more fans than the Browns had the year before; the American League increase was 958,000. The next year a similar process would occur, with Kansas City showing a vast improvement over the Philadelphia A's. Because of the huge success of the Milwaukee franchise which drew two million fans, the National League regularly outdrew the American League. Later in the decade the move to California would increase this National League advantage especially as neither the Baltimore nor Kansas City clubs were successful franchises throughout the 1950s. In their second year in Baltimore and Kansas City, each team's attendance dropped 20 percent as the novelty of Major League baseball wore off. The main difference between the experience of Milwaukee and that of Kansas City and Baltimore was simple: The Braves were a competitive team and a pennant contender every year after their move in 1953.

Television's growth was a fact of life that baseball now dealt with in a variety of ways. Most teams stopped televising home games or televised only selected ones. The worry that television would destroy baseball receded, especially as the revenue from the new medium increased. By the mid-50s Major League teams were getting approximately 20 percent of their total revenue from broadcasting.

Television's major impact was on minor league teams because fans could now watch Major League games in their living rooms. In 1953 minor league attendance was down to 22 million from a high of 41 million in 1949. Some minor league teams tried ingenious methods to overcome television's impact. Earl Mann, owner of the very successful Atlanta Crackers AA franchise, offered his fans season ticket packets. If enough were sold then he would televise home games ("Can Baseball Survive television?" *Business Week*, 12/5/53, pp. 100–103). His method worked in 1953, but it could not circumvent the reach of Major League baseball into the hinterlands, especially once NBC started its Saturday "Game of the Week" series in 1956. CBS followed with a Sunday game televised over its huge network the next year. Major League teams were not hurt by the success of these network broadcasts as they were protected, but the minor league teams were devastated. Branch Rickey suggested that minor league teams be given the right that they had before 1949 to prohibit the telecasting of Major League games in their areas. If not, he predicted, they would be wiped out. He cited what had already taken place in New England as an example of what would happen to the minors. There minor league baseball had been virtually wiped out by the broadcast of Braves and especially Red Sox games. He also wanted some of the revenues from a Game of the Day to go to the minors ("TV Can Kill Baseball," *Newsweek*, 6/9/53, p. 67).

Rickey, one of baseball's great innovators, was always unsympathetic to television but was favorable toward radio, which he believed enhanced appreciation of the game. Television in his view simply made fans stay at home.

Baseball had other financial headaches to confront. The spending of money on the so-called bonus babies had gotten out of control. Over $4.5 million was spent on bonus players in 1952 alone, with the Red Sox spending the most — over $500,000. They paid four teenagers between $77,000 and $100,000. Three of the four, Marty Keough, Jerry Zimmerman and Frank Baumann, made it to the Majors for undistinguished careers. Shortly after Baltimore joined the American League in 1954, it spent over $700,000 on untried talent of whom only two, Wayne Causey and a young infielder named Brooks Robinson, ever made it to the Majors (*SN, Baseball Guide*, 1956, p. 100). In all, the Majors signed 20 players to bonus contracts in 1955. Three became Major Leaguers: Jim Pagliaroni for Boston, Clete Boyer for the Yankees and Lindy McDaniel, who was signed by the Cardinals. This was a terribly inefficient way to develop talent, although it held out the possibility of shortcutting the minors. There were a few success stories: Robin Roberts, Johnny Antonelli, Bill Skowron, Dick Groat, Harvey Kuenn. But overall the money was often wasted on players who never developed.

Various baseball committees were set up to try to stabilize the expenditure of money on untried players, but none worked. A rule was put into effect that Major League teams had to carry certain bonus players on their roster as a way of discouraging them from spending unwisely. It also failed. Every roster in the mid-50s was dotted with players who were simply taking up space. The 1954 Yankees in a battle for the pennant with Cleveland, had to carry an 18 year old, Frank Leja, who got a $50,000 bonus. Billed as the next Lou Gehrig, Leja got to bat five times and played in the field for just six games. In his entire career he got exactly one hit. The Phillies in 1953 carried a pitcher, Tom Qualters, whom they paid $100,000. He pitched a third of an inning. His nickname was "Money Bags." Every roster could duplicate these wasteful practices.

One of the most significant developments for the future of baseball took place in 1954, the creation of the Major League Baseball Players' Association (MLPA). Player representatives from all teams met at the All-Star Game in July and drew up a constitution and bylaws. The players avoided the use of the term *union,* preferring to describe themselves as a social or fraternal organization. This was a wise move given the antilabor mood that prevailed in the Eisenhower years. Most players shared this attitude. Bob Feller, one of the key figures in the organization, summed up the sentiment against unionization: "You cannot carry collective bargaining into baseball" (Dworkin, 28).

The sixteen players constituted a talented collection of Major Leaguers and even included five future Hall of Famers: Robin Roberts, Feller, Stan Musial, Warren Spahn and Ralph Kiner. The major topic of interest was stabilizing the pension program and raising the minimum salary for first-year players from $6,000 to $7,200.

The players' demands were rejected by Major League baseball. The players had hired a lawyer, J. Norman Lewis, to represent them in discussions with the owners, but the owners organization refused to deal directly with him. He was reduced to giving advice to untrained ballplayers about the issues they confronted, in particular how to conduct negotiations. Just in case anyone missed the point, Ralph Kiner defined Lewis's role: "All we want from him is legal advice. We don't want a players' union. Lewis isn't interested in one, and the first hint that he is, out he goes" (Jennings, 14). Ralph Kiner noted the reluctance to confront the owners in the early years of the MLPA. "We were just infants, but we broke the ice" (Helyar, 14).

Although the MLPA failed in most of its demands, it did see an overall improvement in the pension issue, which was the most significant one for most players. When the initial plan of financing the pension lapsed in 1956, the owners offered the players a flat payment of $1 million to finance future pensions. Instead, the players held out for 60 percent of television revenues, even though they were frozen out of all television negotiations. Kiner claimed that it was his idea to use television money to vest the pension program (Peary, 220). This turned out to be a better deal because the televising of baseball generated enormous revenues over the years. Frick estimated that baseball derived $16.3 million from broadcasting between 1947 and 1961 (Jennings, 15).

In 1953 Veeck's problems in St. Louis came to a head. He was losing money, selling off his best players and even selling his ballpark to the newly rich Cardinals as a way of paying expenses. The Cardinals had been purchased early in 1953 by Gussie Busch, owner of Anheuser-Busch, manufacturers of Budweiser beer, for $3.5 million. This effectively meant that the Browns would not be able to compete in the St. Louis market. Veeck also knew that any plan he had for moving to Baltimore depended on the cooperation of American League owners, which he was never going to receive.

Baltimore demonstrated the seriousness of its commitment to Major League baseball throughout 1953 by adding a second tier to its new stadium, by lining up political support and by getting local breweries to promise to back a Major League team through advertising. Baltimore had to overcome complaints that the baseball market in the East would be saturated by putting a club between Washington and Philadelphia. These two cities also feared that a new stadium with almost twice their seating capacity would threaten them. There was also some argument that moving baseball east instead of west and south, where the population growth was greater, was a retrograde step. But the real issue was getting rid of Veeck (Miller, 34).

He was finally bought out by a Baltimore syndicate headed by Clarence Miles and including two popular local breweries for $2.4 million in October 1953. With Veeck out of the way the opposition to Baltimore disappeared. Major League baseball's first year in Baltimore was a huge financial, if not aesthetic, success. The Orioles drew almost 1.1 million fans, a fourfold increase over the Browns' gate in 1953. With an expanded radio and television network the teams made a net profit of $892,000 for the 1954 season (*SNG*, 1955, p. 98). Along with the huge success of the Braves, this opened the eyes of even the most reactionary owner to the profits that awaited the restructuring of the Major Leagues.

Another development of considerable significance for baseball also took place in 1954: the founding of *Sports Illustrated* by the most powerful publisher in America, Henry Luce, of *Time/Life*. *SI* was the first publication that was not just a cheerleader for sports. Its approach was critical and insightful. Along with an emerging generation of younger sportswriters for baseball, Dick Young, Roger Kahn, Jerry Holtzman, *SI* started the process whereby the writer took a jaundiced view of the sport covered. What was important was the inside story, not just what happened on the field. It took a while for this attitude to reshape the coverage of sport; in fact, it was not completed until the 1960s, but it started in the mid-1950s.

Sports coverage in the papers was growing in importance with over 15 percent of space being devoted to it (Voigt, *Baseball*, 255). The largest percentage was given over to baseball, still the number-one sport in America.

Willie's Year

In 1954 fans saw a dramatic change in the pennant race: neither league favorite won. The Yankees and Dodgers, both coming off great years in which they won 99 and 105 games respectively, were overwhelming choices to repeat. According to *The Sporting News*, 60 percent of the members of the Baseball Writers Association of America picked the Yankees to repeat, with Chicago, Cleveland and Boston expected to fill out the first division. The Dodgers were an even more prohibitive favorite: 153 of 197 or 78 percent of the writers picked them to win, followed by the Braves, Cardinals and Giants.

Both the Dodgers and Yankees had good seasons, but the 1954 race demanded exceptional play. The Yankees won 103 games, the highest since Joe McCarthy's 1942 squad, only to finish eight games out of first place. The Dodgers played good ball also, winning 92 games, but fell five games off the pace. The two races also lacked the tension of past seasons. The Indians moved into first place in mid-May and were never really threatened by the Yankees.

The Giants, after a slow start, took over undisputed possession of first place on June 15 and stayed on top the rest of the way. The Giants' performance was remarkable. It was Durocher's atonement for the team's miserable performance the year before. Unlike the Indians, who played good baseball in 1953, the Giants had finished 35 games behind the Dodgers. Many people believed that the Giants had failed to keep pace with the Dodgers and that Durocher's days were numbered (Frommer, 78).

The Giants won for two major reasons: the return of Willie Mays, who got out of the Army in March, and a brilliant trade with the Braves, in which they got Johnny Antonelli, who became a 21-game winner, for Bobby Thomson. The Antonelli-for-Thomson deal was a typical gutsy Durocher move. Thomson had played brilliantly at times for the Giants, and he was only 30. He had driven in over 100 runs for four of the past five years, averaging 27 homers. But Durocher knew that Mays was due back and would take over center field, making Thomson expendable. He was no longer needed at third base now that Hank Thompson had started to hit. Antonelli was 24 and the former bonus baby had a losing record in his career, although he had shown signs of talent in 1953 when he went 12-12 with a low 3.19. Antonelli paid big dividends. He won 21 games for the Giants, including 12 straight victories in the Polo Grounds. He hurled six shutouts, gave up one run six times and two runs six other times (Peary, 256). Durocher made the trade because he saw serious signs of deterioration in his pitching staff in 1953. Larry Jansen looked finished, Jim Hearn was showing signs of wear, and Maglie would be 37 in 1954.

Durocher's managing was not as flashy as 1951, when he had kept the Giants from collapsing in the face of a huge Brooklyn lead. What he did do was maintain the club's balance and focus during the season. He had a hot pinch hitter in Dusty Rhodes, who had shown signs of power in the past. Durocher platooned him in left field with Monte Irvin and used him as a pinch hitter. Rhodes was a hard-drinking Alabamian who believed he could hit any pitcher's fastball and usually did. During spring training Durocher wanted to unload him. "He can't run. He can't field. But...I know one thing he can do. He can drink more whiskey than anyone I've ever known." But Durocher had a soft spot for him because "I like the dirty players. You take those guys nobody else likes, the other players won't talk to. I like them" ("The Lip," *SI*, 11/8/54, p. 15). Rhodes repaid Durocher's faith. He was 15 for 45 coming off the bench. Rhodes hit a phenomenal .341 with 15 homers, 11 of them in the Polo Grounds, and 50 RBI in just 164 at bats. The left-field platoon of Irvin and Rhodes combined for 29 homers and 100 RBI.

Perhaps Durocher's other main accomplishment of the 1954 season was to convince Mays to go for average over power. On July 28 Mays hit his thirty-sixth homer to go two days ahead of Babe Ruth's pace when he hit 60. Durocher told Mays that he wanted him to stop going for the fences and help the team by hitting for an average so that he would be on base when the middle of the lineup including Thompson, Irvin or Rhodes came up. To soften the request, Durocher told Mays that he would have a shot at the batting title (Eskenazi, 274).

It worked. Mays hit only five more homers but raised his average from .320 at the end of July to a league-leading .345, nosing out teammate Don Mueller by 3 points and Duke Snider by 4. He still managed to drive in 110 runs and score 119. Not bad for someone who turned 23 in May.

What won for the Giants was enough offense; they were tied for first with 186 homers, third in runs scored combined with the best team ERA, 3.09, better than a full run lower than the Dodgers. Aside from Antonelli's 21 victories, the Giants got good years from second-year man Ruben Gomez, who went 17-9 and from Maglie, who had a 14-6 year, including four wins in six decisions against the Dodgers. The bull pen duo of Wilhelm and Marv Grissom went 22-11 and saved 26 games. Both men had ERAs in the low twos.

The Dodgers never got untracked in 1954. They started the season with a new manager. Charley Dressen had been let go after the 1953 World Series when he demanded a three-year contract at the urging of his wife. Walter O'Malley had his doubts about Dressen, despite his winning two pennants and the near-miss in 1951. When Dressen made the mistake of insisting it was a long-term contract or nothing, O'Malley let him go. When a few weeks later he heard that Dressen had signed a three-year contract with Oakland in the Pacific Coast League, O'Malley remarked, "I'm sure Mrs. Dressen will be very happy in Oakland" (Golenbock, *Bums*, 368).

The new manager was Walter Alston, who had served a long apprenticeship in the Dodger organization. Alston's hiring was part of the process by which O'Malley was transforming the Dodgers from a Rickey organization to one with his stamp on it. Then just 43, Alston had managed 17 of the players on the 1954 roster. But he had inherited a potentially explosive situation, a veteran team that had won in the past and that had gotten along with the fired manager. It was a situation analogous in many ways to the one in which Stengel found himself in 1949. It took Alston a while to establish himself. He had problems with the veterans, especially Jackie Robinson. It wasn't racism but rather a struggle to see who would control the team (Koppett, 232). Many veteran Dodger players believed that Alston was over his head and was really a minor league manager who couldn't master his roster (Kahn, *Era*, quoting Dick Young on this point, 317–318). For one thing, Alston was a quieter person than Dressen. His baseball philosophy was also to stress the hit-and-run, the sacrifice, whereas Dressen believed that the Dodgers with all their power were better suited to swinging away.

The Dodgers might still have won in 1954 but for a general decline both offensively and in pitching. The 1954 team scored 170 fewer runs, hit 22 fewer homers and saw its batting average drop from .285 to .270. Roy Campanella had the worst year of his career when he suffered nerve damage to his hand and wound up batting just .207. Robinson was beginning to show his age and split time at third and in the outfield, still hitting well but for the first time he was a part-time player. He only batted 386 times in 1954.

Dodger pitching was also a big letdown. They got Don Newcombe back from the Army and expected a return to form. But he struggled all season and wound up just 9-8. Erskine won 18 games but also lost 15. The rest of the staff had ERAs over 4.00. Despite this the Dodgers stayed close to the Giants and even slipped into first place a few days in May and June, but they couldn't get hot and overtake the Giants once and for all.

The Braves dropped back one slot to third in 1954 but continued to show signs of being the team of the future. They won three fewer games than the season before but continued to develop fresh talent. In spring training Bobby Thomson, whom they had counted on to play left field, broke his ankle and was effectively lost for the season. They had to find a replacement and moved up a 20-year-old minor leaguer who hit .362 for Jacksonville in the South Atlantic League. Thus Henry Aaron got his chance a season earlier than expected. They also added a young second baseman, Danny O'Connell, in a big trade with the Pirates. General manager John Quinn unloaded the big salaries of Sid Gordon, Max Surkont and Sam Jethroe plus three other players for O'Connell. Minor league player of the year Gene Conley joined the pitching staff, as did Chet Nichols, ERA champ in 1951, who came out of the service.

The Braves looked so good on paper that some baseball scribes picked them to overtake the Dodgers. Ed Prell of the *Chicago Tribune* argued in *Street and Smith*'s influential survey of the season that the Braves were moving to a peak, whereas the Dodgers had reached theirs in 1953 when players like Snider, Campanella and Erskine had career years (*S&S*, 1954, p. 23). Prell was a little early. The Braves would really peak in 1957.

The Braves' failure to develop could be traced to a slight slippage in offense. They got good years out of Eddie Mathews, who hit 40 homers for the second straight year, and another solid season from Joe Adcock at first. O'Connell was a letdown. He didn't match his 1953 numbers offensively and was poor defensively. He handled the fewest chances of any second baseman in the National League. Nichols was a flop on the mound, winning 9 and losing 11 for the year with a high ERA. Nichols never recaptured his premilitary service form. He went 14-17 the rest of his career and was back in the minors at age 25. Conley, at 6'8" the tallest pitcher in the Majors, won 14 games, and Spahn won 20 games for the sixth time. Bob Buhl, who had pitched so well in his rookie year, hurt his arm and won just two games. If Buhl and Nichols had pitched effectively, the Braves might have won it all.

After the Braves the drop-off in the National League was sharp. There were no other .500 teams. The Phils, Reds and Cards were closely grouped from fourth to sixth place with just three games separating them. The Phils were slowly revamping from their Whiz Kid days, but the nucleus of the team was the stars who had won the pennant in 1950. Robin Roberts won 20 games for the fifth straight year, leading the League with 23 victories. Curt Simmons had a low ERA but had a losing record, 14-15. In an attempt to revitalize the pitching staff, the team had gone out and gotten two starters, Murray Dickson from the Pirates and Herm Wehmeier from the Reds. They went 20 and 28, with Dickson leading the League in losses. Ashburn hit .300 for the fifth time, and Del Ennis drove in 119 runs along with 25 homers. The biggest surprise for the Phils was the hitting of catcher Smokey Burgess. In 108 games he hit a torrid .368, the highest batting average for a National League catcher since 1939 when Don Padgett hit .399.

The Reds showed a six-game improvement, whereas the Cardinals slipped by 11 games in 1954. Big Ted Kluszewski hit 49 homers and drove in 141 runs to lead the National League. Gus Bell, sophomore Jim Greengrass and Wally Post gave the Reds a young, hard-hitting outfield. They accounted for 62 homers and 279 RBI among them. The Reds also had the best double-play combination in the League in Roy McMillan at short and Johnny Temple at second base. What hurt them was an almost total lack of pitching. The team ERA, 4.50, was third worst in the National League.

The Cards' collapse was also connected to their pitching woes. Harvey Haddix and Brooks Lawrence, the latter a rookie, pitched well, winning 18 and 15 games. But Gerry Staley flopped badly to 7 wins after winning 18 games the year before. The Cardinals got Vic Raschi from the Yankees in spring training, and they counted on him to stabilize a young staff. But Raschi's knees were shot, and he was finished as an effective pitcher. They also lost Vinegar Bend Mizell to military service. The Cardinals' hitting was good, and they added a hard-hitting outfielder, Wally Moon, to the cast of Cardinal sluggers. Moon won the job in spring training and enabled the Cards to sell Enos Slaughter to the Yankees. Moon went on to win the Rookie of the Year Award. Finally, Eddie Stanky's style of managing was beginning to grate on the Cardinals. The team was wearying of his constant anger and his aggressiveness. He would be fired after 36 games of the next season. It would take him 11 years to get another managing job.

The Yankee team that won 99 games in 1953, and then handily beat an awesome Dodger club in the World Series, was expected to repeat the next year. On paper the Yankees resembled the big winners of the previous year. But something was missing. George Weiss sensed it from spring training and tried to shake up the club by unloading Vic Raschi, who was 35, bothered by bad knees and noticeably slipping (Golenbock, *Dynasty*, 130). His victory total had dropped from 21 to 16 to 13. Weiss also had at least eight other holdouts to deal with. He wanted to send them a message by getting rid of Raschi. "We've made at least eight of our players independently wealthy," Weiss noted, "and they were acting as if we had to get down on our hands and knees and beg them to play for us"("The Yankees' Real Boss," *SI*, 9/20/54, p. 34).

Weiss's ploy got the other Yankees to sign, but it failed to motivate them as a team. The Yankees, although playing .669 baseball, lacked intensity. Some writers blamed it on the retirement of Johnny Mize and the loss of Billy Martin to military service. But Eddie Robinson filled in capably as a pinch hitter, and along with rookie Bill Skowron and veteran Joe Collins, the Yankees got 22 homers and 114 RBI at first base.

The pitching staff was disintegrating around Stengel. Lopat started the season well by winning seven games in the first two months but then won only five more games the rest of the way. Allie Reynolds was nearing the end of his career. He started only 18 games and relieved in an equal number. He won 13 games, but he wasn't the "Superchief" of old. He hurt his back in a bus accident in 1954 and decided to retire. Fortunately, the Yankees were able to reach into their farm system and produce a big winner in rookie Bob Grim, who won 20. Whitey Ford did a good job and won 16 games. The Yankees had expected a great deal from Harry Byrd, whom they had gotten with Robinson from the A's, but he was a flop, going 9-7 with a high ERA.

The hitting was good, with the Yankees leading the American League in batting average and runs scored and coming in second in homers. They also had four .300 hitters: Berra, Mantle, Irv Noren and rookie third sacker, Andy Carey. But Phil Rizzuto was clearly finished as a regular shortstop. He hit just .195 for the year. Jerry Coleman never regained the form he had displayed before going into the military and hit just .217. Stengel had to scramble and move MacDougald to second, insert Carey at third and even replace the steady Rizzuto at short with Coleman and Willie Miranda.

Despite winning 103 games the Yankees never really challenged for the pennant. After Chicago set the pace for the first month, Cleveland got going in May, winning 22 games against just 7 losses. In fact, they won 20 games each month from May through August to just about wrap up the race. They went into first place on May 16 and held it for the rest of the season, except for a four-day period in mid-June.

Manager Al Lopez did his usual efficient job of managing, but in essence the Indians won because their pitching staff was the best the American League had seen in years. The team ERA of 2.78 was the lowest in the American League since 1919, before the lively-ball era. The big three starters — Lemon, Wynn and Garcia — won 65 games against 25 defeats. The fourth and fifth starters — Feller and Houtteman — went 28-10. In the bull pen Lopez had veteran Hal Newhouser, who made a comeback at 7-2, and rookies Ray Narleski and Don Mossi. Among the three they were 16-6 with 27 saves.

Cleveland pitchers dominated just about every pitching category. They had three of the top five percentage leaders, three of the top four winners, three of the top four in innings pitched and the third highest in saves. Stengel said it was "amazing pitching like I have never seen in six years in the League. And they was well managed" (Creamer, 257).

The Indians had enough hitting, with eight players hitting homers in double figures, led by Doby's league-leading 32 and Al Rosen's 24. Both men drove in 100 runs. For Doby it was one of his greatest seasons, even though he failed to hit .300. His offense combined with great center-field play — he made just 2 errors in 427 chances — made him one of the keys to the Indian victory. Lopez believed that Doby made the offensive difference for the Indians (Moore, 104). Vic Wertz came over from Baltimore in June and took over first base, which was a problem area. Bobby Avila had his greatest year and won the batting title with a .341 average. Stengel was not impressed by the starting lineup. He described the Cleveland infield as three hitters and a shortstop. "Them plumbers," he would mutter as Cleveland's lead grew (Creamer, 256).

Cleveland won by slaughtering the second-division teams plus fourth-place Boston. Their record against them was 95-21. The Indians won 59 games at home and 52 on the road. The last American League team to win 50 games on the road had been the 1941 Yankees. The Indians looked like the best team to play in the American League since the great Yankee clubs of the late 1930s.

The Red Sox, Tigers and Senators were never factors in the pennant chase, and Baltimore and the A's battled for the cellar, with each losing over 100 games. After missing part of the first month, Ted Williams returned to pre-Korea form. He hit .345 with 29 homers but did not qualify for the batting title because he lacked sufficient times at bat. Since he was walked 136 times, giving him 522 plate appearances, this was grossly unfair. The League changed the rule after 1954 so that a batter would not be penalized for bases on balls. The Red Sox had one other solid hitter in 1954, Jackie Jensen, who came over from the Senators in a big trade for Mickey McDermott in December 1953. Jensen hit 25 homers and drove in 117 runs and became a centerpiece of the Red Sox attack for the next few years. But Boston was short on defense, and its pitching staff was thin. Young Frank Sullivan and Tom Brewer showed signs of talent and won 15 and 10 games, but the rest of the staff was shoddy. Kinder was still a top relief pitcher, although at 40 he couldn't have much time left. Parnell was just about finished.

The Tigers and Senators were closely matched in hitting and pitching. They were short in both areas, but there were positive signs if one looked closely. For the Tigers, Harvey Kuenn showed that his rookie year of hitting .300 with over 200 hits was not a fluke by duplicating almost every offensive figure. He was joined by another young regular, Al Kaline, who at 20 played his first full year in the Majors and hit a respectable .276 in 138 games. Detroit's biggest winner was 34-year-old Steve Gromek, having a second career after leaving Cleveland. Gromek won 18 games, hurled the fifth-highest total of innings and had the fifth-lowest ERA in the American League. The rest of the

Tiger staff was made up of untried rookies, like Billy Hoeft, and over-the-hill veterans like Ralph Branca.

The Senators got another good year out of Mickey Vernon, a .290 average, a league-leading 33 doubles and 97 RBI. Roy Sievers rediscovered the power, 24 homers and 102 RBI, that made him rookie of the year in 1949. The Senators were short of pitching. Bob Porterfield was their biggest winner, with 13 victories against 15 defeats. The rest of the staff was dominated by left-handers to take advantage of Griffith Stadium's huge left field, which was 402 feet down the foul line. A couple of good signs appeared in Washington in 1954. Camillo Pascual, a 20 year old fresh from Havana, won the first of many games as a Senator. And on the bench a rawboned bonus player from Idaho, Harmon Killebrew, made his first appearance in the Majors. Both would be heard from.

The Orioles and the A's were awful clubs. Under the conservative leadership of general manager Arthur Ehlers and manager Jimmy Dykes, the Orioles were saved from the cellar only by the total collapse of the A's. Hoping to duplicate the success of the Braves in Milwaukee by moving up in the standings, the Orioles lacked everything. Ehlers wanted to make a profit for the new investors and was reluctant to move Oriole players with trade value (Miller, 41). The team was made up of nobodies scraped together from both Major Leagues: Eddie Waitkus at first from the Phillies, Vern Stephens from Boston via the Chicago White Sox, Cal Abrams from the Dodgers via the Pirates. There were no .300 hitters, no player hit homers in double figures and the team's RBI leader, Stephens, had 46. There was some talent in the pitching staff—Bob Turley, Don Larsen and Joe Coleman—but they all had losing records, with Larsen's 21 defeats leading the American League.

The A's were worse. The management expected to improve over their 59 wins in 1953 by transforming the team at almost every position. They also counted on Bobby Shantz's recovering his 1952 form. Eddie Joost took over as manager, a new uniform was introduced, and young players were installed at second base (Spook Jacobs), at first base (Lou Limmer) and in the outfield (Bob Renna and Vic Power, over from the Yankees in the Byrd-Eddie Robinson trade). The A's also became the first Philadelphia baseball team to field blacks: Power and pitcher Bob Trice. Much was expected of Trice, who won 21 games pitching for Ottawa in 1953 and then went on to win 2 games with the A's late in the season. He started off well but then slumped, finishing the season 7-8. Power played the outfield and hit just .255 and never showed the flash he was later famous for. Shantz continued to be plagued by arm miseries and was on the disabled list from June until the end of the season. He won one game. Gus Zernial, who had hit 42 homers in 1953, fell chasing a fly ball and broke his collar bone and finished the season with just 14 homers. His injury led to one of the incidents that made Philadelphia fans famous or infamous: While he was being carried off the field on a stretcher, he was booed.

The A's were last on merit, losing 103 games and finishing 60 games out of first place, the biggest deficit in the American League since 1939.

The 1954 World Series was a shock. Cleveland was favored. They had easily beaten the Yankees, winners of five Series titles in a row, and had won an American League record 111 games. The four-game Giant sweep ranks with the Braves' victory over the A's in 1914 and the Dodger sweep of the 1963 Yankees as one of the most unpredictable outcomes in Series history. The four games were relatively close: The Giants' margins of victory were 3, 2, 4, 3 runs, but the momentum that the Giants got in game one was never challenged by Cleveland. In game one, with the score tied 2–2 and two men on, Willie Mays made his celebrated back-to-infield catch of Vic Wertz's 440-foot drive to right center. Although Mays and Durocher downplayed the catch, Al Lopez was not as blasé. "I've been in the Major Leagues since 1928," the Indians' manager told reporters after the game, "and that was the greatest catch I ever saw. I believe that was the greatest catch ever made. I'm not even factoring in pressure" (Kahn, *Era*, 321). Two innings later Durocher sent up his favorite pinch hitter, Rhodes, and he hit a pop-fly homer into the short right-field bleachers to win the game.

Cleveland's bats were silent throughout most of the series. Among regulars only Wertz hit higher than .250. Giant pitching was superb, with a team ERA of 1.46, the lowest of any National League team in a World Series since 1918. Cleveland might have had a chance if they could have won game two. But Johnny Antonelli pitched a steady eight-hitter and gave up one run. Rhodes once again was the hero. This time Durocher, in a typical gamble, sent him up to pinch-hit for his cleanup hitter, Irvin, in the fifth inning. Not many managers pinch-hit for their cleanup hitter under any circumstance; the fifth inning is unheard of. Rhodes tied the game and then stayed in to hit a long home run later. Cleveland pitchers gave up just four hits.

The Series moved to Cleveland, and the Giants won game three when Durocher again sent Rhodes up to pinch-hit with the bases loaded for Irvin, this time in the third inning! He drove in two runs to give the Giants a 3–0 lead. Gomez and Wilhelm held the Indians to just four hits. Game four saw the Giants leap off to a 7–0 lead by the fifth inning against Bob Lemon, and the demoralized Indians went quietly.

The Indians failed to pitch or hit. The collapse of the pitching staff was shocking. Lemon's ERA was 6.75, Wynn's 3.86 and Garcia's 5.40. In the meantime, no Giant pitcher in the Series gave up more hits than innings pitched. The bull pen duo of Wilhelm and Grissom, which Durocher had utilized brilliantly all season, pitched five innings, gave up two hits, struck out five and earned one save.

The baseball world was shocked, and Durocher had his one and only world title. He was on top of the world. It proved to be all downhill for the Lip thereafter. But he had given the game something to remember. The 1954 season also saw the final blossoming of Willie Mays, to which Durocher made a major contribution. Mays was the most exciting player to come into baseball since Jackie Robinson. Unlike Robinson, he played with a reckless abandon that indicated he was having fun. With the older generation of stars — Musial, Williams, Robinson — starting to age, baseball was beginning to develop Hall of Fame quality talent — Mays, Mantle, Mathews, Aaron, Banks. The game of baseball was struggling in the mid-50s but the talent on the field was as great as ever. Twenty-five future Hall of Famers played at some time in 1954.

The Boys of Autumn

The brief recession of 1954 ended quickly, and 1955 was one of the most prosperous years in American history. *Time* editorialized that year that anyone "who can't find cause for at least selective optimism is just congenitally morose" (Jones, 45). The two indices that resonated with the American public improved. Unemployment dropped to 4 percent, and instead of inflation's rising slightly it actually dipped by 0.4 percent, the only time that had happened after World War II. Automobile production hit an all-time high of 7.9 million cars sold, a figure that would not be matched for another ten years and 1.3 million better than the next-highest year.

For Major League baseball, 1955 saw the third franchise-move in three years as the sport continued its restructuring. The Philadelphia Athletics, once a dominant franchise in the American League, had been struggling to hold the loyalty of its fans against the better–financed, du Pont–owned, Phillies. Throughout most of the history of the two teams in Philadelphia, the A's had not only been the more successful but also the more popular. When Bob Carpenter bought the Phillies in 1944 and began upgrading the franchise, culminating in the 1950 pennant, fan loyalty in the city passed to the Phillies. They fielded better teams than the A's and consistently outdrew them.

In the early 1950s it was becoming clear that it would be increasingly difficult for any city to support two Major League teams. The failure of the Braves and Browns clearly demonstrated this. Only New York, Chicago and Philadelphia were left with two teams after 1953. The first two cities were huge and could continue to support two teams. It was questionable if Philadelphia in the 1950s could, especially as the city began to change racially and lose population to the suburbs that began to rim the city in that decade. Matters were made worse by the fact that Shibe Park, the home of the A's and Phillies, was in the middle of a rapidly declining neighborhood, still white but moving from lower middle class to working class.

Problems for the A's had been brewing since the end of World War II. After 15 years of truly terrible baseball, the A's revived and beginning in 1947 fielded a competitive team. They were in the thick of the pennant race in 1948 until mid-August and in 1952 had in Bobby Shantz the single most popular athlete in the city. But the team was starved for capital. The Mack family depended on baseball for all its income and did not have the cash to bid for bonus players or to lavish on an extensive farm system.

After the team's terrible collapse in 1950, when it finished last as the Phillies won the pennant and the hearts of the city's fans, 88-year-old Connie Mack was eased out of control of the team. His sons, Earle and Roy, lacked funds, so they mortgaged their biggest asset, the ballpark, to Connecticut General Insurance Company in return for a ten-year loan of $1.75 million. With this money they bought 52 percent of the team's stock (Kuklick, 116). Connie continued to control the remaining 48 percent. Unfortunately, neither man had much grasp of baseball business. Of Earle and Roy it was said they became senile before their father.

For this venture to succeed the A's would have to draw at least 600,000 fans a year. They only did so in one year, 1952, Shantz's phenomenal season. In 1953 attendance dropped to 362,000 and then the next year to 305,000. To make matters worse, the two brothers began feuding. Earle wanted to sell out, but Roy wanted to try to keep the team in Philadelphia. This set off a civil war between the two brothers that doomed any chance, slight as it was, to save the team for the city.

Various Philadelphia businessmen tried to purchase the A's, but they were undercut by the lack of time and by an almost equal lack of interest on the part of the political establishment in the city. Mayor Joseph Clark was not a sports fan and did not lift a finger to try to keep the A's in Philadelphia.

The first serious bid for the A's came in August from a 47-year-old Chicago wheeler-dealer, Arnold Johnson. Johnson entered baseball's financial big league by purchasing Yankee Stadium and the Yankee-owned Kansas City Blues' stadium for $6.5 million in December 1953. Both parks were leased back to the Yankees. At the same time Johnson undertook to bring Major League baseball to Kansas City, despite the fact that it would be the smallest baseball market in the American League. Once Johnson appeared with big money, baseball writers believed that the A's would be on their way out of Philadelphia (*SI*, 8/16/54, p. 111).

The American League met on three separate occasions to work out the complicated transfer of the A's to Johnson. On November 4, 1954, the Macks — Connie, Roy and Earle — closed the deal with Johnson for $3.5 million. The stock, which was worth $2000 a share when Roy and Earle took over the A's in 1950, went for $2,250. In essence, Roy and Earle took in $450,000 each, Connie $604,000, and Johnson absorbed the $1.2 million still owed to Connecticut General and assorted obligations of $800,000 (Kuklick, 123; *SNG*, 1955, pp. 96–97).

What made Johnson so popular with the other American League owners and clinched the deal was a promise to pay off on one million admissions a year, no matter what the real attendance was for the first three seasons in Kansas City (*SNG*, 1955, p. 97). This meant that compared to the 1.2 million fans the A's had drawn between 1952 and 1954, the American League owners would be paid off as visiting team on three million admissions. While the deal was developing, 91-year-old Connie Mack asked the American League to give his sons more time to find local buyers. They turned him down. "Dad was in the League 54 years," Earle said sadly, "and only one time did he ask for a favor. ... He didn't care who owned the club as long as it stayed in Philadelphia. They turned him down. Fifty-four years in the League and they turned him down. That's what put Dad to bed" ("Philadelphia Album," *SI*, 11/8/54, p. 14). Once again, as throughout its history, profit won out over sentiment in baseball.

The Dodger team that began the 1955 season was essentially the dynasty that Branch Rickey had put together in the mid-1940s. The key regulars — Robinson, Campanella, Hodges, Furillo, Reese — were getting older. Robinson was 36 when the season started, and Reese would be 36 before it ended. Only Duke Snider was still in his prime. The pitching staff was younger but lacked depth. The Dodgers knew they didn't have too much time together to prove that they were the best team in baseball.

Although they had failed to catch the Giants the season before, the Dodgers made few changes in 1955. But something happened to them. Alston had won acceptance by challenging some of the veterans, especially Robinson, and the team forgot the complaining that had plagued them in 1954. The Dodgers started the season by breaking the National League record and winning their first ten games. Then after losing two of three they won 11 more in a row. At this point they had an eight-game lead over the second-place Giants. On June 21 their lead had grown to 14 games. The race was effectively over before it ever started.

The Dodgers ran away with the 1955 pennant race because they were so clearly better than any other team in the National League. They led the League in batting average, homers, doubles, runs, slugging average and stolen bases. The only offensive category they did not set the pace in was triples, largely because Ebbet's Field was such a bandbox. The pitching staff had the lowest ERA, struck out the most batters, gave up the fewest runs and paced the National League in saves. Although as a team the Dodgers won seven fewer games than the 1953 squad, they had better pitching depth. Newcombe made a great comeback from a very poor 1954 when he was 9-8 to win 20 games against only 5 defeats. At one point in the season he was 18-1. No other Dodger pitcher threw over 200 innings, but four others pitched over 100 innings, and three hurled between 84 and 99 innings.

Alston was taking a page out of Stengel's book. Beyond Newcombe he recognized he lacked an ace, so he used his starters and relievers intelligently.

Midway through the year with Erskine, Loes and Podres all having problems, the Dodgers reached down to their minor league system and brought up two young arms: Don Bessent and Roger Craig. Working as both starters and relievers they won 13, saved 5 and lost only 4. Both their ERAs were in the twos.

Offensively, the Dodgers got a great comeback year from Roy Campanella. He hit .318, with 32 homers and 107 RBI after his injury-plagued 1954 campaign, earning him his third MVP Award. Hodges, Snider and Furillo chipped in with good years. Hodges hit 27 homers, drove in 102 runs and hit .289, and Furillo had his last big year: 26 homers and 95 RBI. For the third year in a row Snider hit over 40 homers while batting .309 and leading the National League in RBI. Other than Ralph Kiner and Ted Kluszewski, he was the only National League player to hit 40 or more homers in three straight seasons. He would do it two more times to tie Kiner's record of 40 or more homers five years in a row.

Milwaukee again finished second, this time with the fewest wins since their move from Boston. The Braves never got closer than 4½ games to first place. They were hard hit by injuries. Gene Conley, after starting well with 11 wins by the All-Star break, hurt his arm and shoulder and did not pitch after August 17. Joe Adcock's right forearm was broken by a pitch by Jim Hearn and he missed the last two months of the season.

The Braves' hitting held up. Led by Eddie Mathews, who hit 41 homers and drove in 101 runs, they scored the third highest total of runs in the National League. Hank Aaron heralded his arrival as a potential superstar with 27 homers, 106 RBI and a .314 average. Del Crandall continued to hit and catch well, and rookie George Crowe filled in impressively at first for Adcock, with 15 homers and 55 RBI in just 303 times at bat.

The Braves' pitching sagged. Spahn failed to win 20 games, although he led the team with 17 victories. Bob Buhl and Lou Burdette each won 13, and Chet Nichols, for the second year since coming out of the Army, struggled to regain his form. He was 9-8, and the Braves were about to give up on him.

The Giants' collapse from 1954 was almost total. They won just 80 games and were actually under .500 entering July. Aside from Mays who had his second great year in a row, with 51 homers and a .319 batting average, practically every Giant had a poor year. The team that Durocher had put together after taking over the Giants midway through the 1948 season was getting old and losing its sense of purpose. Antonelli, Hearn, and Gomez among the starters had losing records. Maglie, at 38, was 9-5 at the end of July, feuding with Durocher when he was waived to the Cleveland Indians. Durocher had lost his interest in managing and was talking more and more about going into show business, this time television rather than the movies.

No other National League team finished over .500. The Phillies at 77-77 continued to watch the Whiz Kids age. In April 1954 Bob Carpenter had finally recognized that he could not serve as general manager and hired Roy Hamey from the Yankees to oversee the transformation of the Phillies. Hamey's biggest trade for the 1955 season was to send Smokey Burgess and his .368 average to the Cincinnati Reds for Jim Greengrass, Andy Seminick and Glen Gorbous. Gorbous, an outfielder never played consistently, Seminick was 34 and just about finished, and Greengrass had hit 47 homers and driven in 195 runs in the past two seasons. At 27 he had the legs of a man of 60. After the 1953 season he was never a full-time player again. The Burgess-Greengrass trade ranks as one of the worst in the Phillies' long history of giving away talent.

A couple of Phillies had good years. Roberts won 20 games again for the sixth season in a row. Richie Ashburn won a batting title at .338, nineteen points ahead of Mays. Del Ennis had a great year — 29 homers, a .290 average and 120 RBI. But the rest of the Whiz Kids were slipping: Willie Jones, Granny Hamner, Curt Simmons, who was just 12-11. The Phillies had a new manager, an unknown from the Yankee system named Mayo Smith, who was supposed to bring in the Yankee style of play. It didn't work in 1955 — the talent wasn't there.

The Reds under Birdie Tebbetts were showing signs of developing. They won 75 games and were second in runs scored and third in homers, with 181. Two players, Ted Kluszewski and Wally Post hit 40 homers; those two plus Gus Bell drove in 100 runs. Big Klu had established himself as one of the most dangerous power hitters in the National League. The 1955 season was the third in a row that he hit over 40 homers. He also was a surprisingly efficient hitter. He hit .300 for the fourth year in a row. The Reds' problem was an almost total lack of pitching.

The Cubs, Cardinals and Pirates brought up the rear of the National League. Ernie Banks had his first huge season, hitting 44 homers, the most for any shortstop in history. The Cubs lacked depth and had virtually no pitching. The collapse of the Cardinals was shocking. They won just 68 games, and not a single starter was over .500. Musial was still going strong, hitting .319 with 33 homers and 108 RBI — not bad for a 34 year old. The Cardinals also had the rookie of the year for the second year in a row: Wally Moon had been named in 1954; Bill Virdon was picked in 1955. Actually the best of the Cardinal rookies was Ken Boyer, who took over third base, hitting and fielding well.

The Pirates were showing signs of improvement. They lost 94 games but were developing some talent. Bob Friend won 14 games and the ERA title, the first time a last place team had that honor. Roy Face and Vern Law showed signs of becoming good pitchers. In the field, Frank Thomas continued to hit with power and the Pirates had an unheralded rookie in right field named Roberto Clemente that they had stolen off the Dodger roster. He would be heard from.

The '55 Yankee squad won seven fewer games than the previous season

Ted Kluszewski. Prototypical big slugger of the 1950s era, Big Klu hit 40 or more homers for three straight seasons, 1953–1955. He was an excellent average hitter who hit .300 or more seven times. Despite his great power he rarely struck out. In 5929 times at bat he whiffed just 365 times. A bad back ended his power hitting when he was just 32. (Brace Photo.)

and was engaged in one of the greatest dogfights for a pennant in American League history. Four teams—the Yankees, Cleveland, Chicago, and even Boston—battled furiously for the American League flag in 1955. At one point during the season, August 7–9, 1½ games separated the fourth-place Red Sox from first place.

The transformation of the Yankees that had started in the early 1950s was just about completed. Allie Reynolds retired after the 1954 campaign, and Lopat was traded away early the next season. Weiss had negotiated a huge deal with the Baltimore Orioles, now led by Paul Richards, in which the Yankees got two young pitchers: Bob Turley and Don Larsen. Joined with Whitey Ford, then just 26, and rookie 20-game winner Bob Grim, who was only 24, this deal gave the Yankees the youngest group of starters in the American League. Richards was ferociously criticized for trading away his two best prospects. "What concern is it of mine," he answered, "who wins the pennant?...I want to get the Orioles out of seventh place" (Miller, 46–47). It didn't work. The Orioles finished seventh in 1955, but it saved the Yankees.

The Yankees lagged behind the White Sox and Indians throughout most of April and May, but they were never far back. Then on the basis of a 21-7 May they pulled into the lead. By the beginning of July the Yankees led the White Sox by 5½ and the Indians by 7 full games. The Yankees slumped in July going 12-17 while the Indians, White Sox and even Red Sox played great baseball. Each team won 20 games that month and got back into the race. At the end of the Labor Day break, the Yankees trailed the Indians by a ½ game, with the White Sox in third at 1½ back. From this point the Yankees pulled away, as they had so often done in the past, winning 14 of their last 18 games.

The Yankee victory was built around superb pitching as usual. The staff was anchored by Ford, who won 18 games, and surprise comeback lefty, Tommy Byrne, who went 16-5. Turley won 17 games, and Larsen, sent to the minors in midseason to recover from arm miseries, returned in July and won eight of nine games. Jim Konstanty and Tom Morgan solidified a good bull pen.

The Yankees were only fifth in hitting, but they scored the second-highest number of runs and hit 181 homers. They were led by Mantle, who won his first home-run title, with 37; Yogi Berra, who hit 27 homers and drove in 108 runs; and Hank Bauer, who hit 20 homers. Stengel platooned Skrowron, Joe Collins and Eddie Robinson at first with Collins also playing 50 games in the outfield. The three men combined for 41 homers and 148 RBI. Elston Howard became the first black to play for the Yankees. Weiss had been severely criticized by the New York media for dawdling so long in signing a black player. After Howard, as long as Weiss was general manager, no other black player would work his way through the Yankee system and make the Major League roster (Golenbock, *Dynasty*, 141). When Vic Power, who was considered a better prospect than Howard, was traded away, Weiss's justification was that the Yankees needed pitching more than power. But in reality he didn't like Power's reputation of being an "uppity nigger" who drove around in big cars and even dated white women. In Howard the Yankees got a gentleman and fine player. Used in the outfield Howard had a good rookie year, hitting .290.

Stengel came to love him because he was so versatile, but his first comment was a wounding one: "When I finally get a nigger, I get the only one who can't run" (Creamer, 282). Howard fit into Stengel's plans perfectly. He could catch and play the outfield. Later, Stengel, perhaps aware of his earlier cruel comments, noted of Howard, with some players you can substitute but you can't replace. With Howard, he said, "I have a replacement not a substitute" (Golenbock, *Dynasty*, 143).

The Indians did a masterful job to stay close to the Yankees because the team's performance was far below the 1954 standard. The pitching staff did not have a 20-game winner for the first time since 1945. The big three — Wynn, Lemon and Garcia — went 46-34, a drop-off of 19 wins and an adding of 8 losses. The Indians did develop a big winner in Herb Score, whose 16 victories were backed by 245 strikeouts, the most of any rookie in history.

The Indians only outhit the seventh and eighth place teams. Al Rosen, bothered by a bad index finger, hit just .244, with only 21 homers. Bobby Avila saw his average drop by 69 points, and he never again matched his pre-1955 career. He was essentially finished at age 31. Larry Doby and Al Smith had good years in the outfield, and Cleveland tried to milk another season from Ralph Kiner, but the former National League home-run king was at the end of his rope. He hit just 18 homers and retired after the season because of a bad back. Stengel called the Indians' defense "plumbers" but it improved on paper, making the fewest errors in the American League. But none of the four infielders had any great range, as evidenced by their making the third-lowest total of double plays in the American League.

The White Sox, managed by Marty Marion after Paul Richards joined the Orioles, finished a strong third with 91 wins. The White Sox had a very balanced team. They led the American League in batting with a .268 mark, were second in team ERA and tied for the best fielding average. The batting average is deceptive. The White Sox consisted of a bunch of ping hitters who took advantage of their speed. Their best hitter was Nelson Fox at .311, who was second in the American League in hits with 198. George Kell at third, winding down his career, hit .300 but Minoso had an off year for him — .288 average and only 70 RBI. What made the White Sox effective was the pitching staff that Richards had created. Anchored by Billy Pierce, who won 15 games and had a league-leading ERA of 1.97, lowest in the American League since the war years, the White Sox staff gave up the fewest runs. Dick Donovan and Virgil Trucks had good years winning 15 and 13 games apiece, and Sandy Consuega and Dixie Howell anchored a good bull pen.

The Red Sox were in the pennant race until September with a team that nicely balanced hitting and pitching. Williams and Jackie Jensen had their normal solid years, and rookie Norm Zauchin hit 27 homers and drove in 93 runs. Zauchin was one of those one-year wonders the Red Sox often came up with, players like Walt Dropo and Dick Gernert. After 1955 he never played in 100 games again and was out of baseball at age 29. Frank Sullivan, Willard Nixon and Tom Brewer won 41 games among them. But the Red Sox were a player short everywhere in the field, at bat and on the mound.

The remaining teams in the American League never factored in the pennant chase. The Kansas City Athletics played slightly better than the old A's, but they still finished in sixth place. They did succeed in outdrawing the Philadelphia team by over one million fans, making the League owners happy. Baltimore, despite Richards's wheeling and dealing, was pathetic, last in hitting and next to last in team ERA. It wouldn't be long before Richards would begin to work his miracle with the Orioles. Within a couple of years they would emerge as one of the coming franchises in the American League.

The World Series of 1955 is justly famous because it was a first for the Dodgers. "Wait till next year" became this year. Some observers rank the 1955 Dodger squad as one of the great teams in baseball history (see *SI, Baseball's Greatest Teams*). In reality, the 1955 team was inferior to the 1953 squad in almost every offensive category, and they were poorer defensively too, making 15 more errors and turning 6 fewer double plays. The 1955 Dodgers were stronger in most pitching categories, especially depth. But in the final analysis, this Dodger team got over the hump and won the World Series. This explains the emphasis on the 1955 team.

The Dodgers and Yankees matched up nicely in 1955, with the Dodgers having the edge offensively, the Yankees being slightly better defensively and in pitching. In the past the Yankees had beaten the Dodgers because they were the better team, had superior depth in pitching or had the classic hot hand. This time the Dodgers drew the hot hand in the hitting of Duke Snider, who clubbed four homers, and the pitching of young Johnny Podres, who won two games with an ERA of 1.00. Meanwhile the Yankees were hurt by injuries to Mickey Mantle, which limited him to just ten at bats. This time no bench player saved them, although Joe Collins hit two homers and drove in six runs. It wasn't enough.

The Yankees won the first two games at the Stadium behind good pitching by Ford and Tommy Byrne. It looked grim for the Dodgers, but behind Campanella and Snider's hitting and the gutty pitching of Podres, Clem Labine and Roger Craig, Brooklyn won all three games at Ebbet's Field. With Newcombe ailing, Alston gambled when the Series returned to Yankee Stadium for game six by sending young Karl Spooner to the mound. Spooner had come to the Dodgers in September 1954 and wowed everyone with his blazing fast ball, winning two shutouts and striking out 27 batters. But he hurt his arm in spring training and never regained the overpowering fastball. He pitched competently for the Dodgers in 1955, going 8-6, but he was overmatched by the Yankees. They batted him around for five runs before Russ Meyer came in and cooled off the Yankees. This meant a seventh game would be necessary, something Alston had hoped to avoid.

Podres pitched for the Dodgers against Byrne, the Yankees having used Ford in game six to keep the Series alive. In a gut-wrenching close game, the Dodgers won 2-0 because of a remarkable catch by an unlikely substitute, Sandy Amoros. The Yankees got their chance in the sixth inning when, with two men on and one out, Yogi Berra sliced a ball down the left-field line. Amoros had entered the game in that inning, and because he was a left-hander he was able to catch up to Berra's slicing drive. He got the ball to Reese quickly, who doubled off the running Gil MacDougald. Podres set the Yankees down with ease the rest of the way.

The Dodgers were finally world champs, and all Brooklyn went wild. O'Malley had his triumph; he had done what Rickey had been unable to do, and he did it with his man in charge. He was already thinking about the Dodgers' future, and this didn't bode well for Brooklyn.

Mickey's Favorite Year

The 1950s peaked in 1956. It was the year that William H. Whyte published his influential book, *The Organization Man*, which argued that Americans were becoming too conformist. In *The Crack in the Picture Window*, author John Keats launched the first serious attack on the growth of suburbia, lamenting its sameness and its cultural stultification. That year also saw the social critic C. Wright Mills argue in *The Power Elite* that real power had passed out of the hands of the people to the heads of top corporations, the military and the political elite. The thrust of these seminal books was that the American public was growing powerless and had lost its sense of direction.

Meanwhile, a general optimism still prevailed. The birthrate remained at the high level of 25 per 100,000, a figure 20 percent higher than before the war. Consumer debt had risen from $27 billion to over $42 billion as the economy boomed just about everywhere. Two-car families were increasing by 750,000 a year in the mid-1950s. Unemployment dropped to 3.8 percent, the lowest it would be for the rest of the century, and inflation ran at just 1.5 percent. The federal government finished the year with a surplus, something unheard of today. Eisenhower had suffered a heart attack in late 1955, but he recovered fully and announced he would run for a second term. The country still "liked Ike" and the Democratic standidate, Adlai Stevenson, again did not stand a chance. It turned out to be more a coronation than an election, as Eisenhower increased his share of the vote to 57.4 percent, the highest since FDR's massive triumph in 1936.

For baseball 1956 was a down year. Attendance, after rising for two straight years, dipped by 73,000. The National League, with a tight three-way battle for the pennant, experienced a sharp increase as six teams saw attendance rising. Led by the Cincinnati Reds, who went over the one-million mark for the first time, the National League's figure was its highest since 1951. In the American League, where the Yankees ran away from everyone, the decline was almost one million fans. Three teams experienced an increase, but two of them were insignificant: the Yankees, who drew 1654 more fans, and the Senators, whose increase was about 5000. The long-term domination of the American League by the Yankees was killing interest in the pennant chase.

At least baseball was getting something back from television, whose growing hold on the American public contributed to the decline of attendance. Commissioner Frick, following the lead of "Happy" Chandler, negotiated a new deal with the Gillette company on July 2 to continue sponsoring the World Series and All-Star game. With almost 75 percent of the homes in the nation having television and color broadcasting starting, Gillette increased its payment to $16.3 million for five years.

With 60 percent of the money earmarked for players' pensions, Frick was able to stabilize the program. Pensions in those conservative days were the main topic for many ballplayers. By upgrading the pension system, Major League baseball sapped player's criticism of their salaries and playing conditions. Even so, the Major League Players Association was formally organized in 1956, after informally serving the interests of the players for two years. J. Norman Lewis continued as adviser to the MLPA at $15,000 per year. The MLPA, which continued to stress that it was not a union but a fraternal association, sought again to have the minimum salary increased from $6,000 to $7,200. They also complained about scheduling on getaway days. The owners refused to take any action on these issues, preferring the traditional method of stalling by setting up a committee to study the recommendations. By effectively dealing with the pension issue they had undercut player discontent.

For the first time in three years no franchise moved, but O'Malley of the Dodgers sent out more signals that he was unhappy in Brooklyn. He ordered the Dodgers to play seven games in Roosevelt Stadium in Jersey City to show his displeasure with his situation in Brooklyn. The games drew 148,000 fans, or over 12 percent of Brooklyn's attendance for the year. The move was a sign of trouble ahead for the borough's team.

O'Malley constantly pointed to the growing discrepancy in attendance between Brooklyn and the Milwaukee Braves. Since moving to Milwaukee the Braves had drawn almost twice as many fans as the Dodgers, 8 million versus 4.4 million. To O'Malley, this spelled disaster in the future. Eventually, he argued, the Braves will be able to outspend the Dodgers in player development. Of course, this was self-serving because the Dodgers were still making huge profits in Brooklyn, largely from television and season-ticket sales.

The Dodgers' net profit for 1955 was $427,000, almost $20,000 more than the Braves'. The reason for this was simple: the Dodgers' lucrative radio and television contract. The Braves did not televise their games and took in just $130,000 from radio rights whereas the Dodger radio and television package was worth $787,000 (Sullivan, 35, 69).

Even so, O'Malley saw greener pastures in Brooklyn if he could convince the state to provide space for him to build a modern stadium that would hold 50,000. If not, then there was always the possibility of California. The barrier to transcontinental play was rapidly disappearing. Jet travel to California was inaugurated in 1957, making a flight to the West Coast quicker than the overnight train trip to St. Louis.

The National League race was a three-team bloodbath. Coming off their dramatic World Series victory, the Dodgers were the overwhelming choice of the baseball writers to repeat as National League champs, 176 versus 34 for the Braves. The Cardinals and Giants were picked to finish out the first division. But the Dodgers were an aging team, essentially the same group of key players who had come together in the late 1940s. Campenella would be 35 when the season ended and was badly banged up. Robinson was two years older, gray-haired and paunchy, still dangerous in the clutch but no longer capable of playing a full season. He was now a high-class utility player, spending most of his time at third base. Reese would be 38 in midseason. Despite slowing down he had one good season left.

The Dodgers had not made any significant additions to the team in recent years. Junior Gilliam helped out because he was steady and versatile, but he wasn't in the same class with Robinson, Snider, Hodges, Furillo or Campy. Pitchers Roger Craig and Don Bessent contributed in 1955 and were expected to take the place of World Series hero Johnny Podres, who had gone into the military.

In the meantime, the Braves were young and had developed new talent faster than the Dodgers. Hank Aaron had come on nicely in 1955. His .314 average was topped by only one Dodger, Campanella. At 21, Aaron had already hit as many homers as veteran Gil Hodges, 27, and had driven in over 100 runs for the first of 11 times.

The Braves' pitching staff was stronger and younger, with greater depth than the Dodgers'. Spahn, Burdette, Buhl, with the possible return to form of Gene Conley, gave the Braves four solid starters. The Dodgers could only count on Newcombe with Podres gone. They had a reliable reliever in Clem Labine, but Erskine suffered from arm miseries, and the rest of the staff was young and inexperienced.

Fred Haney, like Alston, was a cautious, nonrisk type. He took over from "Jolly Cholly" Grimm in mid-June 1956 when the Braves had failed to challenge the Dodgers. At 58, Haney had a record of second-division finishes with terrible Browns and Pirate teams. He gave the Braves the freedom to play the way they wanted. After he took over from Grimm, the Braves played .630 ball.

The Braves held first place for 121 days in 1956 only to collapse in September and watch the Dodgers edge ahead of them. Except for a short time early in April, the Dodgers didn't make it to first place until it counted, at the end of the season. In all they were in first just 17 days.

For the first two months, five teams — the Dodgers, Braves, Reds, Cards and Pirates — were closely bunched at the top of the National League. When Haney took over on June 17, the Braves suddenly got hot. At this point 24-22, they streaked into first place and held it through late September, except for a short dip in July and another more serious one early in September. The Braves were 18 games over .500 in July and August, three games better than the Dodgers and five better than the surprising Reds.

The Braves' success was built around a balance between pitching and offense. Led by Spahn with 20 wins, Lew Burdette with 19 and Bob Buhl with 18, including an incredible 8 over the Dodgers, the Braves' big three starters were the best in the National League. The problem developed once you got beyond them. Conley did not make a comeback and struggled all season, despite having a good ERA. Sophomore Ray Crone won 11 games but lost 10, and Dave Jolly, who had provided the Braves with a solid reliever in the past, had a disastrous second half.

The Braves' hitting was good: third-best average, third-highest homers, third-most runs scored. These figures, when combined with the staff having the League's best ERA, explain why the Braves were on top for so long. Aaron won his first batting title. Eddie Mathews hit 37 homers, and Joe Adcock hit 38 and drove in 103 runs. Next to Ernie Banks, Johnny Logan was the best hitting shortstop in the National League. Defensively the Braves were weak in the infield. Danny O'Connell never panned out defensively and failed to hit up to expectations. Mathews became a good third baseman, but he was never a polished fielder like Billy Cox or even Willie Jones.

Statistically, the Braves matched the Dodgers in every department, but the Dodgers had one last surge left in them.

The Dodgers played steady, if unspectacular, baseball throughout the 1956 campaign. They did not have a losing month although they only played .500 baseball in May. At the end of June, Newcombe was pitching well, but he was just 9-5. From that point he won 18 games against just 2 defeats. The only other veteran the Dodgers could count on was Erskine, and he had a tender arm most of the year. He did pitch a no-hitter, but he was just a shadow of his overpowering self. He won 13 but lost 11. Second-year man Roger Craig continued to pitch well and won 12 games. Bessent did not perform at the same level as in 1955.

The breakthrough for the Dodgers came in June when they needed another starter. Buzzy Bavasi, the Dodger general manager and general factotum for

O'Malley, checked out the available pitchers. Sal Maglie, at 40, was with Cleveland but hardly getting any work. Bavasi approached Hank Greenberg about a deal. "Take him," Greenberg said. "He's still a hell of a guy" (Honig, '50s, 149).

Maglie, probably the single most hated player in Brooklyn, the famous Dodger killer, became a Bum. It was the most shocking change of uniforms since Durocher went from the Dodgers to the Giants. Maglie took some time to pitch himself into shape, but once he was ready in July, he won 13 key games and was second to Newcombe in efficiency. In 191 innings his ERA was 2.87.

Clem Labine, pitching out of the bull pen, also was a big man for the Dodgers. In 62 games he won 10 and saved 19 to lead the National League.

The real surprise team of the National League was the Reds. Managed by former catcher Birdie Tebbetts, the Reds had been a poor team since their great pennant-winning years in 1939 and 1940, finishing in the second division 11 straight years. Under Tebbetts they began to make slow progress, but no one expected their surge into contention in 1956.

Cincinnati's success was built around tremendous long-ball hitting. The Reds hit 221 homers, tying a Major League record set by the 1947 Giants. They had eight men in double figures in homers, including Kluszewski, Wally Post and sensational rookie, Frank Robinson, with figures in the high thirties. The team's two catchers, Ed Bailey and Smokey Burgess, combined for 40 homers and 140 RBI. The Reds farm system had successfully developed some fine talent — Post, Bailey, Robinson among them — and the Reds had traded wisely, getting players like Gus Bell, Lawrence and Burgess for nothing.

Tebbetts, a great handler of pitchers, worked hard to improve the Reds' pitching, which was the team's major flaw. When he took over in 1954 they had one of the worst staffs in the National League. Every year since, he helped them bring down the staff ERA. At 3.84 it was a reasonable figure.

Tebbetts was still shy on the mound. He got a great season from Brooks Lawrence, who won 19 games, and solid years from Johnny Klippstein and Joe Nuxhall. In the bull pen Hershel Freeman won 14 games and was one of the best relievers in the National League. The problem was that Tebbetts had an unorthodox way of using his staff. He did not draw a clear line between the starters and relievers. Aside from Freeman, whom he used just in relief, he ran his pitching staff based on what he needed at a given time. For example, Lawrence started 30 times and relieved 19 times. For Nuxhall, the figure was 32 and 12, and so on through the staff. This was counter to all the changes that had taken place in the handling of pitching staffs, where the trend was toward four starters and a couple of relievers. Eventually, Tebbetts's approach wore the staff down.

The Reds were in the pennant chase all season, although a couple of key losses to the Dodgers and Phillies in mid-September just about eliminated them. The Reds' 91 wins were the fifth highest in the team's history, and the fans reacted by coming out in record numbers. The 1956 Reds' attendance of 1,126,000 shattered the team's record set in the pennant-winning 1939 season by 144,000.

The top three teams in the National League won 90 or more games for the first time since 1934, indicating that the talent in the National League was concentrated at the top. The drop-off to the fourth-place Cardinals from third-place Reds was 15 games. In 1956 the second division really began with fourth place.

The Cardinals under a new manager, Fred Hutchinson, and a new general manager, "Trader" Frank Lane, won 76 games. The team played competitively for about two months but three losing months in a row, June, July and August, sunk it out of contention. Lane's first trade was a disaster. He sent rookie of the year, Bill Virdon, to the Pirates for center fielder Bobby Del Greco. Virdon hit .319 to finish second in the batting race, whereas Del Greco proved that he could field but not hit. He finished at .215.

Lane's second trade wasn't much better, Harvey Haddix to the Phillies for 39-year-old Murray Dickson. Both men won 13 games, but the nine-year age discrepancy favored Haddix.

The Cardinals had good hitting led by Musial, who hit .310, his lowest average ever but still with 27 homers and a league-leading 109 RBI. Ken Boyer at third also was a .300 hitter. Al Dark stabilized the shortstop position, and rookie Don Blasingame gave the Cardinals a solid second base.

Pitching was the Cardinals' major flaw. The team ERA was the seventh worst in the League. The pitcher with the best record, 13-8, was Dickson who turned 40 in August. Mizell, back from two years in the military, split 28 decisions. There was some young talent in Larry Jackson and Lindy McDaniel, but it was not being used effectively.

No other team in the National League came close to .500. The Phillies, in their second year under manager Mayo Smith, finished 12 games below the .500 mark in fifth place. The team was really aging, and the Whiz Kids, now more like Wheez Kids, were being slowly phased out. The biggest shock of the 1956 season for the Phillies was Robin Roberts's failure to win 20 games for the first time in six years. He finished at 19-18, failing on the last day to win number 20. Six straight years of 300-plus innings had finally taken its toll on Roberts's famous hopping fastball. He gave up a record-breaking 46 homers and finished with an ERA that was .80 higher than any previous year in his career. He never again would be an overpowering pitcher.

Del Ennis and Stan Lopata had good power years, hitting 26 and 32 homers respectively and driving in 95 runs apiece, and Ashburn hit .300 for the seventh time. The rest of the team was terrible and getting old. Jim Greengrass hit just .205 and was finished. Granny Hamner was down to .224, and first base was held by Marv Blaylock, who hit just 10 homers and drove in 50 runs, a miserable performance out of a power position. The Phillies were in need of a full-scale revitalization.

Other than the Reds' great improvement, the closest thing to a surprise in the National League was the performance of the lowly Pirates. The work of Branch Rickey and new general manager Joe Brown started to pay off. The Pirates, after four straight cellar finishes and some of the worst baseball in National League history, rose to seventh but just a game behind the fading Giants. The team's 66 wins were the most of any Pirate club since 1949.

Bobby Bragan, who tutored under Durocher and Rickey, actually had the Pirates in the midst of the pennant race for a month or so. They were only 1½ out of first at the beginning of June. The team then faded, playing 26 games under .500 from that point. The Pirates just missed drawing one million fans, but they put some excitement back in baseball in the Steel City.

Even so, there was reason for optimism. Bob Friend won 17 games and led the League in innings pitched; Roy Face paced all relievers in games, and Ron Kline won 14 games. Offensively the pieces were starting to fall into place. The double-play combination of Dick Groat and Bill Mazeroski was one of the best in the National League. Dale Long at first had a spectacular season, hitting 26 homers, including a stretch where he homered in eight straight games. Two-thirds of the outfield, with Virdon in center and Clemente in right, was set. More significantly, the key players were all young: Mazeroski, 19, when he was called up to the Majors; Groat, not 25 when the season began; Clemente, 21; and Virdon, just 25. The Pirate future looked bright.

The Giants and Cubs were among the worst teams in baseball. Durocher had retired to broadcasting after the 1955 season, and Bill Rigney took over just as the team fell to pieces. The Giants still had Willie Mays and Johnny Antonelli, but aside from them virtually nothing else. Mays had what for him was an off year, 36 homers, 96 RBI and a .296 average. Antonelli won 21 games against 13 defeats with a good ERA. Two young players, first baseman Bill White and outfielder Jackie Brandt showed real ability, but both were lost to military service after the season. Key figures in the Giants' past success had suddenly gotten old: Mueller, Lockman, Rhodes. The team was not drawing in the Polo Grounds, just 600,000 for the year, although television and radio provided them with a profit for the year. The prospects for the future looked grim.

The Cubs finished in the cellar on sheer merit. Aside from Ernie Banks, who had another good year with 28 homers and 85 RBI, the team was truly awful. They had no infield, and the outfield was equally bad although Walt Moryn produced offensively. The pitching staff was led by Bob Rush, with 13 wins. He was the only pitcher to win in double figures. In some ways their best pitcher was "Toothpick" Sam Jones, who went 9-14 but led the National League in strikeouts and was third in fewest hits per nine innings. Jones was the first black to hurl a no-hitter in the Majors. For his services he was traded to the Cardinals after the season in a typical Cub bonehead move for Tom

Whitey Ford. The best left-hander in the American League in the 1950s. At a time when league ERAs were high, Ford wound up with a lifetime ERA of 2.75. Used sparingly by Casey Stengel, Ford did not win 20 games until he was 34. His winning percentage of .690 is the third highest in baseball history. (Brace Photo.)

Poholsky, Jackie Collum and Ray Katt. Poholsky and Collum each won one game for the Cubs in 1957, and Katt was traded away. Meanwhile, Jones won 12 games for the Cardinals and finished fourth in strikeouts. In his next four seasons he won 65 games, more than any Cub hurler in that period.

The 1956 pennant race in the American League was the easiest of Casey Stengel's eight years as Yankee manager. The Yankees ran away from the rest of the League. They were out of first place for a grand total of ten days. The Yankee performance conformed to the views of the BWAA, which before the season began made them the overwhelming choice to repeat as American League champs — 157 writers out of 232 picked them. The Red Sox, Indians and White Sox were named to finish out the first division, but there was virtually no support for any of them to challenge the Yankees.

The season began with the Yankees' winning seven of their first eight games and then, after a mild dip in the last week of April and first week of May, the Yankees broke on top to stay on May 16. From that point the closest any team got was when the White Sox closed to within two games at the end of June. But the Yankees went on a tear, winning 18 of 20 to realistically end the pennant race.

At the All-Star break, July 10, they had a 6½ game lead. The Yankees slowed down in August winning just one more game than they lost, 16-15, but no other team could take advantage of their slide. The White Sox played great baseball in August, winning 21 versus 11 defeats, but that came after a disastrous 9-21 July. With Mantle hitting his fiftieth homer, the Yankees clinched the pennant on September 18, despite the fact that the team played only slightly better than .500 baseball for the last two months of the season.

In a sense the Yankees won because the competition was demoralized by their fast start — they were 67 and 25 by the end of July — and because of the overall weakness of their rivals. For the first time in years only one team, the Yankees, won more than 90 games. Cleveland had its lowest victory total since 1947, just 88 games. The decline for the Indians from their record victory pace in 1954 was 23 games. The slide would continue for two more years, and then, after a slight blip in 1959, the Indians would proceed to become one of the laughingstock teams in the American League. Its golden years 1948–1956, when under Boudreau and Lopez it was one of the most powerful franchises in the League, were over.

The Yankee victory was a testament to the continued development of new talent, this time two new pitchers, Johnny Kucks and Tom Sturdivant, who came out of nowhere to win 34 games between them. Both had broken in with the Yankees in 1955 but contributed little. Now joined with Whitey Ford, who had another great year, 19-6 with a league-low 2.47 ERA, they gave the Yankees a solid starting staff. Bob Turley had an off year, and Larsen was erratic but came on to win big in the second half. The team ERA was second to the Indians.

Weiss and Stengel had presided over the transformation of the Yankees. The DiMaggio-Henrich-Raschi-Reynolds-Lopat winning combination had given way to a new regime led by Mickey Mantle and Whitey Ford. Mantle had his greatest year in 1956. If you cut through the usual New York press hype, his record before the 1956 season was good but not sensational. He had hit 30 or more homers once, driven in 100 runs one time and his best batting average was .311. At a comparable period, Willie Mays had already hit 41 and 51 homers, driven in 100 runs twice and batted as high as .347 to win a title. In 1956 Mantle took his place with the greats.

He won the Triple Crown, one of the most difficult offensive feats in baseball. It had been accomplished in the American League by Hall of Famers Lajoie, Cobb, Foxx, Gehrig and by future Hall of Famer Ted Williams. Mantle did not just win the Triple Crown; he ran away from the League in almost every offensive category. He became the first American League hitter since 1938 to hit 50 homers. In fact, entering September he had 47 and was ahead of Babe Ruth's pace. His margin over the number two home-run hitter, Vic Wertz, was 20, the largest since Ruth hit 54 to Gehrig's 27. Mantle's .353 batting average was the highest in the American League since Billy Goodman hit .354 in 1950. His .705 slugging percentage was one hundred points higher than his nearest competitor. To top his total bases figure you had to go all the way back to 1940. Mantle did not quite carry the Yankees single-handedly, but he came close.

He had help as usual from Yogi Berra, who hit 30 homers and drove in 105 runs, and Hank Bauer, who hit 26 homers with a career high 84 RBI. Bill Skowron had now taken over first base full-time. He hit .308, with 23 homers and 90 RBI. The Yankee total of 190 homers broke their own American League record. The team scored 847 runs and allowed just 631, an enormous margin of victory. The rest of the American League never had a chance.

The Indians finished second with the White Sox just three games back of them. The Red Sox won 84 games but never factored into the pennant race. The Indians had their usual good pitching, leading the American League in ERA. Herb Score, Early Wynn and Bob Lemon were a trio of 20-game winners. But there were problems ahead for all three. Score, whose pitching skills were just blossoming — no less an authority on pitching than Ted Williams labeled him the toughest man to hit against in the American League — would have his career shortened early the next season when he was hit in the face by a line drive off the bat of Gil MacDougald. Lemon would develop arm troubles and win just six more games in his career. Wynn, at 36, had some good years ahead, including one more 20-game season, but for the rest of his career he was just five games over .500.

Cleveland's hitting was a poor .244. No one was close to .300, and aside from Wertz no hitter drove in more than 71 runs. They did, however, produce one potential talent in 1956, Rocky Colavito. He broke in with a bang;

in less than 100 games he hit 21 homers and showed one of the greatest throwing arms in the American League. The Indians seemed directionless. Their pitchers were getting old; they had not solidified their infield, and they were constantly tampering with their outfield. They were a team in trouble.

The White Sox under manager Marty Marion had real possibilities. They had wonderful infield defense with Fox and Aparicio, who in his rookie year led all shortstops in total chances. He also led the League in stolen bases, the first of nine straight years he would accomplish that feat. The White Sox had gotten Larry Doby from the Indians in return for Chico Carrasquel and Jim Busby, and Doby performed at his usual high level: 24 homers and 102 RBI. Minnie Minoso had a fine year, batting .316, with 21 homers and 88 runs driven home. But it was the pitching that really carried the White Sox. Their three top starters, Billy Pierce, Jack Harshman and Dick Donovan won 47 games against 30 defeats. As a team they gave up about the same number of runs as the Yankees.

The Red Sox had good hitting, especially in the outfield, where Jackie Jensen, Jim Piersall and Ted Williams averaged .300. They had only one top-flight pitcher, Tom Brewer, who went 19-10 for his one great season. Ike Delock and Frank Sullivan contributed 13 and 14 wins, but the Red Sox as usual were pitching shy. Detroit surprised many baseball experts. Picked to finish poorly the Tigers had hitting and pitching. Two men, Frank Lary and Billy Hoeft, won 20 games with Lary beating the Yankees five times to gain the nickname "Yankee killer." Three men hit .300, Kuenn, Kaline and Charley Maxwell; Kaline, Maxwell and Ray Boone each hit more than 25 homers. The Tigers had a terrible bench and no first baseman, and Kuenn's range at shortstop was questionable, but they were an exciting team in 1956, finishing ten games over .500 for their best record since 1950.

Baltimore, Washington and Kansas City were sorry teams in 1956. Among them there were just two full-time .300 hitters, Pete Runnels of the Senators and Vic Power of the A's. The Senators had shortened their left-field fence from a ridiculous 402 to 365 feet and two sluggers, Roy Sievers and Jim Lemon, took advantage to crash 56 homers between them. Sievers's 29 homers was the most in Washington history.

The 1956 World Series is one of the best remembered of the decade for one reason — Don Larsen's perfect game victory in the crucial fifth game. It was a typical Yankee-Dodger battle, reminiscent of the 1947 and 1952 Fall Classics. On paper the two teams were closely matched, although the Yankees were younger, and the Dodger dynasty was at the end of the road. The Yankees outhomered the Dodgers, 190 to 179, and turned an incredible 214 double plays, 65 more than Brooklyn's aging infield. In pitching, the Dodgers had a narrow edge with more strikeouts, just 5 fewer saves and slightly lower ERA, 3.57 to 3.63. More significantly, in Don Newcombe, with his 27 wins, the Dodgers had on paper the one overpowering starter, strong enough to start three games if necessary. Unfortunately, for Newcombe, this would be his last chance to lift the onus of not winning the big games. He would fail, and it would haunt him for the rest of his career. After winning 27 games at age 30, he would go downhill, plagued by alcoholism, and finish with just one more winning season before he was washed up at 34. After his big 1956 season he went just 37-42 for the rest of his career.

Alston bypassed Newcombe and started Sal Maglie in game one in Brooklyn against Whitey Ford. Ford suffered the usual fate of lefties in Ebbet's Field. He lasted just three innings and gave up homers to Robinson and Hodges. After serving up a two-run homer in the first to Mantle, Maglie settled down and gave up just one run the rest of the way, another homer to Billy Martin. The Dodgers won 6–3. Game two saw Newcombe again fail to win. He gave up six runs to the Yankees in just 1⅔ innings. The Dodgers rallied for six runs in the second to tie the game and then went on to batter the Yankees 13–8 in a wild and ugly game. After the game, Newcombe got into a fight with a parking lot attendant who accused him of choking up.

When the series transferred to Yankee Stadium, Stengel got a break. Rain postponed game three for a day, enabling him to start Ford again, this time against Roger Craig. Both men pitched well. It was a 1–1 game until the sixth when the Dodgers scored to go ahead, 2–1. In the bottom half of the inning, with two out and two on, one of Weiss's rescue jobs from the National League, Enos Slaughter, came through with a three-run homer into the lower left-field stands. Ford pitched eight-hit ball to win easily. In the fourth game, Stengel went with sophomore Tom Sturdivant, the Dodgers sent Carl Erskine to the mound. At 29, Erskine was just about finished. Too many curveballs had taken their toll on his arm. He had won 13 games in 1956, but he had a high ERA and, for the first time since 1951, allowed more hits than innings pitched. Erskine hung tough for four innings, allowing just three runs and four hits. But the Dodgers couldn't get to Sturdivant, who allowed the leadoff batter to get on for the first six innings. Sturdivant walked six and struck out seven Dodgers. Homers in the sixth by Mantle and seventh by Bauer iced the game for the Yankees, who won by a score of 6–2.

At this point the Series was tied, making game five crucial. Stengel had started Ford, Larsen, Ford, and Sturdivant. Alston had gone with Maglie, Newcombe, Craig, and Erskine. The edge was definitely in the Dodgers' favor. They would play game five with one of their best pitchers, Maglie, ready with four days' rest. Stengel was forced to gamble with Don Larsen, who had been erratic all season and had gotten batted around in game two. The Yankees' charm held up as Larsen pitched a perfect game for the first time in World Series history and the first in the Majors since 1922. Maglie pitched the best game of his World Series career, giving up just two runs and five hits, striking out five and walking just two. It didn't matter. Larsen went into the record books, and the Yankees had the Series lead, three games to two. The rest of

Larsen's career was a study in what might have been. Immensely talented, he never really developed into the pitcher the Yankees expected. Too much of a playboy, he dissipated his great talent, hanging on as a mediocre pitcher for the rest of his career.

In game six Alston bypassed his starters and turned to Clem Labine, one of his best relievers, who had started just three games during the season. It was a terrible indication of noconfidence in Newcombe that a must-win game would be turned over to a reliever when your number one pitcher was well rested. Labine pitched brilliantly, winning 1–0 over Bob Turley in ten innings. Jackie Robinson won the game for Labine with a clutch single over the head of Slaughter, who misjudged the ball.

With the Series tied three games apiece, Stengel gambled on second-year pitcher, Johnny Kucks, an 18-game winner who did not record a victory after September 3. Alston turned the fate of the Dodgers over to Newcombe, now pitching with five days' rest. Newcombe had nothing, giving up two two-run homers to Yogi Berra in the first and third innings. Newcombe left the game behind 4–0, whereas Kucks overcame initial nervousness once he had his lead and held the demoralized Dodgers to just three hits. Later Bill Skowron hit a grand slam as the Yankees breezed to a 9–0 victory.

Once again the Yankees found a way to beat the Dodgers, the sixth time in seven tries dating back to 1941. The Yankees won this time because Stengel gambled and used inexperienced pitchers like Sturdivant and Kucks in critical situations. The Yankee jinx reappeared in the person of Don Larsen, an average pitcher who hurled the best game in World Series history just when the Dodgers' pitcher threw their best game of the Series. Newcombe's failure in two games was also crucial. If he had won just one of the two, the Dodgers would have been home free. But after going 18-2 in the second half of the season, he was beaten by the Yankees twice in less than a week. God must have been a Yankee rooter.

6

California Dreamin', 1957–1958

Baseball Moves West

In January 1957 Dwight Eisenhower, at 67, began serving his second term as president. Unlike his first four years, this term was marked by more problems than successes. Although the nation was still experiencing an economic boom, the great wave of 1950s prosperity had peaked in 1956, the year white-collar workers first outnumbered the blue collars. The consumer price index leaped ahead by almost four points in 1957, a figure greater than its growth in Eisenhower's first term. The country experienced a budget surplus for the second year in a row, but inflation more than doubled over the 1956 figure. Unemployment began a steady rise and would not drop below 5.5 percent for the rest of the decade.

Eisenhower's last great innovation, the National Highway Act, had passed in 1956 and allocated $30 billion for 41,000 miles of superhighways. This program was the most extensive public works project in American history. Among other things, it transformed society by making automobile travel simpler and faster. It was a sign, along with the beginning of jet travel to the West Coast, that the nation was becoming one.

Despite the success of the highway program, there was considerable anxiety in the nation that things were turning sour. The Civil Rights movement pricked the conscience of many white Americans when in September President Eisenhower had to use troops to enable black students to attend high school in Little Rock. The scene of angry mobs of whites chanting hate slogans at black children made many people uneasy and was the start of a process that was going to grow uglier. One month later, the Soviets sent a satellite into space, launching the United States into a race for space supremacy that added to the tensions of the cold war. The success of Sputnik disturbed the

American public because it implied that the United States had fallen behind the feared and hated communist world in science and technology. Things just did not seem to go right in the last years of the 1950s.

Baseball mirrored the economic difficulties and social tensions that plagued the nation in 1957. The single most significant development in the sport's history since World War II took place in 1957: the shift of two premier National League franchises to California. The three previous franchise transfers, including the Braves' move to Milwaukee, were largely cosmetic and did not deeply affect the structure of the sport. An argument could be made that the three cities involved, Boston, Philadelphia and St. Louis, could realistically only support a single team. That was not the case with the New York metropolitan area.

But the shift of the Dodgers to Los Angeles and the Giants to San Francisco was a profound change. From a competitive angle, these two teams were the most successful in National League history. They played in the largest city in America, and they were still prosperous when they pulled up their roots, unlike the Boston Braves, Athletics or Browns. In fact, the Dodgers' profit over the past five years, 1952–1956, was $1.7 million greater than their rival, the Yankees (Sullivan, 68). The move of these two New York area teams sent shock waves through Major League baseball.

At the same time the Majors finally took steps to end the insane competitive bidding for untried talent by abolishing the bonus rule that had plagued the sport since 1946. Prices for so-called bonus babies had been going up for years and often exceeded the $100,000 level, a figure that doesn't seem shocking today in our age of inflated salaries. But in 1957 the average salary of Major League players was approximately $15,000, and only Ted Williams was being paid over $100,000. Other stars like Yogi Berra and Mickey Mantle were earning $60,000, and Stan Musial was the highest paid player in the National League at $80,000 ("Why Baseball Is in Trouble," *USN&WR*, 6/21/57, p. 101–102).

The bonus system, which the owners had tampered with in 1950 and again in 1952, just didn't work. It required teams to carry young players signed for more than $4000 for two years on a Major League roster or be subject to a possible draft. Few developed and most just languished on the bench. In 1957 alone 21 bonus babies were carried on Major League rosters. They included such talents as Bob "Hawk" Taylor, whom the Braves paid $108,000, Johnny DeMerit, Von McDaniel, Bob Miller and Mike McCormick.

Along with the unworkability of the system, which had seen many clubs engaged in cheating, Major League baseball feared alienating Congress, which was involved in one of its fruitless periodic investigations of the game. The owners decided to abolish the bonus rule and institute a draft whereby minor league players with four years' experience would be available for a draft price of $25,000. This was designed to offset criticism that the Major League teams were keeping their minor league talent in a state of near slavery (*SNG*, 1958, p. 110).

The impact of these two changes in the bonus rules and the draft was to make it impossible to protect farmhands by loading up a minor league roster. At some point if the players were not brought to the parent club they could be subject to a draft. As a result there was a greater diversification of talent in the Majors, although the skillful nurturing of the farm system remained a key to success (Davis, 366).

By far the most significant and controversial development in 1957 was the decision of the Dodgers and Giants to pull up stakes and head for California. The roots of this dramatic development go back at least to the early 1950s. The success of Milwaukee, in particular the lucrative stadium deal with parking spaces for 14,000 cars, whetted the appetite of other baseball owners. The Dodgers' lack of parking was obvious — they had space for 700 cars.

Both the Giants and the Dodgers had complained about growing problems with outdated stadiums, lack of parking and assorted ills of declining urban areas. The Giants owned a successful minor league franchise in St. Paul–Minneapolis, an area with a metropolitan population of 1.3 million in the baseball-starved upper northwest. Stoneham's initial thought was that if things did not work out in New York he could transfer the Giant franchise to this virgin territory.

O'Malley did not have that recourse. After the Dodgers won the 1955 World Series he decided to play some home games in Jersey City, where he owned a ballpark. This move was designed to pressure New York officials into taking the Dodgers' complaints seriously. John Lardner of *Newsweek* quipped that the Dodgers were now "1/600th of the way to Los Angeles" (Lowenfish, 77). It appears that O'Malley's basic idea was to stay in the Brooklyn area with a new stadium that he would build on land provided by city-state authorities. It doesn't seem that Los Angeles was on his mind, at least initially. The city fathers of Los Angeles approached O'Malley, not the other way around. Although this does not comport with the "O'Malley as Devil theory" of the betrayal of Brooklyn, it is historically accurate. (The best study of this whole problem is Neil Sullivan, *The Dodgers Move West*, New York, 1987.)

Both the Giants and especially the Dodgers were prospering in the New York area. The decision to move was predicated on changes occurring in the nation that affected baseball, such as the growing power of television revenue, the shifting population from urban to suburban and the enhanced value that a new stadium would bring to a franchise. In the final analysis, both teams believed that they could profit if they moved.

O'Malley's initial plan was to stay in Brooklyn but relocate to a more accessible area close to the confluence of trains and subways. His ideas brought him into conflict with Robert Moses, probably the most powerful nonelected political figure in the state. Moses wasn't against a new deal for the Dodgers, but he was adamantly opposed to the site and plan that O'Malley favored. Moses argued that it was not only overly costly but illegal, and he rejected using slum clearance funds for speculation on baseball (Lowenfish, 77). Moses favored a new ballpark on the site of the 1939 World's Fair in Flushing Meadows, where the Mets currently play. O'Malley rejected that plan. He didn't want a municipal stadium where he would have to share the revenues. He wanted to build the ballpark, thus controlling as many sources of revenue as possible.

Throughout 1956 and 1957 every effort to work out a deal between the city officials and O'Malley collapsed over Moses' opposition and the skill with which he manipulated the political officials of the state and city. Mayor Robert Wagner wanted to cut a deal for the Dodgers, but he lacked Moses' power and was unwilling to spend the political capital necessary to overcome the differences among the various New York City borough authorities.

In contrast, the city officials of Los Angeles, led by their mayor, Norris Poulson, determined to enhance the image of the "City of the Angels" by attracting a Major League franchise (Sullivan, 106). In the final analysis, Los Angeles wanted the Dodgers more than New York.

New York thought that they had plenty of time in 1957 to negotiate a deal with O'Malley and Stoneham, but Los Angeles and San Francisco were determined to act quickly. Stoneham was approached in May by Mayor George Christopher of San Francisco with an offer superior to that of any other city looking for a Major League franchise. Christopher had a $5 million bond issue that guaranteed a new stadium, seating 40 to 45,000 and providing parking for 10,000 to 12,000 cars, to offer the Giants. In return the team would sign a 35-year lease and pay a rent of just $125,000 per year. It was a tremendous bargain for Stoneham, one that guaranteed a profit of anywhere from $200,000 to $250,000 a year versus the $81,000 the Giants made in 1956. Stoneham would also have a monopoly of the lucrative northern California television and radio market, in contrast to the New York area, which he had to share with the more popular Dodgers and Yankees. Contrary to popular belief, Stoneham wasn't dragged to California by O'Malley. He jumped on his own. The Giants were going to leave New York; it was simply a question of where they would go.

Stoneman made the announcement on August 19. "We're sorry to disappoint the kids of New York," he said in a press conference, "but we didn't see many of their parents out there at the Polo Grounds in recent years" (*ibid.*, 133).

In the meantime, the pace of events for the Dodgers also had speeded up. Los Angeles made a major approach during spring training when Mayor Poulson flew into Vero Beach to outline an offer for O'Malley. In February O'Malley signaled his seriousness by cutting a complex deal with Phil Wrigley of the Cubs. The Dodgers bought Wrigley's Los Angeles franchise plus Wrigley Field in the city for $2 million. They also transferred their Fort Worth franchise in the Texas League to the Cubs. This gave the Dodgers rights to the Los Angeles area. What O'Malley wanted from the city was land, approximately three hundred acres in the Chavez Ravine neighborhood, plus a guarantee to upgrade access roads. In return he undertook to finance his own stadium. The latter was regarded as impossible in the mid-1950s. Conventional wisdom held that privately built ballparks were a thing of the past. O'Malley had covered himself. If nothing was forthcoming from New York, he now had a realistic and enormously attractive fallback option in Los Angeles.

The formal offer from Mayor Poulson was made on September 16. It met all of O'Malley's needs. After some political maneuvering by opponents of the deal in the Los Angeles City Council, the Dodgers' stockholders and board of directors voted unanimously to move on October 8.

A half century of National League baseball in New York came to end that autumn. The National League's two most successful teams pulled up roots and left an area where their identity had been forged. It was the end of an era. There were many explanations for this transformation, although at the time the focus was on Walter O'Malley's villainy and sheer greed. Stoneham escaped blame. In reality two teams were acting the way baseball had acted since it became a big-time business — searching for the greatest profit. The New York authorities led by mayor Wagner were not aggressive enough in pursuing the Dodgers, to say nothing of the Giants. Robert Moses really set the pace of events. He was determined that Major League baseball stay in New York but on his terms, which meant in Flushing Meadows.

There are some interesting afterthoughts. The Dodger move was a huge success by any measure, turning an already successful franchise into the most prosperous one in the Majors. Los Angeles adopted the Dodgers, although in a less-emotional and more laid-back California way than Brooklyn had. For the Giants the story was less happy. Despite some fine teams and some huge talents — Mays, Willie McCovey, Orlando Cepeda, Juan Marichal — the City by the Bay has never warmed up to its baseball team. In the meantime, when the National League returned to New York in the form of the Mets, events turned full circle. The Mets eventually moved into Moses' stadium at Flushing Meadows and they became over the years the closest thing to a Dodger-type ballclub for the New York fans. The fans loved their Mets whether bad or good much in the way the Dodger fans adored their "Bums." At any rate baseball would never be the same.

Milwaukee All the Way

After four years of threatening, the Milwaukee Braves finally broke through and won a pennant in 1957. After averaging 89.5 victories in the past four seasons and finishing either second or third, the Braves put everything together to win the pennant by eight full games.

In the preseason polls, the BWAA made them the favorites over Cincinnati, which had surprised everyone in 1956. The Braves were the first choice of 104 of 214 writers, whereas the Reds drew 50 votes. The Dodgers, who suddenly looked like a tired team, received just 42 votes to win, and the Cards were picked by 12 writers. The Dodgers had suffered a grievous blow when after the 1956 season Jackie Robinson was traded to the Giants only to quit rather than change uniforms. Robinson had been an integral part of the great Dodgers' success since his rookie year — six pennants in ten years. Although not a team leader in the sense of Pee Wee Reese, Robinson was an intense, driven perfectionist whose desire to win spread to other Dodger players. He would be hard to replace.

For the first two thirds of the season, there was a close five-team race among the Braves, Reds, Phillies, Cards and Dodgers. No one was able to open a significant lead. As late as July 29, the top five clubs were separated by just 2½ games. After the Braves started off by winning 9 of their first 11 games, they played just .500 ball in May. The Reds got hot in May, winning 21 games against just 7 defeats and took over first place, which they held to the middle of June. From that point on, the Reds played less than .500 baseball and dropped out of the race.

Cincinnati's problem was simple: lack of pitching. Only one starter, Brooks Lawrence, won more than he lost, and he was just 16-13. The rest of the staff was used by Tebbetts in his fashion of alternating starters and relievers with limited success. Hal Jeffcoat, Joe Nuxhall and Tom Acker won in double figures but with very high ERAs. The Reds' hitting was up to par, second in homers and second in team batting average although they couldn't duplicate the 1956 figures. As a team they scored 30 fewer runs and allowed 125 more than they had the season before.

George Crowe, in the only season in which he played regularly, led the team with 31 homers and drove in 92 runs. Frank Robinson showed no sign of the sophomore jinx, hitting .322 with 29 homers. Probably the biggest surprise was the play at third of Don Hoak, whom the Reds got from the Cubs for Elmer Singleton and Ray Jablonski. Once again the Cubs had proven inept in trading: Singleton was 39 and won a grand total of three games in his career with the Cubs. The Cubs moved Jablonski to the Giants for Bob Lennon and the much-traveled Dick Littlefield. For the Cubs Lennon played nine games and hit .143, and Littlefield won just two games. Hoak. meanwhile, hit .293, drove in 89 runs and led all National League third basemen in fielding average, total chances and double plays.

The Phillies and Cards got hot in June. The Cards won 39 games against just 21 defeats in June and July and were in and out of first place from the end of June to early August. They collapsed in August when they could win only

14 of 30 games. The Phillies after a good May and a poor June, went 20-11 in July. On July 14, when rookie Jack Sanford beat the Cardinals, they were briefly in first place for the last time until the 1964 season. The Phillies had won 12 of 14 to forge to the front. But their spurt was shortlived. The team had a disastrous 9-19 August to drop out of the race and begin a slide that would lead to four straight cellar finishes.

The Cards' success was built around good defense at third by rookie Eddie Kasko, a solid outfield of Wally Moon, Ken Boyer, who moved from third to center, and Del Ennis, who came over from the Phillies for Rip Repulski. Ennis had the last good year of his solid career: 24 homers and 105 RBI. Stan Musial, at 36, won his last batting title, at .351, and also drove in over 100 runs. The Cardinals' pitching was much improved. Larry Jackson and Lindy McDaniel won 15 games, Sam Jones 12, and Lindy's brother, Von, broke in with a splash, hurling a one-hitter and a two-hitter among his seven wins. People talked of the best-brother pitching duo since the Deans or the Coopers. Alas, Von would hurt his arm and never win another game after the 1957 season.

The 1957 Phillies finished fifth, but the team finally began the transition from Whiz Kids by adding some new blood. That season the team had eight rookies from the farm system make a contribution and added a new shortstop, Chico Fernandez, from the Dodgers. First baseman Ed Bouchee hit .293 and won rookie of the year laurels, and Jack Sanford won 19 games and led the National League in strikeouts with 188. Two other rookies impressed. Harry Anderson hit 17 homers, and pitcher Dick Farrell won ten games and saved ten others while showing a blazing fastball. The Phillies might have challenged for the pennant but for the near-total collapse of Robin Roberts. The years of throwing 300-plus innings had taken away his fastball, and he was pounded unmercifully, winning just 10 and losing 22. As a big, dominating winner, Roberts was finished. Although he would eventually make the adjustment to becoming a finesse pitcher, Roberts never again would come close to winning 20 games. He would pitch for almost a decade and win less than a hundred games.

The Dodgers were never a factor in the pennant chase. They wound up a distant third, winning the fewest games for a Brooklyn team since 1948. They led the League in ERA largely because 21-year-old Don Drysdale and Johnny Podres pitched well. Drysdale led the team in victories with 17, beginning a career as one of the overpowering right-handers in the National League. The almost total collapse of Don Newcombe hurt the staff. After winning 27 games in 1956, he dropped to 11-12 and was hit hard all season. A typical Newcombe year and the Dodgers would have been right up with the Braves.

What really was shocking was Brooklyn's decline in offense. As a team they only scored 690 runs, their lowest total since 1944 and down almost 170 from their World Series winning year, 1955. Their key figures were getting old. Campanella had a terrible year. His 13 homers and 62 RBI were the lowest since he broke in a decade earlier. Carl Furillo hit .300 but with just 12 homers. Neither Gil Hodges nor Duke Snider drove in 100 runs, the first time that had happened for the Dodgers since 1948. Hodges hit 27 homers and Snider 40 for the last time in his career. Pee Wee Reese played only 23 games at short, with Charley Neal taking over for him. Neal was a good offensive player but a terrible shortstop. No one won the third base job. Ransom Jackson, Reese, Neal and Don Zimmer alternated without much success. The Dodger infield bore little resemblance to the great units that had won them pennants in the past. The entire team needed a thorough restructuring.

After staying at or near the top, the Braves sealed the pennant by getting hot in July and August, winning 37 games against 19 defeats. The Braves' starting eight were probably inferior to past National League pennant winners but were still the best in the League, especially once they got Red Schoendienst from the Giants at the trading deadline, June 15. The Redhead hit .310 for the Braves and shored up their one weak spot, second base. When Joe Adcock got hurt, Frank Torre filled in capably, if without Adcock's power. Johnny Logan was one of the best all-around shortstops, and Eddie Mathews was the best third baseman in the National League. He hit 32 homers and drove in 92 runs. The outfield of Henry Aaron and Bill Bruton was completed when rookie Wes Covington came up from the minors in June to tear the cover off the ball. Covington had a freakish power year. He hit 21 homers although starting just 89 games. He had only 12 other extra-base hits: 8 doubles and 4 triples. Aaron had his greatest year to that point: a .322 batting average, 44 homers and 132 RBI to take his place alongside Mantle, Mays, Banks and Snider as one of the premier power hitters in baseball. Del Crandall was his usual stable self behind the plate.

The Braves' pitching was awesome. As usual Warren Spahn won his 20 games, and the other two big starters, Lew Burdette and Bob Buhl, went 35-16 between them. Big Gene Conley contributed nine victories. This starting four won 65 games, 12 more than their nearest competitor, the Cardinals. Don McMahon saved nine, compiling a staggering 1.54 ERA. In 47 innings he gave up just 33 hits, striking out 46 for as overpowering a performance as any relief pitcher had put on in National League history.

The rest of the National League was a portrait of ineptitude. The Giants were a poor sixth, drawing only 600,000 fans to see a club that had grown old. Only Mays provided any excitement, coming in second to Musial in the batting race with a .333 average. Ruben Gomez won 15 games, but Johnny Antonelli slipped to 12-18. The Giant dynasty that had powered them into contention in the early 1950s was finished. Dusty Rhodes hit .205, Whitey Lockman .248 and Don Mueller .258. The Cubs and Pirates tied for seventh place with 62 wins. Banks had another great power year with 43 homers and 102 RBI, and Walt Moryn hit 26 homers. The only positive development for the Cubs was the emergence of two fine young right-handed pitchers: Dick

Drott and Moe Drabowsky. They won 28 games between them and tied for second place with 170 strikeouts each. In a May game against the future-world-champion Braves, Drott set a Cubs record by fanning 15 batters. Unfortunately, the Cub jinx reappeared, and Drott hurt his arm and never again was a successful pitcher.

The Pirates, after showing signs of emerging from the second division in 1956, unloaded Bobby Bragan and brought in Danny Murtaugh, whose laid-back style suited the young, developing team. The Pirates had the pieces in place; it would just be a case of the players learning to work together. The outfield of Virdon, Clemente and Bob Skinner, who hit .305, was fast and young. Frank Thomas hit 35 homers and played a very shaky third, but in Dick Groat and Bill Mazeroski the Bucs had one of the best double-play combinations in baseball. They already had three fine pitchers in Vern Law, Bob Friend and Roy Face. Murtaugh turned Face into a reliever shortly after he took over as manager. He told Face's wife to make sure he "gets his rest because he's going to do a lot of pitching" (Peary, 364). Face never started another game.

With the development of their outfield, Thomas proved expendable and they sent him after the 1958 season to the Reds in a trade that gave them a catcher (Smokey Burgess), a starting third baseman (Don Hoak) and a veteran pitcher (Harvey Haddix). The Pirates took off from that point.

The American League race was yet another triumph for the Yankees. In many ways it was Stengel's easiest victory despite an injury to Mickey Mantle, which made him miss 15 games. The Yankees led the American League in just about every offensive, defensive and pitching category. The team ERA was 3.00, the lowest of any of Stengel's Yankee teams. The Yankees racked up the most strikeouts and fifteen more saves than their nearest competitor.

Offensively they scored the most runs in the American League and gave up the fewest. They were third in homers but led the League in batting average, triples and slugging average. At the same time they turned the most double plays in the American League.

In spite of this, the team did not look as impressive on paper as past Yankee clubs. No one drove in 100 runs for instance. Mantle, Berra and Skowron were the team leaders with 94, 82 and 88 respectively. Mantle was third in homers with 34, but he walked 146 times and scored 121 runs; the latter two figures led the League. His batting average was .365, the highest of his career, but still 23 points behind Ted Williams, who won his fifth title at .388, just missing the .400 mark by a handful of hits. Mantle suffered from shinsplints the last two months of the season. In fact, he did not hit a homer after August 30. According to Tom Sturdivant, instead of shinsplints, Mantle actually hit his leg in anger with a golf club after he missed a putt (Golenbock, *Dynasty*, 212–213).

As he had done in the past, Stengel manipulated and maneuvered his players brilliantly. He worked two rookies into the lineup, Bobby Richardson

Danny Murtaugh. A mediocre second baseman with the Philadelphia Phillies, Boston Braves and Pittsburgh Pirates, Murtaugh became a highly successful manager in three tours of duty with Pittsburgh. His teams won two World Series and finished first five times. (Brace Photo.)

at second and Tony Kubek at shortstop and the outfield. Both performed brilliant defense and Kubek won the Rookie of the Year Award by hitting .297.

Aside from Mantle and Hank Bauer, who started 135 games, the rest of the outfielders — Enos Slaughter, Elston Howard, Harry Simpson and Kubek — were moved around like chess pieces by Stengel. Howard went behind the plate in 35 games, a sign that Berra was going to be rested in the future. At 33 Berra was beginning to slow down.

Stengel's most masterful performance in 1957 was his handling of the pitching staff. Whitey Ford was hurt for about half the season and only won 11 games. When Ford went down with a tender shoulder, Stengel inserted Bobby Shantz into the rotation. He had come over with Art Ditmar in another trade with Kansas City before the season. Shantz had been bothered by arm troubles since his great 1952 season. Since that time, the most games he had won in a season was five, and the most innings he had pitched was just 125. With the Yankees he won 11 games and led the League in ERA with 2.45, pitching 173 innings. He was a lifesaver. Just before the trade deadline, Weiss made another deal with Kansas City and got Harry Simpson plus a talented minor leaguer, Ryne Duren, for Billy Martin, Ralph Terry and Woodie Held among others. Terry needed seasoning, and some wags said it was better to get it in the Majors than in the minor leagues. Hank Greenberg, Cleveland's general manager, summed up the frustration of the rest of the American League: "It must be nice to have your own farm system in the same league" (Golenbock, *Dynasty*, 193). This wasn't just sour grapes. At one point Kansas City had eight ex-Yankees in their starting lineup, and 16 players on their 25-man roster were Yankee products (*ibid.*, 202).

Between Shantz and Ford, the two lefties won 22 games against just 10 defeats, a record better than any left-hander in the American League. Tom Sturdivant won 16 games, including a crucial eight of nine in August and September, and Bob Turley accounted for 13 wins. Out of the bull pen, Bob Grim won 12 games and saved 19. It was a team performance by a staff that gave up few runs and rarely beat themselves.

The Yankees were never really challenged, but the White Sox were now clearly the next-best team in the American League. Al Lopez had taken over for Marty Marion as manager and brought his expertise in handling pitching staffs to Chicago. He inherited a good staff and made it better. The pitching leader was Billy Pierce, who won 20 games, the only left-hander to do so in the American League and one of two 20-game winners in the League. Dick Donovan and Jim Wilson won 31 games between them. Wilson was a steal from Baltimore in 1956. He cost the White Sox just Dave Philley, who was easy to replace.

As usual the White Sox had little hitting, although they got good seasons from Larry Doby and Minnie Minoso in the outfield. Nelson Fox hit .317 and continued with Luis Aparicio to form the best double-play combination in the American League. They handily led all shortstops and second basemen in total chances.

At one point in June the White Sox led the Yankees by six games, but then the Yankees went 26-6 to take over first place and hold it the rest of the way. Their lead never dropped below 3½ games, and by going 16-9 in September they won the pennant by eight games, the second-widest margin of Stengel's career until that point. The Yankees were equally tough at home and on the road, winning 49 games at the Stadium and 50 on the road.

Three teams other than the Yankees and White Sox played .500 baseball. The Red Sox won 82 games, Detroit 78, and the heretofore pitiful Orioles surprised everyone by going 76-76.

The Red Sox were led by Williams, but he was joined by Jackie Jensen, who had another fine year, driving in 100 runs, and Jim Piersall, who was by far the best defensive center fielder in the American League. Young Frank Malzone took over third, hit .292 and drove in 103 runs. The Red Sox had a couple of capable pitchers in Frank Sullivan and Tom Brewer, but they lacked depth.

Detroit won four fewer games than in 1956, but they moved up a notch in the standings. Their strong suit was pitching. Led by young Jim Bunning, one of two men to win 20 games that year, the Tigers had the fourth-best team ERA at 3.56. Unfortunately, Harvey Kuenn had his first poor year, hitting just .277; and Al Kaline's batting average dropped 19 points, and he failed to drive in 100 runs for the first time in three years. Kuenn's days at short were coming to end. He had the lowest fielding average of any American League shortstop.

The Orioles' performance was truly miraculous. The fifth-place finish and 76 wins was the best performance by the Orioles/Browns since 1945. Richards must have been a genius. The team had virtually no hitting. Bob Boyd hit a soft .318 at first base with just 4 homers and 34 RBI. Only one Orioles regular, second baseman Billy Gardner, got to bat more than 485 times. Richards shifted competent players around, platooned like Stengel without the talent, and nurtured a good pitching staff into making the Orioles tough to beat. The team ERA 3.46 was the third-lowest in the American League although there wasn't a name pitcher on the staff. Connie Johnson was the staff leader, with 14 victories; Billy Loes chipped in 12 wins and Ray Moore 11.

Richards stressed throwing strikes and getting ahead of the hitters. He believed that every pitcher would face a series of crises in every game and that he must have a pitch to bail himself out of the jam. Richards taught the Orioles his version of the change of pace which he called "The Thing." Once the pitchers learned to throw Richards's pitch, they had a good weapon to add to their already existing repertoire of fast balls, curves and sliders. The Orioles of 1957 not only had good pitching going for them, but they were a fine defensive team. They did not make an error in 80 of their games, a good way to keep your team in the game ("New Pitches For Old," *S&S*, 1958, pp. 58–61).

The 1957 World Series was a personal triumph for Lew Burdette, who pitched and won three complete games, including back-to-back shutouts in games five and seven. For once one of Weiss's patented raids of the National League came back to haunt him. Burdette had gone to the Braves in 1951 along with $50,000 for Johnny Sain. Sain made a solid contribution to the Yankees as both a starter and reliever, and Burdette went on to win 203 games in a career that spanned 18 years.

Both the Braves and Yankees were at less than full strength for the Series. Mantle was limping, Bill Skowron had a bad back, Bill Bruton had been lost for the season, and Joe Adcock had not fully recovered from a midseason broken leg. The teams split the first two games at Yankee Stadium, with Whitey Ford outpitching Warren Spahn in game one and Burdette winning game two. When the Series moved to Milwaukee after a day off, the Yankees crushed the Braves 12–3 with hometown hero, Tony Kubek, who hit just three homers all season, slugging two in one game.

Game four was probably the key to the Series. The Braves, behind Spahn, had taken a 4–1 lead into the ninth inning. The Yankees, with two out, tied the score when Elston Howard hit a three-run homer. The Yankees took a 5–4 lead in the top of the tenth. Nippy Jones batted for Spahn against Tommy Byrne to lead off the tenth and claimed he was hit on the foot. After looking at the ball, home-plate umpire Augie Donatelli found a black smudge and awarded Jones first base. Stengel was outraged, but his protests did no good. He went to his bull pen and brought in his best reliever, Bob Grim. Grim came on to try to save the game and give the Yankees a 3–1 Series lead. He had saved 19 games with a low ERA, but he had struggled all through September.

Red Schoendienst moved pinch runner Felix Mantilla to second. Stengel preferred to pitch to Johnny Logan because putting him on would mean the winning run was on first with Eddie Mathews and Hank Aaron on deck. Logan crushed a game tying double. Again Stengel took his chances with Mathews rather than Aaron. Mathews won the game with a booming homer into the right bleachers. Spahn got the win, having pitched all ten innings. Now the Series was tied 2–2, instead of an almost insurmountable 3–1 Yankee lead with one more game in Milwaukee before it returned to New York.

Burdette outdueled Whitey Ford 1–0 in game five. Ford gave up just six hits, but Burdette held the Yankee hitters in check. Mantle only pinch-hit in this game, and Skowron did not play at all. The game's only run scored when Jerry Coleman made an uncharacteristic misjudgment. He underestimated Eddie Mathews's speed on a grounder to second. Mathews legged out a hit, went to second and scored on Joe Adcock's single. One run was all Burdette needed.

With the Series moving back to New York, the Yankees were desperate. They would have to win two games in a row against Bob Buhl and a well-rested Spahn. Having used Ford twice, Stengel would have to go with Turley, Larsen or Sturdivant as his starters.

Turley pitched a beautiful four-hitter to even the Series. It was a touch-and-go game, but the Yankees won on Hank Bauer's homer in the bottom of the seventh off Ernie Johnson, the future announcer for the Braves.

With the Series on the line, Fred Haney, normally cautious, bypassed Spahn for Burdette, who would be pitching with just two days' rest. Stengel chose Don Larsen, a year and five days after his perfect game. This time Larsen

Hank Aaron. Symbolic of the generation of great African American ballplayers who entered the majors after Jackie Robinson broke the color barrier. The greatest slugger of his generation and incredibly durable. He hit 40 or more homers at age 23 and then again at 39. (Brace Photo.)

lasted just 2⅓ innings. There would be no miracle this year. Burdette had already thrown two complete games. If the Braves had lost, Haney would have opened himself to all kinds of second-guessing. But fortunately for him, Burdette was brilliant. He shut the Yankees down on just seven hits, and the vaunted Yankee defense made three errors by the usually sure-handed Berra, MacDougald and Kubek. Mathews drove in two runs, and Del Crandall hit a homer; the Yankees were never in the game.

The Brave victory was richly deserved, although they did not overwhelm the Yanks. The Series was a close match much like the 1952 and 1956 Fall Classics. This time, however, the gods smiled on the National League team. The Yankees' injuries probably hurt more than did the Braves'. The unpredictable, which had usually favored the Yankees, this time helped the Braves. No one could have foreseen the kind of pitching performance that Burdette put on. One had to go all the way back to 1905, when Christy Mathewson hurled three shutouts in five days against Connie Mack's A's, to find a better performance than Burdette's. The fact that Burdette was a former Yankee farmhand made the victory even sweeter.

In some ways, the 1957 Series marked the beginning of the period when the Yankees' domination of the Fall Classic would no longer go unchallenged. The Yankees would be in six more World Series in the next seven years, but their record would be three victories and four losses. This is a far cry from Stengel's record of six world titles in seven tries before 1957. The Yankees were still a great team and would even reach new heights in 1961, but the talent margin was no longer that great. The National League teams had closed the gap and could now play the Yankees at an even level.

1958: The Yankees Bounce Back

Nineteen fifty-eight was a bad year for the United States. The second recession in less than four years raised unemployment to the highest point since World War II, 6.5 percent. But for baseball, especially the National League, it was a very good year. The cost of going to a professional game remained low, making baseball one of the great leisure bargains. In real prices, the average ticket price in 1958, $1.87, was 5 percent lower than in 1946 (Scully, 105). Overall attendance rose by 445,000, but for the National League the improvement was 1.3 million. The total National League figure was the second highest in its history. The American League gate was down by 900,000 because the Yankees so completely dominated during the season.

The key for the National League's success was simple: the move to California of two franchises. The Dodgers broke their attendance record set in 1947 during Jackie Robinson's first year in baseball, drawing 1,845,000 fans. More important, for the first time since 1953 when the Braves moved to Milwaukee, the Dodgers were competitive at the gate with their key rival. The Dodgers' per-game average in Los Angeles was 25,000 versus 13,600 in their last year at Ebbets Field. San Francisco was almost as successful. They doubled their 1957 attendance, drawing 1,272,000 in a ballpark that barely held 25,000.

Overall, four National League teams had gate increases. The Pirates, who drew 450,000 new fans, led the way as they were a factor in the pennant race for the first time since 1948. Even the lowly Cubs boomed at the gate, attracting 300,000 more fans than in the 1957 season. The big losers at the gate were the Reds, who dropped into the second division after being in the thick of two pennant races and who drew 290,000 fewer fans, and the Braves, who despite winning their second pennant in a row, dropped under the two million mark for the first time in five years. The Braves' decline was actually the beginning of troubles for the franchise. As the team grew less competitive, attendance sagged year by year, until by 1962 they reached low levels not seen since the move from Boston.

The Phillies, who wound up in the cellar for the first of four straight years, suffered a decline of 115,000, and the Cardinals, who plunged from second to fifth place at ten games under .500, were down by 120,000. If you subtract the tremendous performance of the California teams, National League attendance would have been unimpressive.

American League attendance problems were linked to the overwhelming success of the Yankees, a team that had so dominated the League that fans were jaded by their success. The 1958 season was particularly boring. The Yankees led the League from day one. There was effectively no pennant race and no other development that season to attract fans. Of the eight American League clubs, six witnessed attendance declines, and only two, the Washington Senators and Kansas City A's, drew more fans than the previous year. In both cases the gains were insignificant, around 25,000. Baltimore had a drop of 200,000, Boston 90,000, and the White Sox lost 340,000 fans, dipping under the million mark for the first time since 1951. Even the Yankees suffered for their success, drawing 70,000 fewer fans than the year before.

In the Yankees' case, this drop-off was offset by the move of their city rivals to California, leaving them with a television monopoly in the huge New York market. According to veteran sportswriter Dan Daniel of the *New York World Telegram and Sun*, the Yankees' television contract guaranteed them $1.7 million for the season (Daniel, "No Third Major League," *S&S*, 1958, p. 7). Even with the highest payroll in baseball, estimated at over $600,000, this meant a massive profit for the Yankees before a game was played.

The success of the Giants and Dodgers in California, which had duplicated the Braves' move to Milwaukee, alerted the baseball establishment to the possibilities of realignment. Although both Baltimore and Milwaukee could be considered sound moves, it was clear that there were greater markets available either in the southern or western part of the United States or possibly in Canada, which had two large urban areas with an interest in baseball, Montreal and Toronto. The move of the Dodgers and Giants had broken the ice of realignment in a way that earlier franchise transfers hadn't. For one thing, the huge New York market, with an estimated population of nearly 17 million, had no National League team to compete with the Yankees. That couldn't last. A temporary expedient in 1958 was to televise Phillies games in New York so that fans there could see National League baseball. Although this gave the Phillies a nice added profit, raising their broadcast revenues for 1958 to the second highest in baseball that year, behind only the Yankees, it was not a satisfactory expedient. The Phillies were a terrible team, and sooner or later the Yankees would threaten retaliation by televising their games in the Philadelphia market. In any head-to-head contest, it was clear who would lose. The Phillies ceased televising their games in New York after one season (Ira Horowitz, "Sports Broadcasting," in Noll, *Government and Sports Business*, 282).

The California experiment of 1958 was a huge financial success by any past baseball standards. But the two California teams had vastly different experiences both on the field and off in 1958. The Giants competed for the National League pennant with a young, exciting team, whereas the Dodgers collapsed, dropping into seventh place for their worst finish since World War II. Off the field the experiences also differed. The Giants' transition to San Francisco was virtually without problems, but the Dodgers faced a series of legal and political headaches that threatened to undermine their move from Brooklyn.

Walter O'Malley discovered that the Dodger relocation was complicated by the political situation that prevailed in California. California had a tradition of progressive politics that enabled voters to place controversial matters on a referendum. Sufficient signatures were gathered in Los Angeles to require the Poulson deal with the Dodgers to go before the public on June 3, 1958, in a measure entitled Proposition B. Initially, public opinion polls showed an overwhelming majority, around 70 percent, in favor of the Dodger deal. But as more information became available to the public, opposition began to form, protesting that the terms of the contract were too favorable to O'Malley and the Dodgers. Shortly before the vote, Mayor Poulson believed the margin was only slightly better than 50 percent (Sullivan, 144).

O'Malley's headaches were mounting. First, he had to find a place to play in 1958. Wrigley Field was out of the question because it was a minor league facility that held only 25,000 and had insufficient parking available. Ford Frick was adamantly opposed to playing Major League baseball there, calling the park a "cow pasture." Interesting choice of words, given that Wrigley Field was right in the middle of Los Angeles.

The only other choices, the Rose Bowl or the Coliseum built for the 1932 Olympics, were not appealing. Both stadia were fine for football, but their layout made them unsuitable for baseball. Early in 1958, after investigating all possibilities, O'Malley eliminated the Rose Bowl and settled on the Coliseum, although it would require extensive modifications for baseball. A deal was struck with the city.

The Dodgers got use of the Coliseum for two years for a rent of $600,000, although $200,000 were required to modify the park for baseball. Overall, it was probably a financial bargain for the city because the Coliseum was empty 300 days a year. Now, it would be in use for 70 days in the spring and summer. The modifications unfortunately were almost impossible to justify for baseball. Because the Coliseum had been built for track and football, it was a narrow oval bowl surrounded by a seating area six stories high. During the season, Duke Snider tried to throw a baseball over the rim of the stadium. The best he could do was the sixtieth row, 19 from the top. He also hurt his arm, for which he was fined $250 by manager Alston (Melvin Durslag, "Hectic Home of the Dodgers," *SEP*, 4/18/59, p. 110). The Coliseum's strange shape meant that one of the foul lines would have to be short, whereas the other would be incredibly long. Because of the preponderance of right-handed hitting on the Dodgers, the modifications created a monstrosity. The left-field foul line was 251 feet from home plate. To compensate for its shortness, a 40-foot-high screen was erected and extended 140 feet into left field. The power alley in left was just 320 feet from home plate, the shortest in baseball. Dead center was 425, but the right-field power alley was 440, and the right-field foul line was 390 feet from home plate (Sullivan, 141–142). Any chance of Duke Snider hitting 40 homers again disappeared when the Coliseum was modified.

The field was a nightmare. In 1958, 193 homers were hit there. Visiting teams outhomered the Dodgers 101 to 92. The next-closest homer haven was Chicago's Wrigley Field, but 20 fewer were hit there than at the Coliseum. Of the 193 homers in Los Angeles, exactly 11 were hit to right field or center, with Duke Snider being the only player to do it more than once. He hit two. The year before he bombed 23 over the short right-field fence in Ebbets Field (*SNG*, 1959, pp. 103–104).

When the restoring of the Coliseum was completed, there was talk that Babe Ruth's feat of 60 home runs in a single season would be in jeopardy. But the fear turned out to be groundless. Charley Neal hit 14 homers in the Coliseum, followed by Gil Hodges with 13 and Carl Furillo with 11. The most by any visiting player was seven by Frank Thomas of the Pirates, hardly a threat to anybody's home-run record.

Criticism of the Coliseum was mitigated by the fact that the Dodgers came from a ballpark that was a bandbox for hitters. The right-field foul line in Ebbets Field was just 297 feet, and the power alley there wasn't much greater than the Coliseum's 320 feet. Yankee Stadium down the right-field line had been devised to suit Babe Ruth. The foul line was just 296 feet away, with a short three-foot fence. The power alley was also in the range of 330 feet. Left field was a huge bowl that swallowed up deep drives with a power alley that measured 402 feet. Leo Durocher once remarked that if Joe DiMaggio had played in Ebbets Field instead of Yankee Stadium, he would have hit 40 to 50 homers a year. As it was DiMaggio was the only right-handed hitter to hit 40 or more homers in the history of Yankee Stadium.

No visiting team complained about playing in California. Their share of the gate receipts soared, making the trip to the West Coast less irksome.

O'Malley's first priority after getting the stadium modifications completed was to see the referendum pass. Support for the Chavez Ravine site was declining. He had originally announced that although all Dodger games would be on radio there would be no television. This was in contrast to Brooklyn, where the Dodgers had the most lucrative television deal in the National League. But O'Malley was looking into the possibilities of pay TV with an organization called Skiatron. The concept proved impractical for both technical and legal reasons. As a way of sweetening the deal for Los Angeles, O'Malley announced that he would televise all 11 games with the Giants in San Francisco. He piously said that this was done to meet requests for shut-ins and those in veterans hospitals. In fact, he was hoping to swing the voters to his side (Sullivan, 144).

The referendum, which drew the most votes other than a presidential race in Los Angeles's history, passed by a 52–48 margin, 24,000 votes out of 667,000 cast. The support of the powerful *Los Angeles Times* was important, as was the backing of prominent Hollywood types, led by actor and baseball fan Joe E. Brown, whose Taxpayers' Committee for Yes on Baseball rallied behind the Dodgers. It was a narrow squeak but a victory nonetheless. As O'Malley noted, few presidents win by bigger margins than 52–48. He still had to survive other court challenges, but the Dodgers were in the City of Angels to stay.

The Braves Again

Milwaukee won again in 1958 by the same margin as the previous season even though their victory total dropped from 95 to 92. Before the season began, they were the overwhelming choice of the BWAA to repeat, with 209 of 240 writers backing them. The Cardinals were a poor second with just 21 votes. There were a few scattered votes for the Reds and Dodgers, but almost every baseball expert figured the Braves were just too good to lose.

The Braves were the class of the National League and were never seriously threatened during the season. They were in first place at the beginning of every month of the season except for May, although they did not pull away from the rest of the teams until after July 4. At that date the Braves were in first place by 1½ games over the Cardinals, and the last-place Dodgers were only seven games out. The close race ended in August when the Braves outpaced everyone else by going 23–11, which put them 8½ games ahead of the Giants and Pirates, who were tied for second. The Giants played poorly in September, whereas the Pirates were one-half game better than the Braves to secure second place.

The Braves' victory was a greater struggle than in 1957 because of injuries to three key players. Red Schoendienst developed TB and appeared in only 106 games. Wes Covington, whom the Braves were counting on as a regular, injured both his knees and was limited to 90 games, and Bob Buhl hurt his arm. His victory total dropped from 18 to 5. To compound their problems, some Braves had poor years. Johnny Logan, at 31, played poorly in the field and hit just .226. Even Eddie Mathews had an off year, batting .252 and hitting just 31 homers with 77 RBI, his worst stats since his rookie year.

As a team the Braves scored 97 fewer runs but also gave up 72 less than in 1957. They won because of their superb pitching staff. The team ERA was almost identical to 1957, 3.21 to 3.22. Spahn and Burdette won 22 and 20 games, and Bob Rush, whom the Braves secured from the Cubs, won 10. Rookies Carlton Willey and Joey Jay, along with second-year man, Juan Pizzaro chipped in to take up the slack of losing Buhl for most of the season. Among them they went 22-16 with very low ERAs. Jay, the first Little Leaguer to make it to the Majors, had a sizzling 2.14 ERA in 97 innings.

Milwaukee's offense was off in almost every category. They hit the same number of doubles but only 21 triples versus 62 the year before. Homers declined from 199 to 167. The offense was led by Hank Aaron, who hit .316 with 30 homers and 95 RBI, and Covington, who was devastating when he played. He hit 24 homers, drove in 74 runs on just 97 hits, batted a torrid .330 and started just 82 games.

Manager Haney platooned wisely and got the maximum out of his squad. Only Logan, Aaron and Mathews were regulars. Haney alternated Frank Torre and Joe Adcock at first and got good production out of them: 25 homers and 109 RBI. He used Felix Mantilla and rookie Mel Roach, who hit .309 in 44 games, to spell Schoendienst at second. Bill Bruton, still bothered by bad knees, played only 96 games in the outfield, forcing Haney to use a variety of players: Andy Pafko was the most active replacement, but Mantilla, Harry Hanebrink, even Adcock spent time in the outfield. Bob "Hurricane" Hazle, who had come up with such a bang in late 1957, was a total flop. After hitting around .170 he was traded to the Detroit Tigers and faded from baseball after 1958.

The Braves' victory was eased by the general lack of competition throughout the National League in 1958. The Pirates in their best year since 1938 came in second with just 84 victories, the lowest total for a second-place team since 1918, when a reduced number of games were played. The Pirates were a young team that had been developing for some years and were coming off eight years of seventh- or eighth-place finishes. The Pirates had been Branch Rickey's one great baseball failure. Although the team eventually benefited from the changes in the organization and farm system that he instituted in the early 1950s after he left the Dodgers, Rickey resigned in 1955 with them buried in the second division. Rickey regarded this as "the biggest disappointment in my baseball life" (Polner, 240).

The pieces fell into place for the Pirates in 1958, and they made a good run at the Braves in the second half of the season, although they never really threatened for the pennant. After a slow start (they were 34-37 at the end of June) the Pirates came on to win 50 of their last 87 games, a .580 percentage. The Pirates had a young, well-balanced team led by some of the best young pitchers in the National League. Bob Friend, who had already won an ERA title, tied with Warren Spahn for most victories with 22. Vern Law won 14 games, Ron Kline 13, and Roy Face saved 20 to lead all National League relievers.

The Pirates had a fast outfield led by Roberto Clemente, who hit .289 and Bob Skinner, who was fifth in batting at .321. In the infield, Bill Mazeroski hit 19 homers and Dick Groat batted .300 on the nose. Midway through the season they brought up Dick Stuart from the minors, and he proceeded to hit 16 homers and drive in 48 runs in just 67 games. He also struck out 75 times and made 16 errors to lead all National League first basemen. He was well on his way to earning the nickname Dr. Strangeglove.

The Pirates lacked depth at catching and pitching, but they were not far from being a solid contender. Danny Murtaugh was the right kind of relaxed, low-keyed manager for this young team that would only get better.

The Giants surprised everyone by moving up from sixth place in 1957 to third, winning 11 more games in the process and becoming the toast of San Franciso. They beat their hated rivals, the Dodgers, 16 of 22 games. Willie Mays showed why he was one of baseball's superstars by hitting 29 homers and almost winning a batting title with a .347 average. He was nosed out by Phillie Richie Ashburn on the last day of the season.

The Giants won while breaking in a talented crew of youngsters led by rookie of the year, Orlando Cepeda, who hit .312 with 25 homers and 96 RBI. Jim Davenport took over at third base, Bob Schmidt behind the plate, and outfielders Leon Wagner, Willie Kirkland and Felipe Alou made their initial appearance in the Majors that season. All three would eventually become regulars with the Giants or some other Major League team, a remarkable performance and a favorable commentary on the strength of the Giant farm system. More would come. In their survey of the Giants' farm teams *Steet and Smith's Baseball Year Book* for 1959 predicted great things for two young talents: Juan Marichal and Willie McCovey, both of whom wound up in the Hall of Fame (*S&S*, pp. 119–120).

The Giants' major flaw was their pitching. Stu Miller, who won only 6 games, had the lowest ERA in the National League, 2.47. Other than Johnny

Antonelli, who won 16 games, the Giants staff was not very impressive, although young bonus baby Mike McCormick emerged to win 11 games in his first full season. Ruben Gomez was 10-12 with a high ERA, and the bull pen was shaky. The Giants were a couple of good pitchers away from challenging for the pennant.

The fourth- through eighth-place teams were separated by just seven games. Cincinnati slipped below .500 for the first time since 1955, and it cost Birdie Tebbetts his job. He was replaced by Jimmy Dykes on August 14, after the Reds had dropped into the cellar.

The Reds' collapse was a team effort. Even Frank Robinson, who hit 31 homers, had a poor year, driving in only 83 runs and batting .269. Gus Bell hit only 10 homers, Ed Bailey 11 and George Crowe just 7, after hitting 31 the year before. Pitching was also a problem area. Young Bob Purkey won 17 games, but Brooks Lawrence had a losing season; and Don Newcombe, whom the Reds secured from the Dodgers for Steve Bilko and Johnny Klippstein, was a flop, splitting 14 decisions. The Reds needed a thorough revamping before they could get back into contention, but they had a couple of good players plus some talent in the farm system, especially a speedy left-hander, Vada Pinson, who hit .343 for Seattle in the Pacific Coast League. They also boasted a couple of young arms, Jim O'Toole and Claude Osteen, who were highly regarded minor leaguers.

The Cubs had been one of the early surprise teams in the National League. They stayed in contention for two months although it was clear that they lacked sufficient pitching to really challenge the Braves. One pitcher, Glen Hobbie, was in double figures, and he only won 10 games. Moe Drabowsky hurt his arm and was useless the last half of the season, and Dick Drott never lived up to what he had shown the previous season. He was 7-11. The Cubs did have a solid reliever in Don Elston, but he couldn't save games for a staff that was consistently behind. Some idea of the Cubs' desperation in pitching is implied in the fact that they used 18 pitchers in 1958, more than any other team in the Majors.

What enabled the Cubs to win 72 games was their hitting. Led by Ernie Banks's 47, the Cubs topped the National League with 182 homers. Four other players — Dale Long, Bobby Thomson, Lee Walls and Walt Moryn — hit 20 or more home runs. The Cubs came up with a good second baseman in Tony Taylor and a good catcher in Sammy Taylor to provide some hope for the future. But the team would live or die by the long ball.

The Cardinals, who tied the Cubs with 72 victories, were, along with the Dodgers, the biggest flops in the National League. After finishing second in 1957, great things were predicted for them, but the pitching staff let them down. The McDaniel brothers turned out to be closer to Marx brothers than the Deans. Lindy went 5-7, and Von wound up back in the minors with a bad arm. Only one starter, Sam Jones, was over .500, and he was just 14-13. Larry

Jackson won 13 games working as a starter and reliever, and Vinegar Bend Mizell failed to come through again as a big winner. He was just 10-14.

The Cardinals' hitting was also off. Musial was his usual self. He hit .337 and came in third in batting. Ken Boyer returned to third where he belonged and hit .307, leading the team in homers with 23 and RBI with 90. Del Ennis, who had given the Cards such a fine year in 1957, suddenly got old, hitting just .261 with only three homers. He never again amounted to much. The Cards had a talented hitter in rookie Joe Cunningham, who hit .312, but they had no place to play him. He was a poor outfielder and a mediocre first baseman and would have been a perfect DH today. The Cardinals unveiled one new talent in 1958: 20-year-old Curt Flood, who had come over to the Cardinals in December 1957 in a trade for three perennial minor leaguers — Marty Kutyna, Ted Wieand and Willard Schmidt. The Reds wanted to avoid an all-black outfield in the future — Frank Robinson, Vada Pinson and Flood — thus their willingness to trade a player with good minor league credentials. None of three players exchanged for Flood ever amounted to anything, whereas he went on to anchor the Cards in center field for over a decade. It took a while before the Cardinals realized what they had in the fleet little outfielder, but by the early 1960s he was recognized as one of the best center fielders in the National League.

The Dodger collapse was almost total. They missed the cellar by just two games. Some of the Dodger players also felt a sense of disorientation in moving to LA. They also had to absorb the loss of Roy Campanella, whose tragic car accident in the winter left him paralyzed and robbed the Dodgers of one of their team leaders. It was a psychological blow according to backup catcher Rube Walker that the entire team felt (Peary, 390).

The team had gotten old in Brooklyn, and there were no replacement parts arriving from the vaunted farm system in 1958. Actually, there was plenty of talent down on the farm, future Major Leaguers like Maury Wills, Don Demeter, Willie Davis, Tommy Davis, Jim Gentile, and Frank Howard, but they were a year or two away. The pitchers had to adjust to pitching in the Coliseum and some, like Don Drysdale, who liked to work inside, feared that the short left-field fence would hurt them. Drysdale won 12 after copping 17 the year before. Johnny Podres finished under .500 at 13-15. Newcombe, after losing his first six games, was traded to the Reds, ending a decade of quality work for the Dodgers. There were some positive signs however. Young Sandy Koufax won 11 games, striking out 131 in 159 innings. He pitched an 11-inning two-hitter against the Braves, a hint of what was to come. Rookie Stan Williams won nine games and showed potential.

The Dodgers, once the most feared hitting assembly in the National League, finished last in batting. Gil Hodges and Charley Neal both hit 22 homers but drove in just 64 and 65 runs. For Hodges that was the lowest total in his career. Carl Furillo led the team in RBI with 83, and Duke Snider, emasculated by the monstrous right-field distance, hit just 15 homers with only 58 RBI. Snider's knees were beginning to bother him, and he would never again get more than 370 at bats in a season. At 32, he was about finished.

The Phils toppled into the cellar and in the process dumped their manager, Mayo Smith. Eddie Sawyer was brought back on July 22 to try to revive the team. It was hopeless. Aside from Robin Roberts, who recovered from two poor years to win 17 games with a low ERA, the pitching staff flopped. Jack Sanford dropped to 10 wins after winning 19 in his rookie year. Curt Simmons went 7-14 and would never again be a winner for the Phillies. Hard-throwing reliever Dick Farrell started the season well and made an impression in the All-Star game when he struck out four batters in two innings, including Ted Williams. But Farrell struggled the second half, winding up just 8-9 with 11 saves.

Richie Ashburn won his second batting title, hitting a career high .350 and leading the League in hits with 215, triples with 13 and walks with 97. Second-year man, outfielder Harry Anderson, hit 23 homers and drove home 97. The Phillies got some wonderful pinch-hitting performances from Rip Repulski and Bob Bowman. Repulski hit four pinch homers, three in a 12-day stretch in August, and the team accounted for a total of 11. The 1957 sensation at short, Chico Fernandez, had a poor year, hitting just .231 and playing spiritless baseball. Willie Jones, at 33, was slowing down, and Stan Lopata managed just nine homers, catching only 80 games. The Phillies were hurt even before the season started when 1957 rookie of the year, Ed Bouchee, was arrested on a morals charge. He missed almost half of the season and never again was the player he seemed to be in 1957. The Phillies would get weaker and weaker for four straight years before any revival could take place.

Over in the American League, the Yankees staged a runaway. During spring training the BWAA made them a near-unanimous pick to repeat as pennant winners, giving them 204 out of 240 votes for first place. The White Sox were a distant second with just 24 votes, and the Red Sox and Detroit were the choice of just 12 scribes.

In effect, there was no pennant race in 1958. The Yankees began the season by leaping into first place, winning 9 of their first 13 games. In the first month of the season, Yankee pitchers threw seven shutouts and gave up one run in eight other games (*SNG*, 1959, p. 55). They were never out of first place, building leads of 6½ games by Memorial Day, 11 games by the All-Star break and reaching a peak of 17 games as early as August 2. It looked at this point as if the Yankees would win by the largest margin in American League history.

Whether from lack of competition or the early onslaught of the problems and injuries that would plague them in 1959, the Yankees began to stumble. Whitey Ford hurt his arm and failed to win a game after August 8. Tony Kubek suffered from an impacted wisdom tooth and didn't hit for the rest of the year. Gil MacDougald and Hank Bauer both hit poorly the last third of the season.

Maury Wills. Along with Luis Aparicio of the Chicago White Sox Wills revolutionized the game of baseball in the late 1960s by reviving the running game when he came to the Majors with the Los Angeles Dodgers. First Major Leaguer to steal 100 bases. He was the first National Leaguer to steal 50 or more bases since Max Carey in 1923. (Brace Photo.)

The team record in August and September was actually one game under .500, 27-28. Stengel was furious. He rode the players unmercifully all season despite their past success. Golenbock suspects that at 68, Stengel had finally lost his patience with young players, the quality that had served him so well in the past. He was becoming increasingly testy and sarcastic, insulting players like the young and nervous second baseman Jerry Lumpe. He looks "like the best hitter in the world until you put him in the lineup" (Golenbock, *Dynasty*, 226–227).

The Yankees clinched the pennant on September 14 and went on to win by ten games over the second-place White Sox. They won despite having only two big winners. Bob Turley had his best year, winning 21 games and leading the League in victories and complete games, finishing third in strikeouts and second in shutouts. Ford won just 14 games but had the lowest ERA in the American League, 2.01, and led the League with seven shutouts. No other Yankee won more than nine games, and Stengel was forced to do his usual job of alternating starters and relievers. He got a great season out of rookie fireman, Ryne Duren. In 44 games Duren won 6 and saved 20 while compiling a low 2.02 ERA. With his thick glasses, blazing speed and uncontrollable wildness, Duren was an intimidating presence on the mound. He gave up just 40 hits in 76 innings, an incredible ratio.

The Yankees led the League in homers, runs scored, batting average and double plays. Eight players hit homers in double figures. Mickey Mantle led the American League with 42, and Yogi Berra hit 22 and drove in 90 runs. Mantle, Norm Siebern in left field and Elston Howard hit .300. It was a fine balanced attack that overwhelmed the opposition by its steadiness. When combined with the lowest ERA in the League, it made the Yankees difficult to beat.

The rest of the American League put on one of the worst performances in recent history. The White Sox won just 82, the lowest total for a second-place team since World War I. The White Sox once again relied on pitching and speed. They had very little hitting and no power at all. Billy Pierce led the team with 17 victories and had the second-lowest ERA in the American League, 2.68. Dick Donovan won 15 but lost 14 after absorbing a terrible first half in which he lost 12 games. Early Wynn won 14 games but lost 16.

Sherm Lollar led the team in homers with 20 and RBI with 84. Jim Landis gave the White Sox 15 homers, but his main contribution was defense in center. Nelson Fox again hit .300. Manager Al Lopez platooned like Stengel at third and first base but he lacked the talent that the Yankee skipper had. The White Sox led the American League in stolen bases with 101, almost double the next highest figure. They also had the fewest homers in the American League.

Third to seventh place was separated by just six games. The Red Sox edged out Cleveland and Detroit by two games, 79–77. Boston had good hitting led by batting champ Ted Williams at .328 and MVP winner Jackie Jensen, who hit 35 homers and drove in 122 runs. Third baseman Frank Malzone hit in the .290s for the second season in a row with 15 homers and 83 runs driven in. Big Dick Gernert led all American League first basemen with 20 homers but hit only .237.

The Red Sox pitching was only adequate. Their four big starters were nine games over .500, with Ike Delock leading the team with 14 victories. The Red Sox were thin at every level. They had talented players at some positions, but once again they lacked the depth to carry them to the top.

Cleveland beat Detroit out for fourth place by losing one less game. The Indians had some potent hitters in Rocky Colavito with 41 homers and Minnie Minoso, who hit 24 homers and batted .302 at 35 years of age. The Indians had no second baseman, shortstop or third baseman to speak of — not exactly what you needed to compete. But they had some great talent on the bench. Vic Power alternated between first base and the outfield and hit .317. Unfortunately, to get Power and infielder-outfielder Woodie Held the Indians sent their fine young outfielder, Roger Maris, to Kansas City. It was not the kind of trade you build a team around.

Cleveland, once the possessor of the best staff in baseball, was short on the mound. Bob Lemon and Mike Garcia were just about finished, and Herb Score, after recovering from the terrible eye injury when he was hit by a line drive off the bat of Gil MacDougald, developed elbow problems and did not win a game in 1958. The team's biggest winner was Cal McLish, with 16 victories. McLish, who had been in and out of the Majors for years, came into his own and would be a big winner for a couple of years. But he was hardly a bellwether or staff leader. He did have baseball's greatest full name: Calvin Coolidge Julius Caesar Tuskahoma McLish, or "Buster" as his teammates called him. There was some hope however as young hurlers, Jim "Mudcat" Grant and Gary Bell won 10 and 12 games. Grant was the only black starting pitcher in the American League at that time, another comment on how far behind the National League the junior circuit was in integration. At that time three American blacks and two Latin blacks were starters in the National League — Juan Pizzaro, Ruben Gomez, Brooks Lawrence, Don Newcombe and Sam Jones.

Detroit finished fifth at .500, and Baltimore and Kansas City were sixth and seventh but separated by only half a game. The Tigers got a comeback year from Harvey Kuenn who moved from shortstop to center field and hit .319. Al Kaline also hit .300, but his power stats were down, just 16 homers and 85 RBI. Detroit's pitching staff was third in the League in ERA and led in strikeouts, but the team's big four — Jim Bunning, Frank Lary, Paul Foytack and Billy Hoeft — were just five games over .500. The Tigers continued to spin their wheels. Aside from some pitchers, their farm system had not produced any young talent since 1953 when Kuenn and Kaline broke into the lineup.

Baltimore won two fewer games than in 1957, but Paul Richards was starting to transform the team. Brooks Robinson played 140 games at third and showed signs of the skills that would take him to the Hall of Fame. Catcher Gus Triandos, one of the players Richards had gotten in the infamous Turley-Larsen trade, hit 30 homers to tie Yogi Berra for most homers by an American League backstop. Richards also performed one of his pitching miracles, getting a 15-11 season from journeyman Arnold Portocarrero, possessor of a career record of 18-37 entering the year. He also broke Milt Pappas, a 19 year old, into the rotation. Pappas would go on to have a highly successful career in the Majors, winning 209 games against just 164 defeats.

Kansas City remained a Yankee extension. Their best player was ex-Yankee Bob Cerv, who had a career year, hitting 38 homers and driving in 104 runs. Roger Maris hit 19 homers in just 400 times at bat to show signs of potential power. George Weiss, always looking to strengthen the Yankees, had his eye on the powerful left-handed hitter with a short sweet stroke. Earlier the Yankees had sent a raw young pitcher, Ralph Terry, to KC to get some seasoning. Terry won 11 games but showed stamina by hurling 217 innings. He would go back to New York the next season.

Washington finished 31 games back of the Yankees. They were last in hitting and last in pitching. The team had two home-run hitters, Jim Lemon and Roy Sievers, two pitchers, Camillio Pascual and Pedro Ramos and virtually nothing else. Little Albie Pearson, just 5'6", came over from the Red Sox in a trade for Pete Runnels and played an acceptable center field. He hit .275 and was named rookie of the year, a sign of how poor the rookie crop in the American League was that year.

For the fourth year in a row the World Series went the full seven games, a sure sign that the two teams were evenly matched. Statistically they were

Yankees	.268 BA	164 homers	ERA 3.22	wins 92
Braves	.266 BA	167 homers	ERA 3.21	wins 92

Defensively the Yankees made more double plays, but the Braves made fewer errors.

A closer look at the two teams gave the Braves a decided advantage. First, unlike other teams playing the Yankees in the World Series, they would not be intimidated, having beaten them once. Second, the Braves had three first-class starters in Spahn, Burdette and Bob Rush, whereas the Yankees had Bob Turley coming off his best year and an injured Whitey Ford.

The Series opened in Milwaukee with Spahn named by Haney to go against Ford, not Turley, Stengel's best pitcher. Stengel was counting on Ford's past success in the World Series. It was a close, well-pitched game by both pitchers, with the Yankees taking a 3–2 lead after five innings on the basis of two homers by Bill Skowron and Hank Bauer. Milwaukee tied the game in the bottom of the eighth on a sacrifice fly by Wes Covington and won it in the tenth when Bill Bruton, injured for part of the season, beat Ryne Duren with a clutch single.

In game two Lew Burdette won his fourth in a row over the Yankees as his teammates gave him a 7–1 lead after one inning. Burdette hit a three-run homer himself and held the Yankees to just seven hits. Bob Turley was knocked out in the first.

After a day off to travel to New York, manager Haney sent ten-game winner Bob Rush to the mound against Don Larsen, who had had an up-and-down year for the Yankees. Larsen, with help from Duren, shut the Braves out 4–0. Rush pitched well, giving up just three hits in six innings. The Yankees iced the game in the seventh against Don McMahon when Bauer hit his second homer of the Series.

Game four was all Spahn. He shut the Yankees out on just two hits and beat Ford, 3–0. Spahn was overpowering, walking two and allowing just four balls to be hit to the outfield. He also stopped Hank Bauer's 17-game World Series hitting streak. The Braves had an apparently insurmountable 3–1 lead. No team had overcome such a deficit since the Pittsburgh Pirates bounced back to beat the Washington Senators thirty-three years earlier.

The Braves were in charge, the Yankees playing poorly at bat and in the field, but there were some disturbing signs. Eddie Mathews was just 3 for 15 with 3 RBI. Hank Aaron was hitting .333 but had no RBI. The Yankees had outhomered the Braves at this point 6–3.

Game five was a rematch of the second game; only this time Turley was overpowering, and Burdette kept the Braves close for five innings only to be raked for six runs in the sixth. Turley struck out ten, the first pitcher since Walter Johnson to strike out ten twice in the World Series. Turley did it against the Dodgers in 1956. Among Turley's victims were Aaron twice and Covington twice.

With the Series returning to Milwaukee, the Braves still seemed in control. Game six would prove the key to the Series. Haney turned to Spahn, who would be pitching with two days' rest against a worn-out Ford. Ford lasted just one inning, and Stengel got superb relief from Art Ditmar and Duren, plus a save from Turley. Spahn pitched into the tenth inning, when the Yanks won the game against him and McMahon with two runs highlighted by a homer by Gil MacDougald. Mathews was 0 for 5 with three strikeouts. The game ended with the Braves down by one run and two men on when Frank Torre's soft liner was nabbed by McDougald.

The Braves counted on Burdette to duplicate his success in game seven in 1957. Despite Turley's having pitched in the previous two games, Stengel decided to go with him again. He and Burdette were tied 2–2 until the top of the eighth, when the Yankees scored four runs, featuring a three-run homer by Skowron.

In some ways this was Stengel's most satisfying win. The Yankees had avenged their loss to the Braves in 1957 and made some Brave players eat crow for taunting that the Yankees couldn't finish third in the National League. Stengel also had won his seventh world championship in nine tries, matching the record held by Joe McCarthy.

There were many reasons for the Braves' collapse after being up three games to one. Turley was overwhelming in the final three games, winning two and saving one. The Yankees also easily outhomered the Braves 10–3, and the Braves played sloppily in the field, making seven errors. The Braves also tallied 56 strikeouts led by Mathews with 11 and Crandall with 10. Mathews hit .160, with 3 RBI, and Aaron drove home two runs. To win a seven-game series a team needs more than five RBI out of its number-three and -four hitters.

7

Baseball Expands, 1959–1960

The Continental League

The late 1950s were a classic time of transition. The nation was developing a growing sense that it was time for a change from the static, satisfied world of President Eisenhower to something more dynamic and adventuresome. There was also an emerging conviction that the United States had lost its sense of direction amidst its great prosperity. Pundits moaned that "Johnny Can't Read" and that Sputnik proved we lagged behind the Soviet Union in science and technology. Authors like John Kenneth Galbraith wrote of the smug stultification of *The Affluent Society*, and politicians eyeing the White House in 1960 spoke of getting the country moving again.

In retrospect the nation was better off than it seemed. But there was a sense of listlessness in American society, perhaps the result of seven years of conservative rule by the oldest man to hold the presidency until Ronald Reagan. America still liked Ike, but they yearned for someone new. It is interesting that all the major political aspirants were young, in their 40s and 50s, symbolizing the passing of power to a new generation, a phenomenon that happens in American society periodically.

Baseball too was in transition. The franchise shifts that began with the Braves in 1953 had shattered the barriers that kept Major League thinking hidebound. When the Dodgers and Giants took the game to sunny California, where it was an instant success, the financial rewards of further changes seized the imagination of even the most reactionary of the magnates.

The baseball establishment acted by consensus. Majority rule in the two leagues or the power of the commissioner since Landis's death were insignificant. The owners, a blend of successful businessmen, amateur sportsmen plus a few old families whose roots went back to the early days of baseball,

179

understood that the events of the 1950s meant that the sport was on the eve of a great transformation.

For years there had been talk of a third or even a fourth Major League. As early as 1952 Ford Frick had predicted that within a decade there would be a third league operating on the West Coast (*SN*, 2/13/52, p. 3). He believed that the Pacific Coast League gradually would be upgraded to Major League status. That didn't happen, and the O'Malley-Stoneman move to California rendered the idea impossible.

In the six investigations of Major League baseball carried out by Congress in the 1950s, the owners defended the game's special league status. They feared what would happen if they lost their antitrust exemption or had the reserve clause declared invalid. The politicians, on the other hand, had a different constituency. They wanted to see more areas of the country, preferably the ones they represented, achieve Major League status. Congress used the threat of removing baseball's antitrust protection as a way of prodding the owners to expand the sport.

Professional baseball was successful in beating back these challenges throughout the decade, but each year the sport's success in avoiding government involvement became more problematic. The move to California took that state's legislators off baseball's back, but others soon replaced them. Senator Estes Kefauver of Tennessee, an old-fashioned populist who disliked monopoly of any kind, joined Representative Emmanuel Celler of New York to press baseball for substantive changes. Allow more cities to have Major League franchises, open new leagues, change the reserve clause — these were some of the suggestions that came from Kefauver and Celler. Kefauver drafted a bill along these lines, which he began shepherding through the Senate in 1959. None of his ideas were palatable to baseball's owners.

Just when the pressure from the politicians became intense in 1959, Major League baseball was threatened from a new direction — the organization of a third Major League, the Continental League. The coming together of these two forces eventually led to baseball's first expansion since the founding of the American League more than a half-century earlier.

The genesis of the Continental League dated back to the flight of the Dodgers and Giants from New York after the 1957 season. Mayor Robert Wagner approached William Shea, a well-connected Manhattan lawyer, to see if New York could find at least one replacement team for the Giants and Dodgers.

At 52 Shea was a handsome, black-haired Irishman, adept at behind-the-scenes maneuvering. Had he been brought in earlier, New York might not have lost the Dodgers or Giants. When he undertook the task of getting a team for New York, he first tied to lure unsuccessful franchises like Cincinnati, or Pittsburgh. When that failed, he approached the National League about expanding to nine or ten teams, with one of them being placed in the New York metropolitan area. His offer included a modern stadium to be built in

Flushing Meadows, on the site of the 1939 World's Fair, one of Robert Moses' pet projects. The National League leadership stalled him, and this got his Irish dander up.

Shea was determined to break the logjam that held up expansion. The Majors had cleared the way for a new league at their May 21, 1959, meeting at the Darby Dan Farm home of John Galbraith, president of the Pirates. This was done partly as a sop to Congress, which continued to talk about ending baseball's antitrust exemption. The owners gave Frick permission to draw up broad plans for a new league. Frick told the press that he would be furnishing to interested cities the rules for setting up a new league. He stressed that the procedure had to be done in an orderly manner "without destroying our present structure and without the bitterness and disruption of a baseball war" (*SNG*, 1960, p. 103). This meant that the Majors were in no hurry to help create a potential rival.

Frick's requirements were relatively straightforward. The cities constituting any new league must have a population equal to that of the smallest of the current Major League teams, Kansas City, which had a city base of 456,000 and a metropolitan total of 814,000. The cities in the League had to provide stadiums with seating for a minimum of 25,000. The new league had also to create a pension program similar to that prevailing in the Major Leagues and had to accept the Majors' minimum salary scale of $7,000.

None of these bothered Shea. He knew that the huge success of Los Angeles, San Francisco, Milwaukee and to a lesser extent, Baltimore, had whetted the appetites of other large metropolitan areas for Major League status. In 1959 he decided to capitalize on that. Having been turned down by current baseball teams to come to New York, he had no other choice but to try to form a new league. Never one for half measures, he protested that he wasn't interested in power or money from the new venture: "I'm no baseball man. ... I'm a lawyer. Once the Continental League is operating, I'm stepping out of the picture" ("Deserving," *New Yorker*, 10/3/59, p. 33).

Shea presented the Majors with the most formidable challenge since the Federal League days. When it became clear he was getting the runaround, Shea got serious. He contacted wealthy business types in those cities that qualified under Frick's criteria. By July 1959 he had established contacts with five cities, heavily bankrolled by rich investors like Jack Kent Cooke, Mrs. Charles Shipman Payson and K. S. Adam of Ada Oil in Texas. A minimum of $3 million was required up front, which was no problem for these people. The initial franchises in the new Continental League, so named by former senator Edwin Johnson of Colorado because it would carry baseball across the nation, were, along with New York, all growing and prosperous communities: Houston, Toronto, St. Paul–Minneapolis and Denver. Their population base was larger than many cities currently in the Majors.

By awarding franchises in four different cities in four different states, Shea shrewdly curried favor with eight senators and a significant number of congressmen who might otherwise be unsympathetic to the new league (Vecsey, 16). Among those whose states would gain Major League status were two of the most powerful Democratic figures in the Senate, majority leader Lyndon Johnson of Texas and Hubert Humphrey of Minnesota. Shea knew how to play the political game.

Both Kefauver and Celler greeted the news of the League's formation enthusiastically. The Tennessee senator called it wonderful news and vowed to help the League anyway he could legislatively. Celler held out a mild threat. If the Major Leagues created any obstacles, he was sure Congress would take the necessary action to overcome them (*NYT*, 7/28/59, p. 30).

At the meeting with the press to announce the formation of the new league, Shea was greeted with skepticism by some baseball writers. One reporter sneered that this was the old Federal League idea all over again: "It died 40 years ago." Shea snapped back: "You're the only one in the room old enough to remember" (Reidenbaugh, *First Hundred Years*, p. 213).

To give the new league further validity and to provide some baseball expertise, Shea brought Branch Rickey on board as president at a salary of $50,000. The 77-year-old Mahatma of baseball had been serving as an adviser to the Pittsburgh Pirates since his retirement in 1955. It was a shrewd move because Rickey knew his way around the dark back alleys of baseball, having done some mugging there himself in the past. Rickey immediately went to work on the press to make the Continental League seem like a fait accompli. "I would never have gone into this thing," he told the reporters when his appointment was announced, "if I had even an iota of doubt as to its ultimate success. Give us five years and we will beat the existing Majors in the World Series" (Dan Daniel, "Third League Is on the Way," *S&S*, 1960, p. 42). Rickey's favorite line to all doubters was simple: "The Continental League is as inevitable as tomorrow morning although not as imminent" (*SN*, 2/3/60, p. 14).

With their financial backing secure, Shea and Rickey met with Frick on August 18 to discuss the terms for acceptance of the new league. Frick spelled out the procedures necessary before the Continental League could be accepted. Rickey spoke for over four hours trying to emphasize how realistic the new league's chances were. He knew his strongest weapon was Congress's threat to baseball's special position in law, but he also appealed to Frick on higher grounds to take the lead in the restructuring of baseball (Polner, 259). Frick was noncommittal because he knew that the owners, his real bosses, were not sure which direction they wanted to move.

The crux of the matter was sufficient players to stock a new league. Rickey recognized that the talent in the Continental League would fall below Major League levels initially. He was careful to point out that unlike the Federal League, the Continental League recognized the position of the Major Leagues and was not interested in raiding. He also cleverly answered the question of where its players would come from. Recruiting managers and coaches would be no problem, but each team in the new league would start with a parity of talent not yet equal to that of the Major Leagues. Rickey argued "that within five years we can compete with the National and American Leagues for... worldwide recognition" (Daniel, *S&S*, 1960, p. 34).

This gradualist approach did not threaten the existing structure of the Major Leagues. The Majors feared two things: a bidding war for talent, as happened with the Federal League and Mexican League, and Congressional legislation limiting the number of players they could control, which could happen if they lost their antitrust exemption. A bidding war would drive up salaries, eating into the owners' profits, as happened later with free agency. The Majors controlled player development through ties to the minors. In 1958 Frick told Congress that of 150 minor league teams, 34 were owned outright by the Majors, and they had working agreements with another 104 ("Can Another Big League Pay Its Way?" *USN&WR*, 9/7/59, p. 51). In effect, this meant that the Majors controlled the best baseball players. There were no truly independent minor league teams as in the past. Unless the Continental League got access to some of these players, their chances of gaining acceptance was virtually nil.

The reaction of Major League players revealed their essential conservatism. Gil Hodges thought the concept of a new league was fine, but it would have problems luring players away from the Majors. Robin Roberts, one of the leaders of the MLPA, agreed with Rickey: It would take four to five years to gain respectability. Neither grasped or spoke publicly about the leverage a new league would give players to raise salary levels ("Can Another League," *USN&WR*, 9/7/59, p. 52).

By the end of 1959 the Continental League had reached eight teams by granting franchisers to Atlanta, Dallas–Ft. Worth and Buffalo. Seven of these eight cities eventually got Major League franchises, so Shea and Rickey had chosen wisely. The eight new teams impinged on the territorial rights of only two Major League teams, the Yankees, who would have to share the lucrative New York television market, and Milwaukee, who would be seriously injured by another team's taking up residence in the Twin Cities. That would cut off Milwaukee's television monopoly for 300 miles to the west. But the real losers were the minor league franchises in the new Continental League cities. They demanded $1 million each in compensation, which was nowhere near what Shea and Rickey were willing to pay (*SN*, 2/3/60, p. 12). This demand would prove a major stumbling block for the Continental League and would also provide Major League owners with justification for denying the new league equal status.

The progress of the Continental League slowed in June 1960 as the legislation that Kefauver had prepared to limit the number of players any team could control to 100 was first gutted and then, after being amended to provide for an unrestricted draft, defeated in the Senate, 45–41. Kefauver's bill was then sent back to committee by an overwhelming vote of 72–12, where it was effectively dead (*NYT*, 7/19/60, p. 32). With Congressional pressure waning, the Majors decided to authorize expansion on their own terms before new legislation was prepared. In July 1960 the American League and National League met separately and decided to expand to ten teams, beginning with the 1962 season. As usual, there were attempts to outmaneuver each other as to the best locations and to the question of timing. Frick was virtually powerless in these maneuverings.

The National League, as in the move to California in 1958, picked off the prime sites for its two teams: New York and Houston. New York was an obvious choice because it would mean the return of National League baseball to a city where it once thrived. There was no way the Yankees would allow another American League team in the city, but they couldn't do anything to reverse this decision (*SN*, 2/24/60, p. 9). Houston was a shrewd choice because it allowed the National League to break into the rapidly growing Southwest market. It also made Lyndon Johnson happy, effectively squelching any chance that the Kefauver approach would be revived.

The American League had been outsmarted for the second time in two years. Their response, partly out of pique, was to move up the deadline for the addition of two teams to 1961, thus beating to expansion the National League by a year. This says it all about how the Majors were administered. Sheer chaos reigned, and the most aggressive side won out.

At the same time that they authorized early expansion, the American League owners voted to allow Calvin Griffith of the Washington Senators to move to the Twin Cities. Griffith had been complaining for years about the lack of support he received in DC and the difficulty of making any money there because of the proximity of the Baltimore franchise. He had been courting the Twin Cities area and knew how deeply the people there wanted Major League baseball. Griffith cut a great deal. The Twin Cities guaranteed him 750,000 attendance for five years, which translated into a yearly profit of $430,000, a figure far beyond anything that Washington had ever made. Griffith also received an offer of a half million dollars for radio and television rights. He had made $180,000 in Washington from radio and television in 1959 (*SNG*, 1960, p. 106).

Griffith blamed his problems on the growing percentage of blacks in Washington, 54 percent according to the 1960 census, the highest of any urban area in the United States. The Senators had drawn just 475,000 fans in 1958, almost 190,000 fewer than the next-lowest team. Even with a gain of 140,000 in 1959, Washington was still last in attendance in the American League by well over 275,000. Later Griffith frankly explained his reasons for moving: "I moved ... to Minnesota when I found out that you people here had only 15,000 Blacks in the state. Black people don't go to ball games, but they fill up rassling rings and put up such a chant it will scare you to death. We came here because you've got good, hardworking white people here" (Harry Edwards, "Sport Within the Veil," p. 125).

The American League granted Washington a new franchise and allowed the new team to keep the name Senators as a way of placating the wrath of Congress. Dan Topping of the Yankees was furious at having his territory invaded by the National League, and he wanted retaliation by having an American League team placed in Los Angeles. Topping blamed Frick for declaring New York an open area and wanted the same designation assigned Los Angeles. But Walter O'Malley was ready for him.

O'Malley pointed out that under Major League Rule 1(c) the American League could locate in Los Angeles only with his approval because he had prior rights there. O'Malley noted that he had paid $450,000 to the Pacific Coast League for the rights to Los Angeles and another $150,000 to refurbish the Coliseum for baseball. He wanted something in return for surrendering his rights. After awarding the Los Angeles franchise to cowboy star Gene Autry, the American League authorized payment of $300,000 to O'Malley. O'Malley also insisted that the new American League team, to be called the Angels, not share the Coliseum but play their games in Wrigley Field, which held only 24,000 fans. This meant that they could not match his attendance figures. He also negotiated a deal whereby when the Dodgers opened the new stadium at Chavez Ravine, the Angels would become his tenants but at what turned out to be a prohibitive rate. Once again O'Malley showed who was the smartest, most devious, baseball owner.

The Yankee Collapse

Although organizational and business matters were the main focus of baseball in 1959, on the field the unexpected happened. The Yankees not only failed to win the pennant, but they were never a factor in the championship race. In the National League the Dodgers came from seventh place to not only win the pennant but also to go on to take the World Series. Not even the wildest prognosticators foresaw these outcomes.

In preseason polls, the BWAA made the Yankees a prohibitive favorite to repeat as American League champs. Of 226 writers, 203 picked the Yankees for first, with seven favoring the Tigers and just five the White Sox. The writers believed that the Yankees, who won both the pennant and World Championship handily in 1958, would have no problems winning again. The team looked sound, and more importantly, the competition seemed weak.

But Stengel was worried. The Yankees had tailed off badly the last two months of the 1958 season, even if they pulled off the World Series. Yogi Berra was getting old, and Stengel wanted to shift him to the outfield. "I can add about three years to Berra's career by taking him away from catching," Stengel told *Sports Illustrated* (*SI*, "The 1959 Baseball Story," p. 22). This meant that Elston Howard would have to take over a greater role behind the plate. At that time no one knew whether he could do so at championship level. He proved he could.

The pitching staff was a problem. Stengel expected a great deal from Bob Turley, who was just 28. But Don Larsen was in and out, and Stengel was losing confidence in him. Whitey Ford had suffered from arm miseries for a couple of years and had been virtually useless the last half of the 1958 season. The Yankees vaunted minor league system didn't have any replacements ready to step forward the way they had in the past when they produced Ford, Grim, Kucks, and Sturdivant at crucial times.

Mantle was a fixture in center and just about irreplaceable. But Hank Bauer in right was 36 and coming off his poorest season as a Yankee. The Yankees hadn't had a left fielder they could count on since Gene Woodling was traded away. Norm Siebern was in Stengel's doghouse for not being aggressive enough. Stengel's great patience with rookies was wearing thin. In the past he might have tried to develop Siebern's skills, but now he just nagged and complained about him. At least the infield seemed set behind Skowron, Richardson, McDougald, Kubek and Carey. No one else had that kind of depth.

When Stengel was told that some writers rated this club the best he had had since taking over in 1949, he said he wouldn't even rate it one of the two best he had managed. He tried to be optimistic: "I have a young ball club with plenty of drive and ambition. They have won four straight pennants and the world championship, but they are not the kind of team that will get careless and beat themselves" (*S&S*, 1959, p. 12). This last point was worrisome. Weiss was concerned that the Yankee players were too involved in outside activities and were not concentrating on the game properly. Mixed in with his usual scare talk of reducing salaries, Weiss believed the Yankees needed to be disciplined and jolted into reality as happened in 1954 (*ibid.*, p. 11). He proved correct.

The rest of the League did seem weak. The Tigers were everybody's second choice because they had the four finest starters in the American League in Jim Bunning, Frank Lary, Billy Hoeft and Paul Foytack. They also had two of the best right-handed hitters in the outfield: Al Kaline and Harvey Kuenn. But they were weak in the infield and behind the plate. The White Sox seemed to have peaked a couple of years earlier. They won just 82 games in 1958 and on paper did not appear to have the quality to match the Yankees or Tigers. But in the last couple of months of the 1958 season, they were the best team in the American League. After June 13 they played .588 baseball, 60–42, four games better than the Yankees.

The White Sox had good pitching, solid defense up the middle and a fine manager in Al Lopez, who had already proved that he knew how to beat the

Yankees. Their hitting ranked among the poorest in the American League especially in power, having been last in the League in 1958. More importantly, there was a feeling that time was running out for the White Sox. They had to win soon or see the team grow old.

Boston and Cleveland were regarded as longshots. Both had some quality players, but both also had serious problems. Ted Williams, although coming off two straight batting titles, would turn 41 in August. Boston's pitching was always a question mark because of the stresses created by having to play in Fenway Park. They lacked the one or two dominating starters that could keep them in a pennant chase.

Cleveland had finished just one game over .500 in 1958, but the team had enormous potential. They got Jimmy Piersall from Boston for next to nothing: Gary Geiger and an aging Vic Wertz. This deal gave Cleveland the best outfield in the American League: Piersall in center surrounded by Rocky Colavito and Minnie Minoso. The Indians also had a pretty good staff anchored by 16-game-winner Cal McLish and young Gary Bell and Jim Grant. They were counting on Herb Score making a comeback to thrust into the heart of the pennant race. Their infield was questionable, but they did have Vic Power, perhaps the best defensive first baseman in the League. They traded for Billy Martin to give them an added spark, but he would never again be the player he was under Stengel.

The rest of the American League — Baltimore, Kansas City and Washington — was of poor quality, although each team possessed a couple of talented players. None of the three had any depth however. They were discounted as factors in the pennant race.

The 1959 season was one of the strangest in a decade. The Yankees were never a factor. Their collapse was a total team effort. Mickey Mantle had the poorest year since his rookie season, driving in just 75 runs. This total led the team, the lowest figure for a Yankee team since 1918. Yogi Berra showed the signs of age as he caught 116 games, the second-lowest total since 1949. He hit 19 homers but drove in only 69 runs. Elston Howard spelled him behind the plate in 43 games and spent the rest of the season at first and in the outfield. Bill Skowron missed half the season with a bad back that would haunt him for the rest of his career. He broke his arm in July on a play at first and was on the disabled list the rest of the year.

The Yankees might have survived the hitters' off year if the pitching had held up. The pitchers other than Whitey Ford were terrible. Bob Turley dropped from 21 wins and the Cy Young Award to just 8 victories. Don Larsen didn't win a game after June 13, and Bobby Shantz had a sore arm most of the year (Golenbock, *Dynasty*, 246). None of the young arms that the Yankees brought up from their vaunted farm system saved them, and the pitching rotation was a shambles, a joke compared to the great Yankee staffs of the past. Ryne Duren pitched well most of the year, but he was now just about a full-blown alcoholic.

On May 20 the Yankees hit bottom. They were in last place for the first time since 1940 on merit. Stengel was at a loss to explain it. "Worst slump we've had since I've been working here," he told the press as he tried to figure out a way to get the Yankees moving. His explanation for the Yankees' flop was succinct: "All I can figure is that they've done a different thing wrong every day" ("Laugh, Yankees," *Newsweek*, 5/18/59, p. 102).

The rest of the League was laughing at the Yankees, and attendance soared as fans around the American League had a chance to enjoy a New Yorkless pennant race and perhaps even watch their local heroes beat the "damn Yankees." By the end of the season, attendance in the American League reached a level not matched since 1949.

The pennant race proved a closely fought battle between the Indians and the White Sox. The two battled until July, when the White Sox finally pulled away from the rest of the League. Cleveland led most of the way behind because of solid hitting. They led the American League in homers. Rocky Colavito shared the League lead with Harmon Killebrew of Washington, who came out of nowhere in his first full season to hit 42 homers and drive in over 100 runs. Cleveland also produced its surprises: "Tito" Francona hit a rousing .363, with 20 homers, and Woodie Held played a decent shortstop and hit 29 homers. Vic Power chipped in by hitting .289, the tenth best average in the American League, and by playing first with his usual finesse.

The Indians had the fourth-best pitching staff in the American League, which probably cost them the pennant in the final analysis. Their key starters were Cal McLish, who won 19 games against just 8 losses and who was 10–2 versus the White Sox and Yankees. He was the only Cleveland pitcher with an ERA ranked in the top 15. The other Indian starters were Gary Bell, who finished 16–11 but with an ERA over 4.00, Jim "Mudcat" Grant, 10–7, and Jim Perry, who came out of the bull pen to finish 12–10. The big letdown for the Indians was the collapse of Herb Score. He looked like the Score of 1956 by winning nine games before the All-Star break. But in the second half he won no games to finish 9–11. He struck out 147 but had an ERA over 4.00. Tragically his career was almost over at 26. He was traded to the White Sox the next year, finishing his career in 1962. Before he was injured by McDougald's line drive he was 38–20, thereafter 17–26. He might have been the Sandy Koufax of the American League with his overpowering fastball combined with a virtually unhittable curve. Ted Williams, no mean authority on pitching, rated his stuff at the peak of his career as among the best he ever faced.

The White Sox played consistently good baseball all season. At no time were they more than two games out of first place. They did it with pitching, defense and speed. Their hitting attack was woefully weak. Of all teams in both leagues they finished sixth in hitting and last in homers, with 97. Led by Luis Aparicio, who stole 56 bases, the most in the American League since George Case pilfered 61 in 1943, the White Sox topped the American League in stolen bases, with 113. They topped their closest rival by 45 stolen bases. For comparison, the Indians had 33 stolen bases, the Yankees 45.

Although five teams scored more runs than the White Sox, none gave up fewer than their 588. The White Sox won the close games all season. In fact, they were 35–15 in one-run games. Their pitching staff was led by Early Wynn, who at 39 won 22 games, and Bob Shaw, who came out of nowhere to win 18 games. Billy Pierce had a sore back and only won 14, and Dick Donovan overcame arm problems to win nine. All four ranked among the top 15 pitchers in the League in ERA. But a major key to the White Sox's success was the work of their relievers. Gerry Staley and Omar "Turk" Lown appeared in 127 games for a combined 17–7 record, recording 29 saves to go along with ERAs under 2.90.

Chicago's defense was another key to their success in 1959. Nelson Fox and Aparicio led all keystone combinations in total chances. Jim Landis in center led all outfielders in putouts with 420. He was the only outfielder in the American League to top 400 putouts. Sherm Lollar behind the plate was superb, handling a pitching staff judiciously. He also led the team in homers with 22 and RBI with 84. You had to go back to the 1916 Boston Red Sox to find a pennant-winning team whose leading RBI man had fewer runs driven in than Lollar. In many ways the White Sox were a throwback to the deadball era of low-run games, stolen bases and hit-and-running.

Once the White Sox took over first place in late July they were never challenged, although their biggest margin over the second-place Indians was only 6½ in early September. What won the pennant for them was a 41–16 stretch in July and August. In fact, they were the only team in the American League to win 20 games in any month. They did it in July and August to lock up the flag.

Like the Indian team he led to victory in 1954, Al Lopez put his stamp on the White Sox. He recognized that he had no dominant starter, no power hitters so he concentrated on speed, which the White Sox had, and juggled his pitching staff brilliantly, getting the maximum out of a rotation that on paper wasn't impressive. His handling of the bull pen, using two men as closers, duplicated Leo Durocher's strategy in the early 1950s with the Giants. But Lopez was a quiet, low-keyed individual who let the players take the credit (Koppett, 182–183). He was also bilingual, which was unusual for the largely uneducated managers of his time. If you look at his record, both with the Indians and the White Sox in the 1950s, it is truly impressive: he never finished lower than second. From 1951 through 1959, he averaged 93 victories, second only to Stengel's 95 wins. Stengel paid him the ultimate compliment: "You ain't going to no picnic when you tangle with them Chicagoans" (Frommer, 128).

In truth, the White Sox had a relatively easy time despite the Indian's tenacity. The Yankee collapse early in the season was psychologically satisfying, removing the fear of another come-from-behind victory by Stengel's team.

No one else in the American League mounted a challenge to the White Sox. Detroit finished fourth, 18 games back and 2 games under .500. The Tigers had a great outfield led by Harvey Kuenn, who won the batting title with a .353 average, a full 26 points ahead of the number-two hitter, his teammate Al Kaline. The third outfielder, Charley Maxwell, hit 31 homers and drove in 95 runs. But Detroit had a poor infield, no catcher and a weak bench. Its pitching staff posted some impressive numbers. The four starters — Bunning, Lary, Paul Foytack and Don Mossi — won 65 games, but they gave up 177 homers, including 37 by Bunning and 34 by Foytack. No offense could overcome those numbers.

Boston and Baltimore finished close to Detroit with 75 and 74 wins apiece. The Red Sox had two good hitters in Jackie Jensen, who led the American League in RBI for the third time and hit 28 homers, and Pete Runnels who hit .314. Ted Williams had a terrible year, hitting just .254, with only ten homers. This was the only time in his long career that Williams hit under .300, and it led to talk of his retirement. But this speculation underestimated his determination to retire on his terms, that is, after a decent season.

As usual Boston was short on pitching. The staff finished with an ERA over 4.00, and its biggest winner was Jerry Casale with a 13–8 record. The Red Sox looked like a team in continued decline.

Baltimore, on the other hand, put new faces in key positions. Brooks Robinson took over as the regular third baseman and showed signs of hitting, finishing with a .284 average. Gus Triandos led the team in homers with 25 and RBI with 70. The pitching staff had the second lowest ERA in the League, 3.56. Paul Richards made Hoyt Wilhelm into a starter, and he not only won 15 games, but he led the American League in ERA with a 2.19, a remarkable feat for a knuckleball hurler. Milt Pappas, just 20 years old, also won 15 games, and Jerry Walker, another of Richards's "Baby Birds" chipped in with 11 wins along with a 2.92 ERA. The future looked bright for Baltimore because, unlike Boston, they had a productive farm system. In the next few years pitchers like Chuck Estrada and Jack Fisher, infielders like Ron Hansen, plus shrewd trades would transform the Orioles into a contender. Richards had laid the groundwork for a first-class Baltimore franchise for the next few years.

Kansas City edged out Washington for seventh place by three games. Of the two teams, Washington showed the most potential. The A's were still the Yankees in a different uniform and continued to serve as training ground for the New York club. The Yankees got back pitcher Ralph Terry, whom they had sent to the A's in 1957 in a May trade. He had gotten his seasoning on the Major League level. It was better and even cheaper for the Yankees than sending him to the minors. Let the A's pay for his development. Along with Terry they also secured outfielder Hector Lopez, who filled in for them at third base and the outfield. Lopez was a nice find. He hit .283 with 22 homers and 93 RBI, more than any other Yankee. Later, in December, the Yankees would pull off another big deal with the A's, sending them sore-arm pitcher Don Larsen, 37-year-old Hank Bauer, Norm Siebern and minor league sensation Marv Throneberry for 26-year-old Roger Maris. No wonder the rest of the American League regarded the A's as a Yankee farm team.

Washington finished in the cellar for the third year in a row. But they showed a great deal of power with Harmon Killebrew tying for the League lead in homers, outfielder Jim Lemon hitting 33 homers and driving in 100 runs and rookie Bob Allison hitting 30 homers. Roy Sievers hit 21 in just 106 games, as the Senators broke their team home-run record with 163, just four behind the League-leading Indians. Washington's problem was their pitching. Camillio Pascual won 17 games, led the League in shutouts with six and was second to Jim Bunning with 185 strikeouts. Pedro Ramos won 13 games but led the American League in losses with 19. For the second year in a row a Senator won the Rookie of the Year Award — Bob Allison in 1959 and Albie Pearson in 1958. The Senators were not that far away from becoming a competitive club.

The Miracle of the Coliseum

The National League race in 1959 was even more unpredictable than the American League's with its Yankee collapse. The Los Angeles Dodgers in just their second year on the West Coast won the pennant with one of the poorest teams to ever cop a title. They did so with the fewest victories of any National League pennant winner since 1918 and against two teams, the Milwaukee Braves and San Francisco Giants, who were clearly superior on paper.

In a preseason poll of the BWAA the Braves were an overwhelming choice to repeat as champs. They received 147 first-place votes from 226 writers. Pittsburgh got 36, San Francisco 34 and Cincinnati 5 votes. The Dodgers were picked to finish 5th, which seemed realistic coming off their poor seventh-place performance in 1958. There was nothing to indicate that the Dodgers had a serious chance at the pennant. The team was old in key spots and still depended on heroes of the Brooklyn era who were getting along in years: Gil Hodges, Duke Snider and Car Furillo. The new talent was not that impressive with Charley Neal, an indifferent infielder, the best of the lot. Dodger pitching also looked weak, with Drysdale and Johnny Podres coming off losing seasons. The team that entered the 1959 pennant chase had made only one significant trade. In December 1958 they sent Gino Cimoli, an average outfielder, to the Cards for former rookie of the year, Wally Moon. It didn't impress anyone at the time. Both men were coming off poor years — Moon had hit .238, whereas Cimoli was just eight points higher. But it turned out to be a great move for the Dodgers. They got a solid left fielder and a hitter who developed the perfect inside-out stroke for the Coliseum with its short left-field screen.

The 1959 pennant race was one of the most dramatic in National League history. It was essentially a three-team struggle among the Giants, Dodgers and the heavily favored Braves, although the Pirates played good ball for the first quarter of the season. Over the past three seasons, the Braves had shown that they were the best team in the National League, winning two pennants, one World Series and finishing one game out of first in 1956. But something seemed missing in 1959. The Braves were flat and played lifeless baseball most of the season. The loss of veteran second baseman Red Schoendienst to tuberculosis hurt them by depriving them of a steady leader. Manager Fred Haney was a careful, cautious man who seemed at a loss for a way to inspire a nonchalant team. He admitted after the season that there were times when his enthusiasm and endurance for baseball were low during the pennant chase (*SN*, 10/7/59, p. 7).

The Braves started off well and held the lead for most of the time from opening day to early July. During this stretch they were 43-35. But they could not pull away from the Dodgers or Giants, both of whom stayed within striking distance of the pace-setting Braves. Pittsburgh was also in the midst of the pennant chase until they collapsed with a July record of 11-16.

The Braves were able to take advantage of off days and rain-outs and really on their three starters in the opening part of the season. Spahn, Burdette and Bob Buhl were 27-20 at the All-Star break. When Buhl developed arm problems in the middle of the season, the second-line Brave pitchers failed to come through. In 1958 Joey Jay, Carlton Willey and Juan Pizzaro had made a major contribution to the Braves victory, winning 22 games versus 16 losses. They flopped in 1959 and finished the season with a combined losing record of 17-22. If only one of the three had come through it might have been enough to put the Braves solidly in first place. Their failure put too much pressure on Spahn and Burdette. Burdette started 39 games to lead the National League and relieved in two others. Even though he won 21 games, he finished the season with an ERA of 4.07 and led the National League in hits allowed, at 312. Spahn started 36 games, and his 21 completions led the National League. Like Burdette, he won 21 but with a much better ERA, 2.96. Between the two, they started almost half the Braves' games.

The Braves had their usual good hitting. Hank Aaron hit .355 to win his second batting title. Eddie Mathews hit 46 homers to lead the National League, and Joe Adcock with 25 homers and Del Crandall with 19 gave the Braves a potent lineup. The Braves were third overall in team batting and first in homers with 177. Wes Covington had a poor year after two good seasons, and Andy Pafko was getting old. The Braves' bench was weak all season.

When the Braves cooled off in early July, the Giants forged to the front and held the lead for two weeks due to a fine blend of power and solid pitching. As a team they finished a close second to the Braves in homers with 167, and the team ERA was the best in the National League. Manager Bill Rigney had the best team in the League on paper. No one could match a starting nine that included Orlando Cepeda, Willie Mays, Willie Kirkland, Daryl Spencer, Jim Davenport and Jackie Brandt. Nor did any other team in the National League have a bench that included reserves like Felipe Alou, Leon Wagner and Andre Rodgers. The Giants were strengthened on July 30 when Willie McCovey was brought up from Phoenix. In his first game he went four for four against Robin Roberts and followed that with six homers in 14 games. McCovey wound up hitting .354 with 13 homers in just 192 at bats. As a first baseman he presented Rigney with a pleasant problem — who to play at first, Cepeda, 1958's rookie of the year, or McCovey, whose potential seemed limitless. The more agile Cepeda played left in 44 games to make room for McCovey.

The Giants' starting four were the best in the National League. Sad Sam Jones had his greatest season, leading the League in ERA at 2.83 and finishing second to Don Drysdale in strikeouts, 242 to 209. Jones was the first National league pitcher to strikeout 200 or more in back-to-back seasons since Dazzy Vance in 1924–25.

Johnny Antonelli won 19 games but lost his last four starts to miss 20 victories. Jack Sanford, who came over from the Phillies in 1958 for Ruben Gomez and Valmy Thomas, won 15 games, and Mike McCormick continued his development, winning 12 games against 16 defeats.

Rigney overused his staff. Jones started 35 games and relieved 15 times. Antonelli started 38 times, Sanford and McCormick 31 times. Among them they started 135 of the Giants 154 games. It is no wonder that the Giants, after holding the lead through most of July and August, collapsed in September, whereas both the Dodgers and Braves played good ball in that crucial month. Rigney had a couple of possible fifth starters in Stu Miller and Alan Worthington. Both were now essentially relief pitchers, but they had been starters in the past. By carefully spotting them, he could have nurtured his big four and had them relatively fresh in the last weeks of the season. In late August the Giants had a four-games lead in the National League. Led by Mays, Cepeda, who drove in 100 runs for the second year in a row, and a red-hot McCovey, they seemed to be the strongest club in the League.

Antonelli traced the Giants' problems to all the young players that the team had brought up the previous year. They had good rookie seasons, but he believed that they "weren't ready for a full year's run at the pennant" (Peary, 432). His explanation has some validity. Third baseman Jim Davenport and catcher Bob Schmidt had poorer offensive seasons in 1959, but overall stats did not bear Antonelli out. The 1959 team scored just 22 fewer runs, hit only two points lower than the previous year and had a much better ERA, 3.47 versus 3.98.

The Giants lacked pitching depth, the kind that Stengel had used so effectively with his successful Yankee teams. Also the Giants' defense was deficient. They led the National League in errors and made the fewest double plays in the League. The team's two shortstops, Andre Rodgers and Ed Bressoud, made 33 errors between them.

But everything turned sour as the wear and tear on the staff began to tell. As it was, the Giants almost won everything. They had a two-game lead as late as September 19 but then lost seven of eight games with Antonelli, McCormick and Sam Jones failing in key situations. Jones not only started two games in a six-day stretch, but he also relieved in one. Antonelli had 18 wins by August 30. In his next seven starts, he won one, lost three and had three no-decisions. His ERA in September was 5.68 (*SN*, 10/7/59, p. 16). Meanwhile, the Dodgers and Braves both were 6-2 to finish in a tie. For the third time in 13 years the Dodgers were in a play-off.

The rest of the National League divided into two parts: four teams, Pittsburgh, Chicago, St. Louis and Cincinnati, who were grouped closely with only seven games separating them and one team, the Phillies by themselves in the cellar for the second straight year.

The Pirates were the best of the first group. They finished over .500 for the second year in a row, the first time they had done that since 1945. They were in the pennant chase until mid-June, when they went into a swoon that left them 7½ games out of first at the end of July. They had the best month of any National League team in 1959 by winning 20 of 29 games to cut a full four games off their deficit. But an awful 8-14 September left them in fourth place, 9½ games behind the Dodgers.

The 1959 Bucs were a good team, and they might have contended for the pennant if Bob Friend hadn't had such a ghastly year. After leading the National League in wins with 22 in 1958, Friend slipped to 8-19, losing his first seven decisions at the beginning of the season. Vern Law won 18 games, and Roy Face won 17 in a row out of the bull pen before he lost to the Dodgers in September. He finished 18-1 with ten saves and a 2.70 ERA. No relief pitcher has topped his victory total. His forkball was unhittable all season. In 93 innings he gave up just five homers.

The Pirate hitters slumped off somewhat from 1958 — they didn't have a .300 hitter. Four regulars — Smokey Burgess, Clemente, Dick Stuart and Don Hoak — hit in the mid-.290s. First base was an effective platoon of Stuart and Rocky Nelson, who between them hit 33 homers and accounted for 110 runs. The Pirates also had great defense. The infield of Hoak, Groat and Mazeroski turned a league-high 165 double plays. The outfield of Skinner in left, Virdon in center and Clemente in right was probably the best defensively in all baseball. The team was still young, and its future seemed bright.

The fifth-place Cubs were a surprise. They won more games, 74, than any Cub team since 1952, but they were essentially a one-man club. Ernie Banks had his second MVP year, hitting 45 homers and leading the National League with 143 RBI. The latter figure was the most of any National Leaguer since Joe Medwick drove in 154 in 1937. Banks only lost the home-run title when Eddie

Mathews hit one in the two-games playoff to finish with 46. Banks accounted for over 21 percent of the Cubs' runs, the third-highest percentage in baseball history.

The Cubs were a mix of veterans like Dale long, Bobby Thomson and Al Dark, all past their primes, plus a handful of youngsters. Two 23 year olds, Bob Anderson and Glen Hobbie, hurled over 230 innings and won 28 games between them and seemed poised for great things. But they never developed and suffered the same collapse as Dick Drott and Moe Drabowsky. Neither Anderson nor Hobbie would have a winning year during the rest of their careers.

The best young player on the Cubs was Tony Taylor, who hit .280 and led all National League second sackers in assists. He was a victim of another Cub tradition. He was traded in 1960, just as he was ready to blossom.

The Reds tied the Cubs for sixth place. They could hit but had no pitching. Only the last-place Phillies had a poorer team ERA. The Reds' biggest winners were Don Newcombe and Bob Purkey, each of whom won 13 games. Unfortunately, Purkey also lost 18 times. Their other starters, Joe Nuxhall (9-9) and Brooks Lawrence (7-12), were ineffective. They had a good reliever in Jim Brosnan who went 8-3 for them.

Cincinnati's hitting was impressive. They led the National League in batting, hit 161 homers and scored 40 more runs than any other team. Frank Robinson, just 23, led them in homers with 36 and RBI with 125, and a rookie whippet in center, Vada Pinson, had an awesome first year. He hit .316, with 20 homers and 84 RBI. Gus Bell had his last good year, with 19 homers, driving in 115 runs. The Reds were hurt when they lost their great defensive cog, shortstop Roy McMillan, to a series of injuries. The Reds had high hopes for Frank Thomas, for whom they gave up three good players, Hoak, Haddix and Burgess, but the ex-Pirate was a terrible flop. He hit just .225, with only 12 homers. The Reds could have used the three players they had given up.

The Reds played better than .500 baseball after Fred Hutchinson replaced Mayo Smith as manager midway through the season. Brosnan credited Hutchinson for the Reds' turnaround. "Who else can it be but Hutch," the reliever said. "He just settled everybody down" (Peary, 387).

The Cardinals' season was set when Stan Musial finally showed signs of slowing up. "The Man" hit .255, the lowest average of his career. The rest of the Cards weren't much better as hitting was a problem for them all season. They scored only 641 runs, just 42 more than the last-place Phillies. Joe Cunningham hit .345 playing first, and the outfield and Bill White hit .302. But the Cards had a problem of where to play them. White was a natural first baseman, as was Cunningham, and Musial had been playing first to save wear and tear on his legs. Until the Cardinals figured out the right lineup, they were in trouble. Their fine third baseman, Ken Boyer, not only hit .300 but did so with power: 28 homers and 94 RBI.

The pitching staff was led by Larry Jackson, who went 14-13, and Lindy McDaniel, who also won 14 games and saved 15 more. Vinegar Bend Mizell was 9-3 on June 25, but he developed back problems and went 4-7 the rest of the way. The Cardinals' ERA was 4.34, the highest in the National League.

The Phillies finished in the cellar for the second year in a row with their poorest record since 1947, 64-90. They had one winning month, July, when the team was 16-13. Just before the season started, John Quinn of the Braves replaced Roy Hamey as general manager. Hamey had made a series of disastrous trades, and Jack Sanford to the Giants for pitcher Ruben Gomez and catcher Valmy Thomas was one of his worst (Westcott & Bilovsky, 487–489). Neither contributed a thing to the Phillies; Gomez was 3-8, with a huge ERA of 6.10, and Thomas hit .200, with seven RBI in 66 games. Sanford went on to pitch effectively for the Giants for five years, winning 89 games for them, while Gomez won exactly two games the rest of his career.

Quinn began transforming the Phillies with a series of trades that broke up the Whiz Kids. Stan Lopata, Granny Hamner and Willie Jones departed. Curt Simmons missed most of the year with a sore arm. Robin Roberts won 15 games but had a high ERA. Jim Owens at 12-12 and Gene Conley at 12-7 with an ERA of 3.00 were the best pitchers. Wally Post drove in 94 runs, and third sacker Gene Freese hit 23 homers including five as pinch hitter. Richie Ashburn had his worst year as a Phillie, hitting .266 with just 20 RBI in 153 games. He would be the next Whiz Kid to go in Quinn's housecleaning after the 1959 campaign. In January 1960 he sent Ashburn to the Cubs for Al Dark and two youngsters, pitcher John Buzhardt, 23, and third baseman Jim Woods, just 20.

The tie between the Dodgers and Braves forced a best-of-three play-off. The first game was played in Milwaukee, with game two and (if necessary) game three to follow in Los Angeles. Neither team had its best pitchers ready, and both were forced to use second-line hurlers. Haney had been forced to use Bob Buhl in the last game of the season against the Phillies to gain a tie with the Dodgers. After he became the Braves' manager, Charley Dressen questioned Haney's use of Buhl. Dressen left himself wide open for Haney's response. "Maybe Charles shouldn't have brought Ralph Branca from the bullpen to pitch to Bobby Thomson in 1951" (*SN*, 2/3/60, p. 14). The Dodgers sent Danny McDevitt, 10-8, to the mound against Carlton Willey, who was just 5-9. Attendance was just over 18,000, a sign that Milwaukee's love affair with the Braves was on the wane.

The game was tied 2-2 when Alston brought in rookie Larry Sherry in relief. Sherry had come up from the minors in early July, lost his first two games and then reeled off six victories in a row. Once he took over in the second inning, he shut the potent Braves lineup down on just four hits and no runs in 7⅔ innings. Catcher John Roseboro won the game with a homer in the sixth inning.

The two teams flew to Los Angeles, and the next day, before a disappointing crowd of 36,500, Lew Burdette took the mound against the Dodgers' biggest winner, Don Drysdale. Burdette pitched a gem of a game for eight innings. He entered the ninth with a 5-2 lead and it appeared that the play-offs would go the full route. But Burdette never got another out. The Dodgers tied the game with three runs. Moon, Snider and Hodges singled, loading the bases and driving Burdette from the mound. McMahon relieved and promptly gave up a two-run single to Norm Larker. Spahn then came on to face Furillo, who tied the game with a sacrifice fly. The Dodgers won it in the twelfth when, with Gil Hodges on third, Felix Mantilla, filling in for shortstop Johnny Logan, threw a ball past first baseman Frank Torre. The Dodgers, who had played in all three National League play-offs, finally won one. Alston was thrilled. "We never wore anybody out," he said after the play-off. "We didn't win half a dozen easy games all year. We had to scramble and scratch for everything we got. But I've never been around a ball club that could equal this one for spirit" (Roy Terrell, "From Obscurity to Near Miracle," SI, 10/5/59, p. 18).

The 1959 World Series seemed lifeless, anticlimactic. For many fans a World Series meant the Yankees against the Dodgers. The Go-Go White Sox seemed like a poor replacement for the New York Bombers. The White Sox were the stronger of the two teams. The oddsmakers made them a 6–5 favorite. They were rested having clinched the pennant on September 22, whereas the Dodgers had only one day off after beating the Braves.

The Series opened in Chicago, and the White Sox made it look easy, beating the Dodgers 11-0 behind 22-game-winner Early Wynn, and Ted Kluszewski hitting two homers. The Dodgers used five pitchers and made three errors. They now had been shut out in their last two World Series games, losing game seven in 1956 to Johnny Kucks, 9-0. But, as they had all season, they bounced back and evened the Series in game two as Johnny Podres, with a save from Larry Sherry, beat the White Sox and Bob Shaw, 4–3.

The Series moved to Los Angeles, and after a day off for traveling, the Dodgers took the lead as Don Drysdale pitched out of jam after jam. Drysdale gave up 11 hits but was the winner when Carl Furillo hit a pinch bases-loaded single. Furillo's "hit" was a simple ground ball that hit a clump of dirt and bounced over Aparicio's shoulder. The Dodgers' luck had changed. Once again Sherry got a save. Chicago pitcher Dick Donovan gave up just 2 hits in 6⅔ innings but was beaten when he walked the bases loaded in the seventh and Furillo singled in two runs to break a scoreless tie.

The Dodgers were winning the close games, a bad sign for the White Sox, who had dominated the American League in that category. In game four the Dodgers knocked out Wynn with a four-run third. Chicago tied the game in the seventh when Sherm Lollar, their only power threat, hit a three-run homer. Sherry came on again to pitch two scoreless innings and won the game when Gil Hodges hit a homer in the eighth inning.

With the Dodgers up 3–1, game five was crucial for the White Sox. Bob Shaw opposed young Sandy Koufax in the best-pitched game of the Series. Koufax and Stan Williams combined for a five-hitter but lost 1–0 as Shaw and Gerry Staley shut down the Dodgers. Ahead three games to one Alston gambled on winning with a relatively untried pitcher. He could afford a loss because he would have Podres and Drysdale ready for games six and seven if needed. Lopez had to win every game to stay alive — he couldn't afford a gamble.

The Series returned to Chicago after a day off. Wynn started for the third time in eighteen days. Wynn had lasted just 2⅔ innings in his last start before the Dodgers knocked him out. He was a big, strong bull of a man, but it was asking a great deal of a 39 year old to pitch three times in so short a span.

Alston countered with Johnny Podres, who was pitching with five days' rest. Los Angeles took a 2–0 lead into the fourth inning and then broke the game wide open with six runs. Snider, Wally Moon and Chuck Essegian all hit homers for the Dodgers. When Kluszewski got the White Sox three runs with his third homer, Alston brought in Sherry for the fourth time. He pitched 5⅔ shutout innings to wrap up the Series for the Dodgers.

The 1959 World Series wasn't a particularly interesting one, and there are no incidents that make it memorable. The Series' only real hero was Sherry, who won 2 games and saved 2 others while compiling an incredible 0.71 ERA. Bob Shaw pitched well for the White Sox, and Ted Kluzewski showed flashes of the great power that had made him a feared hitter. Charley Neal led the Dodgers with two homers and six runs driven in. Interestingly, all the stars of the 1959 World Series faded quickly. Sherry hung around for ten more years and had a couple of average seasons, but he never again was the overpowering pitcher of the last half of 1959.

Neal also slumped badly after the 1959 campaign. He had shown signs of power for an infielder accumulating 60 extra-base hits in 1959, but he went into rapid decline. He was out of baseball at 32 and never again matched his 1959 stats. Ted Kluzewski suffered the same fate. A bad back had robbed him of much of his power, and he played two more years before retiring after the 1961 season. Bob Shaw had an 11-year career that saw him win 108 games, but he never matched his 1959 season.

Statistically the two teams were evenly matched in batting and ERA. The Dodgers won because of their players, eight to be precise, had been through the special tension of a World Series before. The World Series was a new experience for the White Sox, and they were off their game. The Go-Go Sox actually were outrun by the Dodgers, who stole five bases to Chicago's two. The defensively superior White Sox also were outplayed by the Dodgers, who turned seven double plays to just two for the Aparicio-Fox duo.

Alston also deserves some credit. He took a team in transition and guided them through a tight pennant race and then made all the right moves in the World Series. He won his second world championship in five years, not bad for a manager often derided for being dull and colorless. He handled his pitchers brilliantly and had the Dodgers ready for a seventh game if necessary.

The Dodgers were an unusual World Series winner. Their most successful pitcher won 14 games. They had only two .300 hitters, and their leading home-run hitter (Snider) had just 23. Still, they beat two stronger teams in the National League for the pennant and then whipped a superior White Sox team in the World Series. Baseball is indeed a strange game.

One question arises from Lopez's handling of his staff. Why did he only use Billy Pierce in relief? Pierce was a crafty veteran who was coming off a mediocre season by his standards, 14-15 and an ERA of 3.62, but he was the kind of pitcher who might have excelled in a World Series. His 1959 record was better than Donovan's, and he would have given left-handers like Moon, Roseboro and Snider fits.

Because three games were played in Los Angeles before crowds in excess of 92,000, the 1959 Series set an attendance record for a six-game series. It also was the biggest payoff for players in history, $11,200 for the winners and $7,250 for the losers, quite a sum in those days of average salaries around $4,500.

Casey's Last Hurrah

Nineteen sixty witnessed the passing of power to a new generation in American politics as 70-year-old President Eisenhower was replaced by a dynamic, 43-year-old senator from Massachusetts, John F. Kennedy, who promised among other things to "get this country moving again." The country was tired of government by old men and yearned for excitement, something new. Kennedy capitalized on that feeling and launched a cult of youth and "vigah" in the process.

That year the first group of baby boomers entered high school. When they graduated from college eight years later, the country had undergone a revolution: civil rights marches, urban riots, the war in Vietnam and a wave of assassinations unmatched in American history.

Nineteen sixty also marked an important turning point for baseball. Another 70 year old, Casey Stengel, was given his walking papers by the Yankees and replaced by a younger man, Ralph Houk, just 41. George Weiss, the penny-pinching, guiding genius of the Yankees, also was let go. Under Houk and Weiss's successor, Roy Hamey, the Yankee dynasty would go on to win four more pennants in a row. But then neglect of the farm system, age and injuries would turn the Yankees into a run-of-the-mill team.

Major League baseball looked forward to 1960 with both optimism and trepidation. The nagging worry about the Continental League bothered the owners and was a constant problem until the Majors took the mater into their own hands and decided to expand. The sense of optimism was grounded in signs indicating that baseball was entering a new, prosperous decade.

For the fourth year in a row attendance rose, to 19,911,000, the third-highest figure in Major League history. The overall gain was just 4 percent, but the National League set a new mark, bettering the 1947 record of 10,388,000 by almost 300,000. A total of six National League clubs showed increases in attendance, with three National League teams setting attendance records. The Dodgers, despite a disappointing fourth-place finish, eclipsed Milwaukee's National League attendance record by drawing 2,254,000 fans to the Coliseum. The Giants, in their first year in Candlestick Park, attracted 1,795,000 fans, almost 200,000 more than they had ever drawn in the Polo Grounds. The Pirates, in winning their first pennant since 1927, shattered Pittsburgh's record by over 200,000. The only National League club to suffer a sharp drop in 1960 was Milwaukee, where the decline since the golden days of the mid-1950s continued. The Braves drew just 1,497,000, a decline of 250,000 from 1959 and almost 800,000 since their peak year in the Beer Capital of America.

The American League's performance lagged behind the senior circuit largely because of a great pennant race in the National League and the opening of a brand new ballpark in San Francisco. Even so the American League figure of 9,227,000 was its best since 1950. Five teams experienced improved attendance. The Orioles, who became a contender for the first time since moving from St. Louis, drew 1,188,000, a new Baltimore record. Even the White Sox topped their 1959 record and led all American League teams with 1,644,000 despite falling to third place. The Yankees showed a modest improvement but finished with their best figure since 1952. Baseball seemed to be booming.

Even the old nemesis of television was now showering baseball with untold wealth. Early in 1960 Ford Frick signed a new television deal, good until 1966, with the Gillette Safety Razor company and NBC. Gillette would continue to serve as the sole sponsor of the World Series and the All-Star game, and NBC would retain television rights. The package was valued at $31,250,000. Sixty percent of this money was to go to finance the Major League pension program, which in 1960 was extended to managers. Frick was pleased because the deal eased many of baseball's financial problems (*SN*, 3/2/60, p. 9).

Television Age magazine reported that 29 different sponsors would spend $39,000,000 on baseball in 1960, making it by far the most lucrative sport in the nation. Individual teams also cut rich deals with television stations. The Yankees received $900,000 from a variety of sponsors including Ballantine Beer and Camel cigarettes. The Indians, Tigers and Red Sox got $500,000, and even the lowly Senators received $250,000 from television.

In the National League the biggest beneficiary was the Dodgers, who derived $600,000 from TV despite televising only 11 away games with the Giants from San Francisco. The Cubs got $450,000, the Cards $400,000, with the Phillies receiving the least in the National League, $300,000. Two National

League teams, the Braves and Giants, did not televise their games, a mistake they would rectify in the near future (*SN*, 4/13/60, p. 26).

What these figures mean is simple. The Yankee payroll was estimated at $700,000, and the Dodgers' figure was $468,000 for 1960. Both teams would pocket a profit in 1960 from television before a game was played. This was probably true even for teams like the Phillies, whose television revenue was low, because their payroll was low. For example, only Robin Roberts of the Phillies commanded a major salary, $40,000, in 1960. The rest of the Phillies were mostly rookies making the Major League minimum.

Baseball also was drawing its television sponsors from solid businesses. Beer companies led the way: Hamm's, National Bohemian, Carling Black Label, Schlitz, Ballantine and Anheuser-Busch were among the biggest sponsors of baseball, helping to identify baseball and beer in the minds of another generation of young men. Cigarettes, car dealers and oil companies were a distant second. Baseball was a man's world on television in the late 1950s and early 1960s.

The Yankees were embarrassed by their performance in 1959, the worst since 1925, the year of Babe Ruth's big stomachache. Weiss had negotiated a major trade in December 1959 to strengthen the outfield when he talked his country cousins, the Kansas City A's, into giving up Roger Maris for Norm Siebern, 37-year-old Hank Bauer, Don Larsen and Marve Throneberry. The A's also threw in Joe DeMaestri, a good reserve shortstop. It was Weiss's fifth major deal with KC and his best by far (Golenbock, *Dynasty*, 249).

It was a fine trade for the Yankees because it gave them a 25-year-old solid outfielder who had already shown signs of considerable power. Maris had hit 28 homers in 1958 and had the perfect compact swing to take advantage of the short right-field fence in Yankee Stadium. The trade would also enable Stengel to alternate Berra in left field with Hector Lopez while Mantle patrolled center. It should give the Yankees one of their best outfields in years and stabilize the lineup at every position.

Not everyone thought the Yankees got the best of the deal. "Trader" Frank Lane told anyone who asked him that Norm Siebern was a better player than Maris. Lane was also willing to bet anyone that Siebern would outhit Maris in 1960 (*SN*, 2/3/60, p. 12). Lane was wrong on all counts. Siebern was a good player for two seasons, Maris a great one who helped establish another Yankee dynasty that would win five straight pennants.

One thing was clear: The Yankee organization had not stood still. Of the 37 men who played for Casey Stengel in his first year as manager, 1949, only one, Yogi Berra, took the field in 1960 (Koppett, 153). Weiss's farm system would continue to generate talented players for a couple of more years, but then the scrimping to save money, as the owners, Topping and Webb, got older and began planning to sell the team, began to tell. By 1964 the vaunted Yankee farm system was dry and capable of producing only marginal players like Roger Repoz.

The White Sox were the choice of the BWAA to repeat as American League champs. They secured 120 votes from 266 writers to finish first versus 70 for Cleveland and 66 for the Yankees. Over the winter the White Sox had revamped the team to make up for the lack of hitting in 1959. Without hurting the current team but taking a long-term risk, they secured Gene Freese from the Phillies to play third, Roy Sievers from Washington to play first and Minnie Minoso from Cleveland to complete their outfield. The total cost to the White Sox was heralded rookie Johnny Callison to the Phillies; Earl Battey, Don Mincher and $150,000 to the Senators; and John Romano, Bubba Phillips and Norm Cash to the Indians. It was a disastrous trade in the long run because five of the six players the White Sox gave up became solid Major Leaguers: Callison, Battey, Romano, Mincher and Cash. Minoso was 38, Sievers 33. Only Freese, at 26, seemed to have a future. These three helped the White Sox to lead the American League in hitting in 1960, raising the team batting average 20 points. Sievers hit .295 with 28 homers and 98 RBI. Freese hit .273, 17 homers and drove home 79 runs, and Minoso had a great year: .311, 20 homers and 105 RBI. Unfortunately, what the White Sox needed in 1960 was the kind of pitching that won the pennant for them in 1959. They didn't get it. The staff collapsed. Also Freese was a disaster at third. He had the second-lowest fielding percentage of any third baseman in the American League. His throwing made it dangerous to sit in the stands behind first base. After one season, Lopez had enough of him, and he was sent back to the National League, to Cincinnati for two pitchers, Cal McLish and Juan Pizzaro.

Frank Lane tried to strengthen the Indians, who had played so well in 1959 for the pennant chase, by giving up local hero and slugger Rocky Colavito for batting champ Harvey Kuenn of the Tigers. The trade made no sense. It was another example of Lane's trading for trading's sake. Since coming to Cleveland he had made 55 trades, both significant and minor. Among those he got rid of were Early Wynn and Al Smith in 1957. They helped the White Sox win the pennant in 1959. He send Roger Maris to KC for Vic Power and Woody Held, which helped the Indians in two positions. He sold Hoyt Wilhelm to Baltimore when Wilhelm still had many good years ahead of him. A deal with Boston, Jimmy Piersall for Gary Geiger and Vic Wertz, didn't make sense. Piersall brought his problems and quirky personality to Cleveland and was more trouble than he was worth. Lane's trades show no pattern of building.

The Kuenn-Colavito trade fits that description. Cleveland had led the American League in batting average and homers in 1959 so that Kuenn added nothing to their attack. He was only an average outfielder. Colavito was a fine right fielder, and at 27 one of the best power hitters in the American League, who had a half dozen good years ahead of him. Kuenn was three years older and never again was the player he had been in the mid-1950s.

Later in the season, with Cleveland struggling, Lane outdid himself—he traded managers, sending Joe Gordon to Detroit for Jimmy Dykes. It didn't matter. Dykes couldn't revive the Indians. In fact, they played poorer for him than they had for Gordon: 27-32 versus 49-46 under Gordon.

The 1960 season was a three-way race among the Yankees, the White Sox and the surprise team of the American League, the Baltimore Orioles. The Orioles had been picked to finish fifth but were a consistent challenger for the pennant all season.

Cleveland stayed in the hunt for a couple of months but then collapsed in the second half because of injuries and general poor play.

The Yankees started slowly and didn't reach the .500 mark until June 4. But then a 21-8 month featuring good hitting by Maris, Mantle and Skowron put the Yankees right in the middle of the pennant race. From June on they were never far from first place, but they couldn't shake the White Sox or the Orioles.

Chicago's hitting made them a threat all season, but the vaunted White Sox pitching collapsed. Early Wynn and Bob Shaw, the team's two big winners in 1959 with 40 victories between them, never got untracked. By the All-Star break, they were just 10-15, and Wynn in particular was getting hit hard. His ERA was 4.98, next to last in the American League among starters. Billy Pierce won 14 games with a good ERA, and Frank Baumann, a lefty Lopez picked up from Boston, not only won 13 games but led the American League with an ERA of 2.68. Bauman, a former Boston bonus baby, had never amounted to much in Beantown. After one good season in Chicago he reverted to form and ended his career five years later, having gone 19-24 after 1960. The White Sox were an enigma, finishing third with 87 victories, seven less than 1959. The team ERA rose over the League-leading 3.29 in 1959 to 3.60, but the defense was still solid except for Freese at third; and the hitting was the best in the American League. Lopez could never seem to get the team untracked. They didn't play badly, but they never played consistently well. Shaw's collapse was devastating, as was the failure of Gerry Staley out of the bull pen in the last two months of the year. After having gone 9-3 with a 1.80 ERA before the All-Star game, he was just 4-5 the second half of the season when the White Sox needed him the most. He pitched well and won 13 games, saving 10 others, but he was useless in August and September. His bull pen partner, "Turk" Lown, also had a poor year, with only two wins and five saves along with a high ERA.

The team that gave the Yankees fits most of the year was the surprising Orioles. Paul Richards's crop of "Baby Birds" finally matured in 1960. The club had been consistently losing money as huge sums were poured into player development, close to a million dollars in 1959 (Miller, 75). The planning began to pay off in 1960. Although picked to finish fourth or fifth, the Orioles, after a .500 April, came alive in May and June to challenge for first place. They were 45-35, in third place, just four games behind the League-leading Yankees at the All-Star break.

The team was young and suddenly jelled. The infield was anchored by

Brooks Robinson, who at 22 had the most experience. Rookies Ron Hansen at short and Marv Breeding at second took over as the double-play combination. At first base Richards installed Jim Gentile, whom he got from the Dodgers for nothing. Gentile had put together tremendous minor league stats but had been unable to oust Gil Hodges from first. Gentile was frustrated when the Orioles took a chance on him. Once Richards began to use him, he proved that not only could he hit, and hit with power, but also he was a superb defensive first baseman. By the All-Star break he was second in the American League at .328, with 12 homers and 59 RBI in only 186 times at bat. His RBI total was second in the American League behind only Roger Maris, who had 69 but in 83 more times at bat. Gentile finished with 21 homers and 98 RBI, the most in Orioles history at that point.

The Orioles' outfield was anchored by eccentric Jackie Brandt in center, whom Richards had gotten from the outfield-rich Giants for Billy O'Dell. Gene Woodling played left and Richards platooned in right. Gus Triandos was the catcher.

The real surprise of the Orioles was their pitching staff. Richards believed that his young arms were ready, thus his willingness to deal O'Dell, the first Orioles bonus baby. The Oriole staff tied the Yankees for the best league ERA and led the American League in complete games. Chuck Estrada, at 22 and in his first year, tied with Jim Perry for the American League lead in wins, with 18. Two other rookies were also starters and consistent winners: 21-year-old fire-balling Steve Barber was 10-7, and another 21 year old, Jack Fisher, went 12-11. The "dean" of the starters was Milt Pappas, also 21, but with two full years under his belt. He won 15. Hoyt Wilhelm and Skinny Brown also won in double figures. In all, the Orioles had six pitchers with ten or more victories.

By any standard it was a great year for the Birds. They won the most games in the team's history; they were young and talented and seemed to have their futures ahead of them. In 1960, despite a club payroll of $500,000 and another million spent on player development, the Orioles turned an after-tax profit of $315,000 (Miller, 76). For the next 20 years, the Orioles would be one of the most successful franchises in the American League. Richards had done his work well, and when he left to take over the new Houston franchise in the National League, he did so knowing that he had put the Orioles on the right path. He would never again duplicate the success he had with the White Sox and Orioles in the 1950s.

After staying close to the top for the first half of the season, Baltimore sagged in the month of July. But a strong August during which the team won 22 games, including one stretch of 13 out of 14, put them back in the race. Just before Labor Day, the Orioles' season peaked. In a three-game series in Baltimore, they swept the Yankees with Pappas and Fisher shutting out the Bombers, and Estrada managing a no-hitter until the seventh before winning 6-2. The sweep put Baltimore two games in front.

But the Yankees weren't dead. Beginning September 15, they got hot, first taking four in a row against the Orioles in Yankee Stadium and then continuing on to win their final 11 games of the season to finish with a 15-game winning streak. Their final margin over Baltimore was eight games. In effect, the Yankees won the pennant the way they had in the past. Beat your main competition and play your best ball when it counts. From August through the end of the season, the Yankees were 44-18, an incredible .710. For comparison the Orioles were 35-20, the White Sox 30-27.

The Yankees won because they were clearly the best team in the American League. They hit a record 193 homers, led the League in runs and had the lowest team ERA — an unbeatable combination. Maris had a great year and won the MVP award for hitting 39 homers and leading the American League with 112 RBI. Mantle hit 40 homers to lead the American League and drove in 94 runs. Skowron was the team's only .300 hitter, and he hit 26 homers and drove in 91 runs. Berra caught 63 games and played 36 in the outfield. He hit 15 homers and drove in 62 runs. The Yankees' defense was solid, and the pitching was surprisingly good. They led in team ERA, with 3.52, although no one won more than 15 games. Art Ditmar won 15 with a low ERA and Whitey Ford 12, also with a low ERA. Jim Coates went 13-3, starting and relieving. The Yankees lacked the kind of starters that characterized the team in the early 1950s, the Raschis, Reynolds, Lopats, but they had tremendous depth in 1960. They led the American League in shutouts and had the most saves in the League. They were a superb professional team and didn't beat themselves.

Cleveland finished fourth, and the Senators in their last year in Washington won 73 games, their highest total since 1953. The Senators were developing a fine, young team. Harmon Killebrew, after a sluggish first half, hit 27 homers in the second part of the season to finish with 31. Earl Battey, who came over in the Sievers trade, proved a fine receiver and hit 15 homers. Jim Lemon drove in 100 runs and hit 38 homers. Bob Allison slipped from his rookie of the year numbers in 1959 but was still a fine outfielder. The Senators had some talent down on the farm ready to blossom — Don Mincher, Jimmie Hall, Jim Katt and Zorro Versalles. The team was short on pitching but was primed to contend in the near future. Unfortunately, it wouldn't be in Washington but in the Twin Cities.

Detroit, Boston and Kansas City rounded out the American League. The Tigers had some talented long-ball hitters — Kaline, Colavito, Maxwell and Norm Cash — who enabled them to finish second to the Yankees in homers. But the team batting average, .239, tied the hapless Phillies for the lowest in the Majors. The Tigers also made the second-highest number of errors and turned the fewest double plays in the American League. The pitching staff had a good ERA, but their two biggest winners, Frank Lary and Jim Bunning, finished 26-29.

Boston finished seventh on merit. The team had the highest ERA in the

American League and failed to hit up to past Red Sox teams. Ted Williams ended his career on an up note with a homer in his last at bat. He had 29 for the year along with a .316 batting average, not bad for a 42 year old. Another veteran, Vic Wertz, had a good year, driving in 100 runs. Bill Monbouquette was the team's big winner, with 14 victories, and Mike Fornieles was solid in relief—14 saves, 10 wins and an ERA of 2.64. The rest of the staff was awful.

Kansas City continued to be staffed by ex-Yankees, most of whom were underachievers or over the hill. Norm Siebern was their best hitter, finishing with 19 homers and a .279 average, but he didn't top Maris's figures as Frank Lane had predicted. Lefty Bud Daley started brilliantly, winning 12 of 16 decisions by the All-Star break, but finished just 16-16. Ray Herbert, who finished 14-15 with a low 3.28, was KC's best pitcher. He went 11-6 during the second half of the year. In 1960 Charley Finley purchased control of KC, and the team's days of serving as a training ground for the Yankees ended. Finley began the process of reviving the franchise, signing talented prospects and pouring money into player development.

Stengel looked forward to the World Series, which he was sure would be his last. He wanted to top Joe McCarthy, with whom he was tied for winning the most World Series, seven. It looked possible as the Yankees were a clear favorite to beat the surprising National League champs, the Pittsburgh Pirates.

Beat 'em Bucs

Over the senior circuit the Giants were an overwhelming choice to win the pennant. They had been in the chase until the last week of the 1959 season, and they would have Willie McCovey for the whole season; plus they had added Billy O'Dell and Billy Loes to provide pitching depth. They also got Don Blasingame from the Cardinals to help the infield defensively, as well as to add speed to the lineup. Of 266 sports writers, 131 picked the Giants to win; 88 chose the Braves, with the Dodgers coming in third with 34 first-place votes. In fourth place with just 11 votes were the Pirates, the eventual surprise winner in 1960 (*SNG*, 1961, p. 57).

For the third year in a row, a different team won the pennant in the National League, a testament to the senior circuit's better balance. The Dodgers had gone from seventh to first in 1959, whereas the Pirates would rise from fourth to first in 1960. Interestingly, this balance would continue until the development of a new Sandy Koufax–led Dodger team in 1963. The Reds would bounce from sixth to first in 1961, and the Giants would win in 1962—five different winners in five years for the National League.

Although never running away with the race, the Pirates won handily. At the beginning of every month in the season they were in first place, with their margin growing slowly but steadily during the season. They went into first place May 30 and stayed except for one day, July 24, for the rest of the season. They were challenged at different times by the Giants, Cards and Braves and beat back each one despite disbelief in Pittsburgh's talents. The Bucs had the uncanny habit of pulling lost games out. They won 21 games in their last at bat and an incredible 12 with two out in their last at bat (*S&S*, 1961, p. 15).

The 1960 Pirates were a true Cinderella team, a club that had been developing over a couple of years and then jelled solidly in one season. Only Dick Groat at short had a career year, winning the batting title with a .325 average. And even he came close to that figure a couple of times in his career. The Bucs had a number of good, not great players, who came together for a good, not great, year. The only Hall of Famer on the team, Roberto Clemente, hit .314, a figure he topped nine times in his career.

The Pirates had a great infield of Don Hoak at third, Groat at short, Mazeroski at second and Dick Stuart and Rocky Nelson alternating first. Defensively Hoak and Mazeroski were the best in the National League at their positions, and Groat was an able if unspectacular fielder. Stuart had concrete hands, but Nelson was a fine fielder. Hoak hit well in 1960, .282 with 79 RBI, many of which came late in key games. Stuart and Nelson combined for 30 homers and 118 RBI.

The outfield of Clemente in right, Virdon and Gino Cimoli in center, and Bob Skinner in left was one of the fastest in the National League. Along with hitting .300, Clemente also led the Bucs with 94 RBI, and Skinner drove in 86 runs. Lefty Smokey Burgess and right-handed hitter Hal Smith handled the catching. Between them they hit 18 homers and drove in 84 runs.

Pirate pitching was second in ERA only to the Dodgers and issued the fewest walks in the Majors. They also allowed the fewest homers in the National League, 105. Bob Friend bounced back from a disastrous 8-19 year to win 18 games, and Vern Law won 20. Lefty Harvey Haddix chipped in with 11 wins and Vinegar Bend Mizell, who came over from the Cards in a trade for Julian Javier (who couldn't oust Mazeroski from second base), was 13-5 for the Pirates. Roy Face led the National League with 68 appearances and won 10 games, saving 24 others.

Danny Murtaugh was the perfect manager for this blend of young players and vets. He didn't interfere that much, never panicked and handled his pitching staff just about perfectly. According to Vern Law, Murtaugh was not only a fine communicator, but he also knew what his players were capable of. He believed in his team and they trusted him (Law to author, 5/19/95). It was a fine, low-keyed job of managing, nothing flashy but always having the right person at the right spot. He deserved the honor of Manager of the Year given him by *The Sporting News*.

The Braves, under new manager Charley Dressen, gave the Pirates a battle. Eventually they wound up second, but they won two more games than in 1959. A slow 16-16 start left them 4½ games out at the beginning of June. Warren

Spahn struggled with a 4-4 record at this point, and there was talk that at 39 he was finally finished. He suddenly got straightened out and went 17-6 from June 1 on to put the Braves in contention. Instead of being finished he won 96 games after his thirty-ninth birthday. Led by Spahn, Burdette and Bob Buhl, the Braves got to within two games by the end of July. These three won 56 games versus just 32 defeats, but the Braves were done in by the failure of their second-line pitchers. At the All-Star break, Carlton Willey and Juan Pizzaro were 9-5, and along with Joey Jay, they should have provided the depth to overtake the Pirates. But all three collapsed in the second half of the season. Willey and Pizzaro went 3-9 after the All-Star break, and Jay was just 11-11 overall. The danger for the Braves was that not only was Spahn 39, but Burdette would be 34 at the end of the year and Buhl 32. They had failed to develop the younger arms to replace their big three. Haney had been criticized for overusing his three key starters in 1959, but Dressen wound up using them almost as much. They started 98 games for him versus 100 for Haney.

Don McMahon's failure out of the bull pen was another factor in the Braves' collapse. From 5-3 and a 2.97 ERA in 1959 he dropped to 3-6, with just ten saves and an inflated ERA of 5.94.

The Braves still had a potent offense. Led by Eddie Mathews's 39, Hank Aaron's 40 and Joe Adcock's 25, they hit 170 homers, just seven less than the year before. They also scored the same number of runs, 724, as in 1959, but there were too many holes developing in the lineup. For the third year in a row, Wes Covington flopped, hitting just .249 with 10 homers and only 35 RBI. Red Schoendienst only got to bat 257 times, and Johnny Logan hit .245 in his last year as a regular.

The Braves had gotten old. They had more ten-year men in their lineup than any team in the National League: ten. The team that won the World Series in 1957 and the pennant the next season had been put together by John Quinn in the early 1950s. The farm system that produced Eddie Mathews, Hank Aaron, Warren Spahn, Bob Buhl, Del Crandall and Johnny Logan developed nothing of value after 1954, when Aaron entered the Majors. Milwaukee's farm system products on a Major League roster in 1960 included such names as Don Nottebart, Chuck Cottier, Ed Haas, Felix Mantilla, Al Spangler. None of them helped to sustain the Braves the way the Yankee farm system kept the Yankee dynasty alive.

During the 1960 pennant chase, Aaron had predicted that by August the Braves would pass the Pirates like a jet. The plane never got off the ground, and 1960 marked a turning point for the Braves, as they were not a factor in any pennant race until their surprise victory in the National League West as the Atlanta Braves almost a decade later in 1969.

The Cardinals, led by manager Solly Hemus, surprised everyone by finishing third with 86 wins, rising from a seventh-place finish in 1959. After a slow start that found them 9½ games out by the end of June, the Cardinals played some of the best baseball in the National League the second half of the season. They were 53-33 from July on, which was one game better than the Pirates. The Cardinals' hitting was not up to par. Only Ken Boyer hit over .300, and he led the team with 32 homers and 97 RBI. But Stan Musial bounced back from a poor 1959 to hit .275, with 17 homers, playing mostly in left field. Bill White took over first base and not only fielded the position brilliantly but showed signs of hitting, with a .283 average and 16 homers. Curt Flood was still struggling to find his batting stroke, but he had the highest fielding percentage of any National League outfielder.

The Cardinals did well because of their pitching. Ernie Broglio, who had come over to them from the Giants after the 1958 season, started poorly but finished with 21 victories, 20 after Memorial Day, to tie Spahn for most wins in the National League. Lindy McDaniel won 12 and saved another 26 games and was even better coming out of the bull pen than Elroy Face in 1960. Larry Jackson won 18, rookie Ray Sadecki won 9 and Curt Simmons, whom the Cards picked up when the Phillies released him, chipped in with 7 wins, but had a low 2.66 ERA.

The Dodgers finished fourth and were never a factor in the pennant race. They had losing records in May and June and played just .500 baseball in August and September. Their failure was a team effort. Gil Hodges got hurt and was finished as a full-time player. He hit .197 and only played in 92 games in the field. Carl Furillo hurt his leg and was released after playing eight games. Duke Snider got to bat just 235 times and hit .243, with 14 homers. The Brooklyn dynasty was over, and the LA one had not yet arrived. The Dodgers were a team in transition.

Frank Howard, LA's most heralded newcomer, had a good year, leading the team with 23 homers and finishing second with 77 RBI to first baseman Norm Larker's 78. This was enough to win Howard Rookie of the Year laurels. Another rookie, Tommy Davis, hit .276 but showed signs of talent at bat. Don Demeter, who had helped lead the Dodgers to a pennant with a great first half in 1959, struggled all year and eventually lost his job. John Roseboro had a terrible year, hitting only .203.

The Dodgers had the best starting pitching in the National League. They led in ERA and for the second year in a row recorded over 1000 strikeouts. Don Drysdale, with 246, led the National League and went 15-14. Johnny Podres was 14-12, Stan Williams and Larry Sherry both 14-10. The Dodger bull pen recorded just 20 saves, second lowest in the National League, and this crippled the Dodgers all season.

Sandy Koufax was struggling to gain control and finished just 8-13, but he was on the brink of overpowering stardom. Early in 1961 catcher Norm Sherry convinced him that he did not have to try to strike out every hitter. Koufax went on to have six of the greatest years in pitching history: three Cy Young Awards, six straight years of 200 or more strikeouts, three years of

300-plus strikeouts and 129 victories. All this despite having chronic arm, finger and elbow problems.

The most dramatic development of the 1960 season was the near-total collapse of the heavily favored Giants. Nothing worked for them, including the opening of Major League baseball's first all-new ballpark since Yankee stadium, Candlestick Park. There were complaints right from the beginning about the playing conditions. Winds whipped off the bay, making every fly ball an adventure, and at night temperatures plunged to near frigid levels. Day games were bearable, but in late afternoon the winds began to build slowly as temperatures dropped. The Giants seemed demoralized, and the players complained about the conditions. Still, the Giants played .584 ball at home, .442 on the road. Where you saw a major difference was in homers. The powerful Giants had the fewest home runs at home, 46, but led the National League with road homers, 84.

But it wasn't the ballpark that beat the Giants. It was a breakdown at nearly every level of play. Willie McCovey suffered from the sophomore jinx and wound up back in the minors. He hit just .238 for the season. Don Blasingame hit a career low .235 and proved a defensive liability instead of an asset. The trade for Billy O'Dell and Billy Loes was also a flop. O'Dell went 8-13, and Loes was 3-2 with just five saves. The rest of the staff was equally useless. Johnny Antonelli was just 6-7, and Jack Sanford, Sam Jones and Mike McCormick went 45-40 among them.

Manager Rigney was fired with the Giants eight games over .500, 33-25, and superscout Tom Sheehan took over. Rigney had been a marked man because of his handling of the pitching staff in September 1959.

Sheehan was a poor choice. He was out of touch with the modern player, and the Giants went into a complete nosedive, winning just 46 of 96 games under him. After the season, Al Dark was hired to revive the team.

The Reds, Cubs and Phillies brought up the rear. Of the three only the Reds showed any promise. Vada Pinson and Frank Robinson had poor years for them. Pinson hit .287, 20 homers and only 61 RBI; Robinson hit .297, with 31 homers and 83 RBI. Gus Bell faltered, hitting .262, with only 12 homers and just 62 RBI. At 31 he was washed up. Wally Post over from the Phillies put up some good numbers in about half the games he played: .281 with 17 homers. The failure of the Reds' pitchers really hurt them. The team ERA, 4.00, just nosed out the cellar-dwelling Phillies for sixth place. Bob Purkey led the Reds with a 17-11 record, and young Jim O'Toole showed potential in splitting 22 decisions. Don Newcombe was about finished and Cal McLish, who had won 19 games for Cleveland in 1959, went 4-14 for the Reds.

The Cubs narrowly beat the Phillies for seventh place by winning 60 games to the Phillies' 59. The Cubs had the worse team ERA and the League's biggest loser in Glen Hobbie, who went 16-20. Ernie Banks continued to hit, topping the 40 mark in homers for the fifth and last time with 41. He also drove in 112 runs. Rookie third sacker Ron Santo showed flashes of talent. He hit nine homers and drove in 44 runs in about two thirds of a season. Everyone predicted great things for him.

The Phillies finished last for the third year in a row under a new manager, Gene Mauch, who took over for Eddie Sawyer. Sawyer quit after one game, uttering the memorable quote, "I'm 49 and I would like to live to 50." The implication was that the Phillies would be terrible. They were. Only KC in the American League lost more games. The Phillies were being retooled by John Quinn, and he brought in a slew of young players to try to find the right mix. Some of the new Phillies showed flashes of talent. Johnny Callison looked like he might prove a good outfielder and a potential home-run hitter. Tony Gonzalez, whom Quinn got from the Reds, hit with occasional power, and Tony Taylor, who came over from the Cubs for Ed Bouchee and pitcher Don Cardwell, led the Phillies in batting with a .287 average. He also fielded his position well. Rookie Ruben Amaro won the shortstop job and formed a fine double-play combination with Taylor. Aside from relief pitcher Dick Farrell, who won ten games, the Phillies' staff was awful. Robin Roberts was 12-16, Gene Conley feuding with Mauch was 8-14 and Jim Owens, who had won 12 games in 1959, dropped to 4-14. The short-term future looked grim for the Phillies.

The Yankees entered the World Series as a prohibitive favorite. They had won 15 games in a row at the end of the season to blow away the Orioles, and there seemed no reason why they shouldn't continue to play this kind of baseball. But the 1960 World Series was strange. The Pirates were a gutty blend of veterans and young players who showed during the National League campaign that they didn't give up. And Stengel made an uncharacteristic blunder that set the stage for the Yankees' defeat. He passed over Whitey Ford to open the Series in Pittsburgh so as to have him ready for game three in Yankee Stadium, where Ford was virtually unbeatable (Golenbock, *Dynasty*, 259). His choice to open for the Yankees was Art Ditmar, a 31-year-old journeyman right-hander who came to New York in one of Weiss's rapes of KC. Ditmar once lost 22 games in a season. For the Yankees in 1960 he was the leader in victories with 15 but had a total of 9⅔ innings of World Series experience. This decision was to cost the Yankees dearly. The Pirates responded by starting their ace, Vern Law, a 20-game winner and easy choice for the Cy Young Award.

Law won 6–4, with Face getting a save even though he gave up a ninth-inning two-run homer to Elston Howard. The game wasn't as close as the score. The Pirates built up a 6–2 lead, and the Yankees made uncharacteristic errors in the field. Stengel pinch-hit in the second inning for his starting third baseman, Clete Boyer, in hopes of breaking the game open. The tactic didn't work, and neither did much else that Stengel tried in the 1960 Series.

The Yankees, behind Bob Turley, who had pitched only 173 innings in 1960, bounced back and bombed the Pirates 16–3 in game two. It was the start of a pattern that defied reason. The Pirates would win the close games, and the Yankees would win by scoring in double figures.

The Series transferred to New York for game three, which Ford won easily, shutting out the Pirates on just four hits, 10–0. It looked like the Yankees were back in the driver's seat. But in game four, Law, pitching on two days' rest and with another save from Face, won 3–2. Ralph Terry pitched well for the Yankees in a losing cause.

The fifth game, always crucial in a short series, went to the Pirates as Harvey Haddix outdueled Ditmar. Again Face got a save with 2⅔ inning of hitless relief. The Pirates were now in command, with the Series finishing back in Pittsburgh. Ford, on two days' rest, pitched his second shutout as the Yankees again massacred the Pirates 12–0. Bob Friend was beaten for the second time. In two starts against the Yankees he had lasted six innings with an ERA of 13.50.

The seventh and deciding game saw Law start for the third time but with three days' rest. He was given a four-run lead but couldn't hold it as the Yankees strafed Law and Face. Going into the eighth inning the Yankees had a seemingly insurmountable 7–4 lead, when the Pirates showed the combination of grit and luck that made them National League champs.

Bobby Shantz was entering his fifth inning in relief. The 35 year old had not pitched that long all season. He never retired a batter in the eighth. Cimoli singled, and then Bill Virdon hit a sure double-play grounder to Kubek at short. The ball hit a clump of dirt in the rock-yard Pittsburgh infield, bounced up and hit Kubek in the throat. Kubek had to leave the game. Instead of two out, there were two on. Groat singled in one run. Jim Coates, 13-3 in 1960 but another journeyman, came on for Shantz. Skinner bunted the runners up to second and third. The Yankees maintained a two-run lead, and all Coates had to do to get them out of danger was get one out. Clemente bounced to Skowron at first, but Coates failed to cover as the Pirates made the score 7–6. With runners at first and third and the game on the line Coates threw a 3-2 fastball to catcher Hal Smith, a former Yankee, who hit it over the left-field fence to give the Pirates a 9–7 lead. Chants of "Beat 'em Bucs" rained down on the Yankees as the Pirates had done the impossible — scored five runs off the Yankee bull pen.

The Yankees weren't finished. Friend came on to get the final three outs for the Pirates. He got none. After two hits, Haddix replaced him. Haddix got three outs, but the Yankees scored the tying runs on a single by Mantle and an infield ground-out by Berra. In the bottom of the ninth, Stengel turned the ball over to Terry, and Mazeroski hit his second pitch far over the left-center fence and won the Series. It was the first time that a World Series had ended on a home run.

The impossible had happened. The Pirates, with a team ERA of 7.11, had beaten the Yankees, whose ERA was 3.54. The Yankees hit .338, the Pirates

.256. Kubeck hit .333, Mantle .400 with 3 homers, Berra .318, Skowron .375 and Bobby Richardson got 11 hits for a .375 average. The Yankees should have won easily. But questionable decisions by Stengel and some gutty pitching by Law, Face and Haddix had done the Yankees in. Too many Yankees struck out, 40 versus just 26 Pirates who went down on strikes. The vaunted Yankee defense had holes, making eight errors to four for the Pirates.

For the fifth time in seven World Series, the National League had won. Beginning after World War II the American League won seven of ten World Series. In the last five years of the 1950s the National League won three of five. It looked as if the tide had turned in favor of the National League after years of American League (read Yankee) domination. Great Yankee teams would win two in a row, 1961 and 1962, but then the National League would assert itself as the better talent, especially black players, would push the senior circuit to the fore. From 1963 to 1969 the National League would win five times to just two American League victories.

Shortly after the Series, Stengel and Weiss were let go, and an era had come to an end. The 15 years following World War II had witnessed many changes in American life. Baseball was not able to avoid change itself, despite the traditionalism and hidebound qualities that had characterized the game. Both the country and baseball were better off as the result of the events of this generation.

Conclusion:
Baseball Survives
by the Skin of Its Teeth

The 15 years from the end of World War II to the first expansion in 1960 constitutes a paradoxical period in the history of baseball. For some, like Harold Rosenthal in *The Ten Best Years of Baseball* or Roger Kahn in *The Era*, it was baseball's Golden Age, the last time when the original 16 teams still played in the same 11 cities where modern baseball emerged in 1903. Others, like the reigning baseball statistic guru, Bill James, see this period as "the most one-dimensional, uniform, predictable version of the game that has ever been offered for sale"—get on base and wait for someone to hit a home run (Bill James, *Historical Baseball Abstract*, 206).

For the fan, this 15-year period saw some of the most unforgettable moments in baseball history — Bobby Thomson's homer to win the 1951 play-offs, Don Larsen's World Series perfect game, Willie Mays's unbelievable catch of Vic Wertz's drive in the 1954 World Series, Ted Williams's homer in his last at bat. In fact, during these years many of baseball's most exciting moments did take place. In preparing a selection for *The Sporting News* of *Baseball's 50 Greatest Games*, Lowell Reidenbaugh chose a dozen from this era, more than any comparable period in baseball history.

Despite the excitement generated on the field in the decade and a half after World War II, the game lurched from one crisis to another off the field. But just as in the past, when baseball had been challenged by new threats — the founding of the American League in 1903, the threat from the Federal League on the eve of World War I, the economic devastation caused by the Great Depression, the possibility that professional baseball would be closed down for the duration of World War II — the game survived somehow. Each crisis generated its own solution, which the leaders of baseball were forced, often reluctantly, to accept. One thinks of public opinion's forcing the National League to accept the equal status of the American League in 1903 or the resort to such "gimmicks" as the All-Star game, night baseball and radio broadcasting to survive problems in the past.

The generation after World War II saw the game of baseball deal with an equally grave set of economic, social and game-related problems. Some were handled creatively, some clumsily, but by the beginning of John F. Kennedy's aptly named "New Frontier," baseball was ready to enter a new era of growth, development and prosperity. This new era was rooted in the changes that baseball successfully underwent between the end of World War II and the first expansion of the game in 1961.

One of the most intractable and embarrassing flaws in baseball's claim to be America's Game was the existence of racial segregation. That came to an end in the aftermath of the war. In 1947 baseball was integrated, ending an 80-year period when a significantly talented proportion of the population, the African American, was banned from the Majors. The ending of the misnamed "Gentlemen's Agreement" to keep blacks out of baseball by the Major League owners took most of this period to complete. The process was a painful one and took a terrible personal and psychological toll on Jackie Robinson, the man who broke the color barrier. Gradually, over a dozen years — one is tempted to say "with all deliberate speed" — baseball was integrated. In 1957 the Phillies became the last National League team to field a black in their lineup. The Tigers added a black player the next year. The Boston Red Sox had the ignominious distinction of being the last team in the Majors to have a black player, the forgettable Pumpsie Green. It took them 12 years and 3 months after Jackie Robinson joined the Dodgers to do so.

On the eve of expansion in 1960, African Americans constituted 14.5 percent of the 400 players on the Major League rosters, a figure slightly higher than their percentage in the United States population. Baseball had often lagged in the past in coming to grips with the social and economic problems that plagued the game, but at least in integration it was ahead of most other sectors of the nation. What other branch of American society could show this degree of integration by 1960 — certainly not industry, politics, the universities or even the churches. Seven years before *Brown vs. the Board of Education*, Jackie Robinson had proved that "separate but equal" was a joke.

Whereas some teams had only undertaken token integration — the Yankees come to mind — others like the Dodgers, Giants, Indians had made themselves into successful franchises by recruiting talented black players. The Negro Leagues were destroyed in the process, but it was a price African Americans were willing to pay. By 1960 great black players had proven themselves in all phases of baseball. During the 1950s they were particularly influential in the

National League, where they won eight Most Valuable Player Awards and seven Rookie of the Year Awards. Between 1949 and 1960 blacks won four batting championships and led the National League in homers four times. Progress in the American League was slower. The first African American to win an MVP Award there was Elston Howard in 1963. No black in the American League won a batting title in these years, and only one, Larry Doby, captured a homer title.

The African American contribution to baseball was significant in other ways. Black players were responsible for restoring the element of speed to the game. The stolen base had been a dying art in baseball for over three decades. For example, in 1950 Dom DiMaggio led the American League with 15 stolen bases. In the Negro Leagues, where African Americans honed their talents, base stealing was a vital part of the game. Beginning with Jackie Robinson in 1947, blacks led the National League in stolen bases for 12 of 14 years. Willie Mays became the first player in the National League to steal 40 bases since 1929, and Maury Wills's 50 steals in 1960 represented the highest figure in the National League since Max Carey in 1923. African Americans brought back the running game, and both leagues began to open up baseball in the late 1950s. In the American League Luis Aparicio, who played against blacks in Latin America, led the League in steals for nine straight years, a record not likely to be broken soon.

The slowness of the American League to integrate may explain why the talent edge had passed to the National League by the late 1950s. The American League, really the Yankees, dominated the World Series in the years after World War II. American League teams won the World Series seven years in a row, 1947–1953. But from 1954 to 1960 the edge swung to the National League, which won in five of the next seven years. Even the All-Star game saw the National League creep up on the American League, which had a huge edge up to the end of World War II, winning 12 of 16 games. During the 1950s the National League won seven times, the American League four. There were two games in 1959. Great black players, especially Willie Mays, Ernie Banks and Hank Aaron, played a part in this swing to National League domination.

Another way of examining African American influence in the National League as explanation for the senior circuit's dominance is to look at the players who entered the Majors from 1954 to 1960, when the pace of integration quickened. Twenty-eight blacks joined the National League, 11 the American League. More significant, among the National League black players were Hank Aaron, Roberto Clemente, Bob Gibson and Frank Robinson, all future Hall of Famers. None of the American League black players were of that caliber.

After World War II baseball confronted other challenges that mirrored changes experienced by the nation as it adjusted to a new postwar reality. As David Voigt has noted, baseball played a major role in reconciling the country to the bewildering pace of change that occurred after the war. As it had in the past, baseball and the traditions that surrounded the game helped the American public accept changes sweeping the country, of which those connected to the transformation of the nation's urban areas were the most intractable.

America's population was shifting both internally and externally. The core urban areas were losing population to the exploding suburbs. At the same time the fastest growing parts of the nation were in the South and the West. Major League baseball confronted the consequences of this reality in the 1950s.

Baseball stadiums had been located in the center of the major cities since the game's formative period early in the twentieth century. Fifteen ballparks opened between 1909 and 1923 — all along the axis of streetcar or subway lines in the heart of the city. By the mid-1950s the rising popularity of the automobile threatened Major League baseball. People were reluctant to drive to games because of a lack of parking, as well as a fear of vandalism and crime. In 1960 baseball was on the eve of a new ballpark-building boom. Beginning that year with the opening of Candlestick Park in San Francisco and lasting for 17 years, new stadiums would open in fifteen cities. They were all designed to accommodate cars and in most cases were built either in the commercially prosperous downtown areas or on the fringes of the cities, with easy access to the suburbs.

Baseball had to find a way to reach its new audience. One way was to begin to move franchises from markets that could not support them. The Major League franchises after World War II were located in the same general areas as they had been when Theodore Roosevelt ran for president in 1904. The modern game emerged at a time when the nation's population was just over 70 million. By the 1950s it was rising past 150 million, and the shift to the South and West was becoming noticeable. California and other parts of the far West had begun to boom during World War II as the aircraft and ship-building industries thrived there. After the war the Pacific Coast League requested Major League status. That was rejected by baseball's leadership, but Commissioner Ford Frick in 1952 stated that before a decade passed, Major League baseball would reach California. What he didn't specify was whether the form it took would be a third league or just expansion.

Expansion was the result of baseball's internal dynamics. In 1953, with little warning, the sanctity of traditional baseball was broken when Lou Perini moved the Boston Braves to Milwaukee. His success fueled similar franchise shifts to Baltimore and Kansas City in the next two years. Neither Baltimore nor Kansas City matched Milwaukee's financial or baseball success. They were poor teams and in the case of KC badly administered. Baltimore only became a serious Major League contender in 1960, six years after Paul Richards had begun the transformation of the St. Louis Browns. KC failed at all levels, and eventually the team was taken out of the city in 1967 by Charles O. Finley.

But the lesson of expansion was simple: The unthinkable had now become thinkable, and there were profits to be milked from these virgin areas.

The real shock to baseball came with the move to California in 1958 of two of the most successful franchises in the National League, the Brooklyn Dodgers and the New York Giants. Interestingly enough, it was Bill Veeck, one of baseball's secular saints, not Walter O'Malley, who first gave serious consideration to taking a Major League team — in his case, the lowly St. Louis Browns — westward. Veeck's reason was the same capitalist one as O'Malley's: He could make more money in California than in St. Louis, which had long been a Cardinals town. When Gussie Busch of Budweiser bought the Cardinals in 1953 and pledged his huge fortune to building a contender, Veeck knew he couldn't survive in the Gateway City. Veeck's role in opening baseball to a move to California may not fit into the "O'Malley as devil" theory but it does suit the facts.

O'Malley and Horace Stoneham were the innovators of the move to California because the situation in New York was enmeshed in city and state politics. As Neil Sullivan points out in his fine study *The Dodgers Move West*, O'Malley would have stayed in the New York area if he had gotten the land on which to build his new ballpark with his own money. Stoneham had been thinking about moving the Giants for some time but to Minneapolis, where he owned the baseball rights, not to San Francisco. It is hard to see how California could be denied Major League baseball when the state possessed in Los Angeles one of the fastest-growing metropolitan areas in the nation and had powerful friends in Washington like Vice President Nixon and Senate minority leader William Knowland.

Baseball in California was an immense financial success, especially for the Dodgers. The Giants' situation was more problematic. San Francisco lured Stoneham with the offer of a state-of-the-art ballpark. What he got with Candlestick Park was a disaster by the bay. Despite one of the most productive farm systems in baseball, San Franciscans have never embraced the Giants with the same fervor that the Angelinos did the Dodgers. The other teams in both leagues that have followed the Dodgers and Giants westward — the Angels, Oakland, San Diego and later Seattle — have not duplicated their success. But each franchise except Seattle won pennants and in the case of Oakland produced one great dynasty in the early 1970s and a fine club in the late 1980s. Baseball belonged in the West. It was tragic that the move there was at the expense of New York and Brooklyn, areas that had been so fiercely loyal to their teams in the past.

The franchise moves of the 1953–1958 period generated the last serious attempt to form a new league. The Continental League was born in 1958, fathered by a New York power broker, William Shea, and god-fathered by baseball's great innovator, Branch Rickey. Building on the growing public demand for expansion and the mounting political pressure exerted by powerful politicians such as Senator Estes Kefauver and Representative Emmanuel Celler, the Continental League threw a scare into Major League baseball. Eventually the Majors responded not by granting the Continental League equal status as they had done with the American League in 1903 but by undertaking expansion. They undermined the appeal of the Continental League by expanding to four new cities among the eight founding members of the new league: Minneapolis–St. Paul, New York, Los Angeles and Houston. Eventually seven of the eight cities that made up the Continental League received Major League franchises — the exception was Buffalo — testifying to the groundwork that Shea and Rickey had laid. In a sense expansion was Rickey's last contribution to Major League baseball. It was not as important as his role in ending racial segregation in baseball, but it ranked with the development of the farm system concept as among the game's great innovations.

Baseball also confronted a new challenge with the dramatic emergence of television in the years after World War II. A tiny cloud in 1947, television was perceived as a serious threat to the game by the mid-1950s. At first baseball's leadership was at a loss as to how to deal with television, whether to view it as a deadly enemy or as a possible boon. Rickey, it is interesting to note, differentiated between radio and television. The former he believed created new fans; the latter satiated them by making it too easy to follow their team. He was wrong, but his argument seemed unanswerable in the early 1950s.

After a decade of near panic, baseball finally made its peace with television. First Commissioner Chandler and then his successor, Ford Frick, discovered that television could be made to pay for some of baseball's problems. The pension program, the foundation of an arrangement between owners and players that kept peace for twenty years, was financed by television revenues derived from the All-Star game and the World Series. In the meantime other owners discovered that there were enormous profits to be made from televising their games. By 1960 most Major League clubs were meeting the costs of their player payrolls out of television revenues. Baseball was on the eve of a great boom in television income, a boom that would start slowly in the 1960s and then rise enormously in the 1970s and 1980s, before leveling off in the early 1990s.

The game of baseball survived its various challenges in the generation after World War II. Some of the solutions were arrived at intelligently, some clumsily, but by the early 1960s baseball was a stronger, healthier, better balanced institution than ever before. The 1946–1960 era had been dominated by two teams, the Yankees in the American League and the Dodgers in the senior circuit. Between them they won 17 pennants and 10 World Series. Baseball was seriously unbalanced. In the next comparable generation, 1961–1975, 12 teams won pennants, and 9 different clubs won World Series.

The generation after World War II witnessed some of the most exciting baseball in the game's history and one of the most innovative eras administratively and structurally. Major League baseball went through an era of crisis as dramatic as any in its long, complex history. In spite of a leadership that often was puerile, mean spirited and even cowardly, the game survived. Bismarck once remarked that God looked after children, drunkards and the United States of America. He might have added Major League baseball in the years 1946–1960.

Appendix 1:
Statistics

1946

National League

Club	Won	Lost	Pct	Games Back
St. Louis	98	58	.621*	
Brooklyn	96	60	.615	2
Chicago	82	71	.536	14.5
Boston	81	72	.529	15.5
Phila	69	85	.448	28
Cin	67	87	.435	30
Pitt	63	91	.409	34
NY	61	93	.398	36

includes a St. Louis victory over Brooklyn in a playoff, 2 games to 0.

Batting title	Hits	Runs	Doubles	Triples
Musial .365	Musial 228	Musial 124	Musial 50	Musial 20
St. Louis	St. Louis	St. Louis	St. Louis	St. Louis

Home Runs	RBIs
Kiner 23	Slaughter 130
Pitt	St. Louis

Victories	ERA	Strikeouts	Walks	Percentage
Pollet 21	Pollet 2.10	Schmitz 135	Kennedy 116	Rowe .733
St. Louis	St. Louis	Chicago	NY	Phila

American League

Club	Won	Lost	Pct	Games Back
Boston	104	70	.675	
Detroit	92	62	.597	12
New York	87	67	.565	17
Wash	76	78	.494	28
Chicago	74	80	.481	30
St. Louis	66	88	.429	38
Phila	49	105	.318	55

Batting Title	Hits	Runs	Doubles	Triples
Vernon .353	Pesky 208	Willimas 142	Vernon 51	Edwards 16
Wash	Boston	Boston	Wash	Cleve

Home Runs	RBIs
Greenberg 44	Greenberg 127
Det	Det

Victories	ERA	Strikeouts	Walks	Percentage
Feller & Newhouser 26	Newhouser 1.94	Feller 346*	Feller 153	Newhouser .743
Cleve & Det	Det	Cleve	Cleve	Det

all-time major league record

World Series: St. Louis defeated Boston, 4–3

1947

National League

Club	Won	Lost	Pct	Games Back
Brooklyn	94	60	.610	
St. Louis	89	65	.578	5
Boston	86	68	.558	8
NY	81	73	.526	13
Cin	73	81	.474	21
Chicago	69	85	.448	25
Phila	62	92	.403	32
Pitt	62	92	.403	32

Batting Title	Runs	Hits	Doubles	Triples
H. Walker .363	Mize 137	Holmes 191	Miller 36	Walker 16
Phila	NY	Boston	Cin	Phila

Home Runs	RBI
Kiner & Mize 51	Mize 138
Pitt NY	NY

Victories	ERA	Strikeouts	Walks	Percentage
Blackwell 22	Spahn 2.33	Blackwell 193	Higbe 122	Jansen .808
Cin	Boston	Cin	Brk-Pitt	NY

American League

Club	Won	Lost	Pct	Games Back
NY	97	57	.630	
Det	85	69	.552	12
Boston	83	71	.539	14
Cleve	80	74	.519	17
Phila	78	76	.506	19
Chicago	70	84	.455	27
Wash	64	90	.416	33
St. Louis	59	95	.383	38

Batting Title	Runs	Hits	Doubles	Triples
Williams .343	Williams 125	Pesky 207	Boudreau 45	Henrich 13
Boston	Boston	Boston	Cleve	NY

Home Runs	RBI
Williams 32	Williams 114
Boston	Boston

Victories	ERA	Strikeouts	Walks	Pct.
Feller 20	Haynes 2.04	Feller 196	Marchildon 141	Reynolds .704
Cleve	Chicago	Cleve	Phila	NY

World Series: New York defeated Brooklyn 4–3

1948

National League

Club	Won	Lost	Pct	Games Back
Boston	91	62	.595	
St. Louis	85	69	.552	6.5
Brooklyn	84	70	.545	7.5
Pitt	83	71	.539	8.5
NY	78	76	.506	13.5
Phila	66	88	.429	25.5
Cin	64	89	.418	27
Chicago	64	90	.416	27.5

Batting Title	Runs	Hits	Doubles	Triples
Musial .376	Musial 131	Musial 230	Musial 46	Musial 18
St. Louis	St. Louis	St. Louis	St. Louis	St. Louis

Home Runs	RBI
Kiner & Mize 40	Musial 131
Pitt & NY	St. Louis

Victories	ERA	Strikeouts	Walks	Percentage
Sain 24	Brecheen 2.24	Brecheen 148	VanderMeer 124	Brecheen .741
Boston	St. Louis	St. Louis	Cin	St. Louis

American League

Club	Won	Lost	Pct	Games Back
Cleve	97	58	.626	
Boston	96	59	.619	1
NY	94	60	.610	2.5
Phila	84	70	.519	12.5
Det	78	76	.506	18.5
St. Louis	59	94	.386	37
Wash	56	97	.366	40
Chicago	51	101	.336	47

Batting Title	Runs	Hits	Doubles	Triples
Williams .369	Henrich 138	Dillinger 207	Williams 44	Henrich 14
Boston	NY	St. Louis	Boston	NY

Home Runs	RBI
DiMaggio 39	DiMaggio 155
NY	NY

Victories	ERA	Strikeouts	Walks	Percentage
Newhouser 21	Bearden 2.43	Feller 164	Wight 135	Kramer .783
Det	Cleve	Cleve	Chicago	Boston

Cleveland defeated Boston in a one-game playoff.

World Series: Cleveland defeated Boston 4–2

1949

National League

Club	Won	Lost	Pct	Games Back
Brooklyn	97	57	.630	
St. Louis	96	58	.623	1
Phila	81	73	.525	16
Boston	75	79	.487	22
NY	73	81	.474	24
Pitt	71	83	.461	26
Cin	62	92	.403	35
Chicago	61	93	.396	36

Batting Title	Runs	Hits	Doubles	Triples
Robinson .342 Brk	Reese 132 Brk	Musial 207 St. Louis	Musial 41 St. Louis	Musial 13 St. Louis

Home Runs	RBI
Kiner 54 Pitt	Kiner 127 Pitt

Victories	ERA	Strikeouts	Walks	Percentage
Spahn 21 Boston	Koslo 2.50 NY	Spahn 151 Boston	Wehmeier 117 Cin	Roe .714 Brk

American League

Club	Won	Lost	Pct	Games Back
NY	97	57	.630	
Boston	96	58	.623	1
Cleve	89	65	.578	8
Det	87	67	.565	10
Phila	81	73	.526	16
Chicago	63	91	.409	34
St. Louis	55	101	.344	44
Wash	50	104	.325	47

Batting Title	Runs	Hits	Doubles	Triples
Kell .343 Det	Williams 150 Boston	Mitchell 203 Cleve	Williams 39 Boston	Mitchell 23 Cleve

Home Runs	RBI
Williams 43 Boston	Williams & Stephens 159 Boston

Victories	ERA	Strikeouts	Walks	Percentage
Parnell 25 Boston	Parnell 2.77 Boston	Trucks 153 Det	Byrne 179 NY	Kinder .793 Boston

World Series: New York defeated Brooklyn 4–1

1950

National League

Club	Won	Lost	Pct	Games Back
Phila	91	63	.591	
Brooklyn	89	65	.578	2
New York	86	68	.558	5
Boston	83	71	.539	8
St. Louis	78	75	.510	12.5
Cin	66	87	.431	24.5
Chicago	64	89	.418	26.5
Pitt	57	96	.373	33.5

Batting Title	Runs	Hits	Doubles	Triples
Musial .346 St. Louis	Torgeson 120 Boston	Snider 199 Brk	Schoendienst 43 St. Louis	Ashburn 14 Phila

Home Runs	RBI
Kiner 47 Pitt	Ennis 126 Phila

Victories	ERA	Strikeouts	Walks	Percentage
Spahn 21 Boston	Hearn 2.47 NY	Spahn 191 Boston	Wehmeier 135 Cin	Maglie .818 NY

American League

Club	Won	Lost	Pct.	Games Back
NY	98	56	.636	
Detroit	95	59	.617	3
Boston	94	60	.610	4
Cleve	92	62	.597	6
Wash	67	87	.435	31
Chicago	60	94	.390	38
St. Louis	58	96	.377	40
Phila	52	102	.338	46

Batting Title	Runs	Hits	Doubles	Triples
Goodman .354 Boston	DiMaggio 131 Boston	Kell 218 Det	Kell 56 Det	Doerr & DiMaggio Boston Evers Det 11

Home Runs	RBI
Rosen 37 Cleve	Dropo & Stephens 144 Boston

Victories	ERA	Strikeouts	Walks	Percentage
Lemon & Raschi 21 Cleve & NY	Wynn 3.20 Cleve	Lemon 170 NY	Byrne 160 NY	Raschi .724

World Series: New York defeated Philadelphia 4–0

1951

National League

Club	Won	Lost	Pct	Games Back
NY	98	59	.624*	
Brooklyn	97	60	.618	1
St. Louis	81	73	.526	15.5
Boston	76	78	.494	20.5
Phila	73	81	.474	23.5
Cin	68	86	.442	28.5
Pitt	64	90	.416	32.5
Chicago	62	92	.403	34.5

New York defeated Brooklyn 2 games to 1 in a playoff.

Batting Title	Runs	Hits	Doubles	Triples
Musial .355	Musial 124	Ashburn 221	Dark 41	Musial 12
St. Louis	St. Louis	Phila	NY	St. Louis

Home Runs	RBI
Kiner 42	Irvin 121
Pitt	NY

Victories	ERA	Strikeouts	Walks	Percentage
Maglie & Jansen	Nichols 2.88	Spahn & Newcombe	Spahn 109	Roe .880
NY 23		Boston & Brk 164	Boston	Brk

American League

Club	Won	Lost	Pct.	Games Back
NY	98	56	.636	
Cleve	93	61	.604	5
Boston	87	67	.565	11
Chicago	81	73	.526	17
Det	73	81	.474	25
Phila	70	84	.455	28
Wash	62	92	.403	36
St. Louis	52	102	.338	46

Batting Title	Runs	Hits	Doubles	Triples
Fain .344	DiMaggio 113	Kell 191	Mele Wash	Minoso 14
Phila	Boston	Det	Kell Det	Cleve/Chi
			Yost Wash 36	

Home Runs	RBI
Zernial 33	Zernial 129
Chi/Phila	Chi/Phila

Victories	ERA	Strikeouts	Walks	Percentage
Feller 22	Rogovin 2.78	Raschi 164	Byrne 151	Feller .733
Cleve	Chi/Det	NY	NY/St. Louis	Cleve

World Series: NY (AL) defeated NY 4–2

1952

National League

Club	Won	Lost	Pct.	Games Back
Brooklyn	96	57	.627	
NY	92	62	.597	4.5
St. Louis	88	65	.571	8.5
Phila	87	67	.565	9.5
Chicago	77	77	.500	19.5
Cin	69	85	.448	27.5
Boston	64	89	.418	32
Pitt	42	112	.273	54.5

Batting Title	*Runs*	*Hits*	*Doubles*	*Triples*
Musial .336	Musial 105	Musial 194	Musial 42	Thomson 14
St. Louis	St. Louis	St. Louis	St. Louis	NY

Home Runs	*RBI*
Sauer & Kiner	Sauer 121
Chicago & Pitt 37	Chicago

Victories	*ERA*	*Strikeouts*	*Walks*	*Percentage*
Roberts 28	Wilhelm 2.43	Spahn 183	Mizell St. Louis	Wilhelm .833
Phila	NY	Boston	Wehmeier Cin 103	NY

American League

Club	Won	Lost	Pct	Games Back
NY	95	59	.617	
Cleve	93	61	.604	2
Chicago	81	73	.526	14
Phila	79	75	.513	16
Wash	78	76	.506	17
Boston	76	78	.494	19
St. Louis	64	90	.416	31
Detroit	50	104	.325	45

Batting Title	*Runs*	*Hits*	*Doubles*	*Triples*
Fain .327	Doby 104	Fox 192	Fain 43	Avila 11
Phila	Cleve	Chicago	Phila	Cleve

Home Runs	*RBI*
Doby 32	Rosen 105
Cleve	Cleve

Victories	*ERA*	*Strikeouts*	*Walks*	*Percentage*
Shantz 24	Reynolds 2.04	Reynolds 160	Wynn 132	Shantz .774
Phila	NY	NY	Cleve	Phila

World Series: NY defeated Brooklyn 4–3

1953

National League

Club	Won	Lost	Pct.	Games Back
Brooklyn	105	49	.682	
Milwaukee*	92	62	.597	13
Phila	83	71	.539	22
St. Louis	83	71	.539	22
NY	70	84	.455	35
Cin	68	86	.442	37
Chicago	65	89	.422	40
Pitt	50	104	.325	55

*The Boston Braves had moved to Milwaukee shortly before the 1953 season began.

Batting Title	Runs	Hits	Doubles	Triples
Furillo .344	Snider 132	Ashburn 205	Musial 53	Gilliam 17
Brk	Brk	Phila	St. Louis	Brk

Home Runs	RBI
Mathews 47	Campanella 142
Mil	Brk

Victories	ERA	Strikeouts	Walks	Percentage
Spahn, Mil	Spahn 2.10	Roberts 198	Lindell 139	Erskine .769
Roberts, Phila 23	Mil	Phila	Pitt/Phila	Brk

American League

Club	Won	Lost	Pct.	Games Back
NY	99	52	.656	
Cleve	92	62	.597	8.5
Chicago	89	65	.578	11.5
Boston	84	69	.549	16
Wash	76	76	.500	23.5
Det	60	94	.390	40.5
Phila	59	95	.383	41.5
St. Louis	54	100	.351	46.5

Batting Title	Runs	Hits	Doubles	Triples
Vernon .337	Rosen 115	Kuenn 209	Vernon 43	Rivera 16
Wash	Cleve	Det	Wash	Chicago

Home Runs	RBI
Rosen 43	Rosen 145
Cleve	Cleve

Victories	ERA	Strikeouts	Walks	Percentage
Porterfield 22	Lopat 2.24	Pierce 186	Parnell 116	Lopat .800
Wash	NY	Chicago	Boston	NY

World Series: NY defeated Brooklyn 4–2

1954

National League

Club	Won	Lost	Pct	Games Back
NY	97	57	.630	
Brk	92	62	.587	5
Mil	89	65	.578	8
Phila	75	79	.487	22
Cin	74	80	.481	23
St. Louis	72	82	.468	25
Chicago	64	90	.416	33
Pitt	53	101	.344	44

Batting Title	Runs	Hits	Doubles	Triples
Mays .345	Snider & Musial	Mueller 212	Musial 41	Mays 13
NY	Brk & St. Louis 120	NY	St. Louis	NY

Home Runs	RBI
Kluszewski 49	Kluszewski 141
Cin	Cin

Victories	ERA	Strikeouts	Walks	Percentage
Roberts 23	Antonelli 2.30	Roberts 185	Gomez 109	Antonelli .750
Phila	NY	Phila	NY	NY

American League

Club	Won	Lost	Pct.	Games Back
Cleve	111	43	.721	
NY	103	51	.669	8
Chicago	94	60	.610	17
Boston	69	85	.448	42
Det	68	86	.442	43
Wash	66	88	.429	45
Baltimore*	54	100	.351	57
Phila	51	103	.331	60

*St. Louis moved to Baltimore for the 1954 season.

Batting Title	Runs	Hits	Doubles	Triples
Avila .341	Mantle 129	Fox & Kuenn	Vernon 33	Minoso 18
Cleve	NY	Chi & Det 201	Wash	Chicago

Home Runs	RBI
Doby 32	Doby 126
Cleve	Cleve

Victories	ERA	Strikeouts	Walks	Percentage
Lemon & Wynn	Garcia 2.64	Turley 185	Turley 181	Consuegra .842
Cleve 23	Cleve	Balt	Balt	Chicago

World Series: NY defeated Cleveland 4–0

1955

National League

Club	Won	Lost	Pct	Games Back
Brooklyn	98	55	.641	
Mil	85	69	.552	13.5
NY	80	74	.519	18.5
Phila	77	77	.500	21.5
Cin	75	79	.487	23.5
Chicago	72	81	.471	26
St. Louis	68	86	.442	30.5
Pitt	60	94	.390	38.5

Batting Title	Runs	Hits	Doubles	Triples
Ashburn .338	Snider 126	Kluszewski 192	Aaron & Logan	Mays 17
Phila	Brk	Cin	Mil 37	NY

Home Runs	RBI
Mays 51	Snider 136
NY	Brk

Victories	ERA	Strikeouts	Walks	Percentage
Roberts 23	Friend 2.83	Jones 198	Jones 185	Newcombe .800
Phila	Pitt	Chicago	Chicago	Brk

American League

Club	Won	Lost	Pct.	Games Back
NY	96	58	.623	
Cleve	93	61	.604	3
Chicago	91	63	.591	5
Boston	84	70	.545	12
Det	79	75	.513	17
KC*	63	91	.409	33
Balt	57	97	.370	39
Wash	53	101	.344	43

Philadelphia moved to Kansas City in 1955.

Batting Title	Runs	Hits	Doubles	Triples
Kaline .340	Smith 123	Kaline 200	Kuenn 38	Carey & Mantle 11
Det	Cleve	Det	Det	NY

Victories	ERA	Strikeouts	Walks	Percentage
Ford NY	Pierce 1.97	Score 245	Turley 181	Byrne .762
Lemon Cleve	Chi	NY	NY	NY
Sullivan	Boston			
18				

World Series: Brooklyn defeated NY, 4–3

1956

National League

Club	Won	Lost	Pct	Games Back
Brooklyn	93	61	.604	
Mil	92	62	.597	1
Cin	91	62	.591	2
St. Louis	76	78	.494	17
Phila	71	83	.461	22
NY	67	87	.435	26
Pitt	66	88	.429	27
Chicago	60	94	.390	33

Batting Title	Runs	Hits	Doubles	Triples
Aaron .328	Robinson 122	Aaron 200	Aaron 34	Bruton 15
Mil	Cin	Mil	Mil	Mil

Home Runs	RBI
Snider 43	Musial 109
Brk	St. Louis

Victories	ERA	Strikeouts	Walks	Percentage
Newcombe 27	Burdette 2.70	Jones 176	Jones 115	Newcombe .794
Brk	Mil	Chicago	Chicago	Brk

American League

Club	Won	Lost	Pct.	Games Back
NY	97	57	.630	
Cleve	88	66	.571	9
Chicago	85	69	.552	12
Boston	84	70	.545	13
Det	82	72	.532	15
Balt	69	85	.448	28
Wash	59	95	.383	38
KC	52	102	.338	45

Batting Title	Runs	Hits	Doubles	Triples
Mantle .353	Mantle 132	Kuenn 196	Piersall 40	Lemon Wash,
NY	NY	Det	Boston	Jensen Bost,
				Minoso Chi
				Simpson KC 11

Victories	ERA	Strikeouts	Walks	Percentage
Lary 21	Ford 2.47	Score 263	Turley 177	Ford .760
Det	NY	Cleve	NY	NY

World Series: NY defeated Brooklyn 4–3

1957

National League

Club	Won	Lost	Pct	Games Back
Mil	95	59	.617	
St. Louis	87	67	.565	8
Brk	84	70	.545	11
Cin	80	74	.519	15
Phila	77	77	.500	18
NY	69	85	.448	26
Chicago	62	92	.403	33
Pitt	62	92	.403	33

Batting Title	Runs	Hits	Doubles	Triples
Musial .351	Aaron 118	Schoendienst	Hoak 39	Mays 20
St. Louis	Mil	Mil 200	Cin	NY

Home Runs	RBI
Aaron 44	Aaron 132
Mil	Mil

Victories	ERA	Strikeouts	Walks	Percentage
Spahn 21	Podres 2.66	Sanford 188	Drott 129	Buhl .720
Mil	Brk	Phila	Chicago	Mil

American League

Club	Won	Lost	Pct	Games Back
NY	98	56	.636	
Chicago	90	64	.584	8
Boston	82	72	.552	16
Det	78	76	.506	20
Balt	76	76	.500	21
Cleve	76	77	.497	21.5
KC	59	94	.386	38.5
Wash	55	99	.357	43

Batting Title	Runs	Hits	Doubles	Triples
Williams .388	Mantle 121	Fox 196	Gardner Balt	Bauer NY
Boston	NY	Chicago	Minoso Chicago 36	Simpson NY/KC
				McDougald NY 11

Victories	ERA	Strikeouts	Walks	Percentage
Bunning Det	Shantz 2.45	Wynn 184	Moore 103	Dononvan Chicago
Pierce Chicago 20	NY	Chicago	Balt	Sturdivant NY .727

World Series: Milwaukee defeated NY 4–3

1958

National League

Club	Won	Lost	Pct	Games Back
Mil	92	62	.597	
Pitt	84	70	.545	8
SF*	80	74	.519	12
Cin	76	78	.494	16
St. Louis	72	82	.468	20
Chicago	72	82	.468	20
LA*	71	83	.461	21
Phila	69	85	.448	23

NY moved to San Francisco and Brk to Los Angeles for the 1958 season.

Batting Title	Runs	Hits	Doubles	Triples
Ashburn .350 Phila	Mays 121 SF	Ashburn 215 Phila	Cepeda 38 SF	Ashburn 13 Phila

Home Runs	RBI
Banks 47 Chicago	Banks 129 Chicago

Victories	ERA	Strikeouts	Walks	Percentage
Friend & Spahn 22 Pitt & Mil	Miller 2.47 SF	Jones 225 St. Louis	Jones 107 St. Louis	Spahn & Burdette .667 Mil

American League

Club	Won	Lost	Pct	Games Back
NY	92	62	.597	
Chicago	82	72	.532	10
Boston	79	75	.513	13
Cleve	77	76	.503	14.5
Det	77	77	.500	15
Balt	74	79	.484	17.5
KC	73	81	.474	19
Wash	61	93	.396	31

Batting Title	Runs	Hits	Doubles	Triples
Williams .328 Boston	Mantle 127 NY	Fox 187 Chicago	Kuenn 39 Det	Power 10 Cleve & KC

Home Runs	RBI
Mantle 42 NY	Jensen 122 Boston

Victories	ERA	Strikeouts	Walks	Percentage
Turley 21 NY	Ford 2.01 NY	Wynn 179 Chicago	Turley 128 NY	Turley .750 NY

World Series: NY defeated Milwaukee 4–3

1959

National League

Club	Won	Lost	Pct	Games Back
LA	88	68	.564*	
Mil	86	70	.551	2
SF	83	71	.539	4
Pitt	78	76	.506	9
Chicago	74	80	.481	13
Cin	74	80	.481	13
St. Louis	71	83	.561	16
Phila	64	90	.416	23

**LA defeated Milwaukee in a playoff 2–0.*

Batting Title	Runs	Hits	Doubles	Triples
Aaron .355	Pinson 131	Aaron 223	Pinson 47	Neal & Moon
Mil	Cin	Mil	Cin	LA 11

Home Runs	RBI
Mathews 46	Banks 143
Mil	Chicago

Victories	ERA	Strikeouts	Walks	Percentage
Burdette & Spahn Mil	Jones 2.83	Drysdale 242	Jones 109	Face .947
Jones SF 21	SF	LA	SF	Pitt

American League

Club	Won	Lost	Pct	Games Back
Chicago	94	60	.610	
Cleve	89	65	.578	5
NY	79	75	.513	15
Det	76	78	.494	18
Boston	75	79	.487	19
Balt	74	80	.481	20
KC	66	88	.429	28
Wash	63	91	.409	31

Batting Title	Runs	Hits	Doubles	Triples
Kuenn .353	Yost 115	Kuenn 198	Kuenn 42	Allison 9
Det	Det	Det	Det	Wash

Home Runs	RBI
Colavito Cleve	Jensen 112
& Killebrew Wash 42	Boston

Victories	ERA	Strikeouts	Walks	Percentage
Wynn 22	Wilhelm 2.19	Bunning 201	Wynn 119	Shaw .750
Chicago	Balt	Det	Chicago	Chicago

World Series: LA defeated Chicago 4–2

1960

National League

Club	Won	Lost	Pct	Games Back
Pitt	95	59	.617	
Mil	88	66	.571	7
St. Louis	86	68	.558	9
LA	82	72	.532	13
SF	79	75	.513	16
Cin	67	87	.435	28
Chicago	60	94	.390	35
Phila	59	95	.383	36

Batting Title	*Runs*	*Hits*	*Doubles*	*Triples*
Groat .325	Bruton 112	Mays 190	Pinson 37	Bruton 13
Pitt	Mil	SF	Cin	Mil

Home Runs	*RBI*
Banks 41	Aaron 126
Chicago	Mil

Victories	*ERA*	*Strikeouts*	*Walks*	*Percentage*
Spahn Mil	McCormick 2.70	Drysdale 246	Buhl 103	Broglio .700
Broglio St. Louis 21	SF	LA	Mil	St. Louis

American League

Club	Won	Lost	Pct	Games Back
NY	97	67	.630	
Balt	89	65	.578	8
Chicago	87	67	,565	10
Cleve	76	78	.494	21
Wash	73	81	.474	24
Det	71	83	.461	26
Boston	65	89	.422	32
KC	58	96	.377	39

Batting Title	*Runs*	*Hits*	*Doubles*	*Triples*
Runnels .320	Mantle 119	Minoso 184	Francona 36	Fox 10
Boston	NY	Chicago	Cleve	Chicago

Home Runs	*RBI*
Mantle 40	Maris 112
NY	NY

Victories	*ERA*	*Strikeouts*	*Walks*	*Percentage*
Perry & Estrada 18	Baumann 2.67	Bunning 201	Barber 112	Perry .643
Cleve & Balt	Chicago	Det	Balt	Cleve

World Series: Pitt defeated NY 4–3

Appendix 2:
Attendance Figures

American League Attendance Figures, 1946–1960

Year	St. Louis	Boston	Chicago	Cleveland	Detroit	Wash.	N.Y.	Phila.	Totals
1946	526,435	1,416,944	983,403	1,057,289	1,722,590	1,027,216	2,265,512	621,793	9,621,182
1947	320,474	1,427,315	876,948	1,521,978	1,398,093	850,758	2,178,937	911,566	9,486,069
1948	335,564	1,558,798	777,844	2,620,627	1,743,035	795,254	2,373,901	945,076	11,150,099
1949	270,936	1,596,650	937,151	2,233,771	1,821,204	770,745	2,283,676	816,514	10,730,647
1950	247,131	1,344,080	781,330	1,727,464	1,951,474	699,697	2,081,380	309,805	8,832,866
1951	293,790	1,312,282	1,328,234	1,704,984	1,132,641	695,167	1,950,107	465,469	7,570,392
1952	518,796	1,115,750	1,231,675	1,444,607	1,026,846	699,457	1,629,665	627,100	7,267,050
1953	297,238	1,026,133	1,191,353	1,069,176	884,658	595,594	1,537,811	326,113	6,928,076
Baltimore									
1954	1,060,910	931,127	1,231,629	1,335,472	1,079,847	503,542	1,475,171	304,666	6,861,454
								Kansas C.	
1955	852,039	1,203,200	1,175,684	1,221,780	1,181,838	425,238	1,490,138	1,393,054	8,942,971
1956	901,201	1,137,158	1,000,090	865,467	1,051,182	431,467	1,491,784	1,015,154	7,893,503
1957	1,029,581	1,181,087	1,135,668	722,256	1,272,346	457,079	1,497,134	901,067	8,196,218
1958	829,991	1,077,047	797,451	663,805	1,098,924	475,288	1,428,438	925,090	7,296,034
1959	891,926	984,102	1,423,144	1,497,976	1,221,221	615,372	1,552,030	963,683	9,149,454
1960	1,187,849	1,129,866	1,644,460	950,985	1,167,669	743,404	1,627,349	774,944	9,226,526

National League Attendance Figures, 1946–1960

Year	Boston	Chicago	Cincinnati	Brooklyn	Phila.	Pitts	St. Louis	N.Y.	Totals
1946	969,673	1,342,970	715,751	1,796,824	1,045,247	749,962	1,061,807	1,219,873	6,339,264
1947	1,277,361	1,364,039	899,975	1,807,526	907,332	1,283,531	1,247,913	1,600,973	10,388,650
1948	1,455,439	1,237,792	823,386	1,398,967	767,429	1,517,021	1,111,440	1,459,269	9,770,743
1949	1,081,795	1,143,139	707,782	1,633,747	819,698	1,449,435	1,430,676	1,218,446	9,484,718
1950	944,391	1,165,944	538,794	1,185,896	1,217,035	1,166,267	1,093,411	1,008,878	1,320,616
1951	487,475	894,415	588,288	1,282,628	937,658	980,590	1,013,429	1,059,539	7,244,022
1952	281,278	1,024,826	604,197	1,088,704	755,417	686,673	913,113	984,940	6,339,148
	Milwaukee								
1953	1,826,397	763,658	584,086	1,163,419	853,644	572,757	880,242	811,518	7,455,721
1954	2,131,388	748,183	704,167	1,020,531	738,991	475,494	1,039,698	1,155,067	8,013,519
1955	2,005,836	875,800	693,662	1,033,589	922,886	469,397	849,130	824,112	7,674,412
1956	2,046,331	720,118	1,125,928	1,213,562	934,798	949,878	1,029,773	629,179	8,649,567
1957	2,215,404	670,629	1,070,850	1,028,258	1,146,230	850,732	1,185,575	653,923	8,821,601
				Los Angeles				*San Fran.*	
1958	1,971,101	979,904	788,582	1,845,556	931,110	1,311,988	1,063,730	1,272,625	10,164,596
1959	1,749,112	858,255	801,298	2,071,045	802,815	1,359,917	929,953	1,422,130	9,994,525
1960	1,497,799	809,770	663,485	2,253,887	886,205	1,705,828	1,096,63?	1,795,356	9,612,330

Selected Bibliography

Periodicals

Baseball History
Baseball Research Journal
Business Week
The Diamond
The Journal of Sports History
Life
The New Republic
Newsweek
New York Times (NYT)

The Saturday Evening Post
Sports Illustrated (SI)
The Sporting News (SN)
The Sporting News Guides (SNG)
Street & Smith's Baseball Yearbook
  (S&S)
Time
U.S. News and World Report
  (USN&WR)

Books and Articles

Anderson, Dave. *Pennant Races: Baseball at Its Best.* New York, 1994.

Berkow, Ira (ed.). *Hank Greenberg: The Story of My Life.* New York, 1989.

Boudreau, Lou. *Boudreau: Covering All the Bases.* Champaign, 1993.

Cairns, Bob. *Pen Men.* New York, 1992

Carmichael, John (ed.). *Who's Who in the Major Leagues, 1945–1951.*

Clayton, Skip. "Seminick." *Phillies Report* (November 10, 1983).

Creamer, Robert W. *Stengel: His Life and Times.* New York, c. 1984.

Crissey, Harrington E. *Teenagers, Graybeards and 4F's.* 2 vols. Privately published, 1982.

Davis, Lance. "Self Regulation in Baseball, 1909–71." In Noll.

Durocher, Leo, with Ed Linn. *Nice Guys Finish Last.* New York, 1975.

Dworkin, James B. "Owners vs. Players." *Baseball and Collective Bargaining.* Boston, 1981.

Edwars, Harry. "Sport Within the Veil: The Triumphs, Tragedies and Challenges of African-American Involvement," *American Academy of Political and Social Science, Annals*. vol. 445, 1979, 1.

Eskenazi, Gerald. *The Lip: A Biography of Leo Durocher*. New York, 1993.

Frommer, Harvey. *Baseball's Greatest Managers*. New York, 1985.

Gilbert, Bill. *They Also Served: Baseball and the Home Front, 1941–45*. New York, 1992.

Golenbock, Peter. *Bums: An Oral History of the Brooklyn Dodgers*. New York, 1984.

______. *Dynasty: The New York Yankees, 1949–64*. Englewood, 1975.

______. *Fenway: An Unexpurgated History of the Red Sox*. New York, 1992.

Gould, Paul. "Unionism's Bid in Baseball." *New Republic*, August 5, 1946.

Halberstam, David. *The Summer of '49*. New York, 1989.

Helyar, John. *The Lords of the Realm*. New York, 1994.

Henrich, Tommy, and Bill Gilbert. *Five O'Clock Lightning*. New York, 1992.

Higbe, Kirby, with Martin Quigley. *The High Hard One*. New York, 1967.

Holland, Gerald. "Who in the World but Larry?" *Sports Illustrated*, August 17, 1959.

Honig, Donald. *Baseball Between the Lines*. New York, 1976.

______. *Baseball in the '50s. A Decade of Transition*. New York, 1987.

James, Bill. *Historical Baseball Abstract*. New York, 1988.

______. *The Politics of Glory. How Baseball's Hall of Fame Really Works*. New York, 1994.

Jennings, Ken M. *Balls and Strikes: The Money Game in Professional Baseball*. New York, 1990.

Jones, Landon Y. *Great Expectations: America and the Baby Boom Generation*. New York, 1980.

Jordan, David. *A Tiger in His Time: Hal Newhouser and the Burden of War Time Ball*. South Bend, 1990.

Kahn, Roger. *The Boys of Summer*. New York, 1972.

______. *The Era, 1947–1957: When the Yankees, the Giants and the Dodgers Ruled the World*. New York, 1993.

Kleinknecht, Merl. "Integration of Baseball after World War II." *Baseball Research Journal* (1983).

Koppett, Leonard. *The Man in the Dugout*. New York, 1993.

Kuklick, Bruce. *To Everything a Season: Shibe Park and Urban Philadelphia*, Princeton, 1991.

Langford, James. *The Game Is Never Over*. South Bend, 1982.

Linn, Ed, with Leo Durocher. *Nice Guys Finish Last*. New York, 1975.

Lowenfish, Lee. *The Imperfect Diamond: The Story of Baseball's Reserve System and the Men Who Fought to Change It*. New York, 1980.

Manchester, William. *The Glory and the Dream: A Narrative History of America, 1932–1972*. Boston, 1974.

Markham, Jesse, and Paul Teplitz. *Baseball Economics and Public Policy.* Lexington, 1981.

McGowen, Roscoe. "Commissioner A.B.C." *Pic Quarterly Baseball* (spring 1949).

Mead, William B. *Even the Browns.* Chicago, 1978.

Miller, James E. *The Baseball Business: Pursuing Pennants and Profits in Baltimore.* Chapel Hill, 1990.

Moore, J. Thomas. *Pride Against Prejudice: The Biography of Larry Doby.* New York, 1988.

Noll, Roger (ed.). *Government and the Sports Business.* Washington, 1974.

Parrott, Harold. *The Lords of Baseball.* New York, 1976.

Patterson, Robert. *Only the Ball Was White.* New York, 1984.

Peary, Daniel (ed.). *We Played the Game.* New York, 1994.

Polner, Murray. *Branch Rickey: A Biography.* New York, 1982.

Powell, Douglas S. "Is Big League Baseball Good Municipal Business?" *The American City,* vol. 72, November 1957.

Quirk, James, and Rodney D. Fort. *Pay Dirt: The Business of Professional Team Sports.* Princeton, 1992.

Rader, Benjamin. *American Sports: From the Age of Folk Games to the Age of Televised Sports.* Englewood, 1990.

______. *In Its Own Image: How Television Transformed Sports.* New York, 1984.

Reidenbaugh, Lowell. *Baseball's Fifty Greatest Games.* St. Louis, 1986.

Reidenbaugh, Lowell. *The Sporting News: The First Hundred Years, 1886–1986.* St. Louis, 1985.

Robinson, Jackie, as told to Alfred Duckett. *I Never Had It Made.* New York, 1972.

Rosenblatt, Aaron. "Negroes In Baseball: The Failure of Success." *Transaction,* vol. 4, September 1967.

Rosenthal, Harold. *The Ten Best Years of Baseball: An Informal History of the Fifties.* New York, 1979.

Salsinger, H. G., and Don Black. *Major League Baseball: Facts and Figures.* New York, 1953.

Scully, Gerald W. *The Business of Major League Baseball.* Chicago, 1989.

Smith, Robert. *Illustrated History of Baseball.* New York, 1973.

Sommers, Paul M. *Diamonds Are Forever: The Business of Baseball.* Washington, 1992.

Steinberg, Cobbett. *Reel Facts: The Movie Handbook.* New York, 1982.

Sullivan, Neil J. *The Dodgers Move West.* New York, 1987.

Turner, Frederick W. *When the Boys Came Back: Baseball and 1946.* New York, 1996.

Tygiel, Jules. *Baseball's Great Experiment: Jackie Robinson and His Legacy.* New York, 1983.

Vecsey, George. *Joy in Mudville.* New York, 1970.

Veeck, Bill. *Hustler's Handbook.* New York, 1985.

Voigt, David Q. *American Baseball,* vols. 2 & 3. University Park, 1970.

_____. *Baseball: An Illustrated History.* University Park, 1987.

Warfield, Don. *The Roaring Redhead, Larry MacPhail: Baseball's Great Innovator.* South Bend, 1987.

Westcott, Rich, and Frank Bilovsky. *The New Phillies Encyclopedia.* Philadelphia, 1993.

Wiggins, David. "Wendell Smith, the *Pittsburgh Courier-Journal* and the Campaign to Include Blacks in Organized Baseball, 1933–1945." *The Journal of Sports History,* X, no. 2, Summer 1983, 5–29.

Williams, Peter (ed.). *The Joe Williams Baseball Reader.* Chapel Hill, 1989.

Wolff, Rick, et al. *The Baseball Encyclopedia.* 9th ed. New York, 1993.

Index